Memoirs of
a Mask Maker

Kathryn Graven

LEAF BY LEAF

Published by Leaf by Leaf
an imprint of Cinnamon Press,
Office 49019, PO Box 15113, Birmingham, B2 2NJ, United Kingdom.
www.cinnamonpress.com

Print Edition ISBN 978-1-78864-954-4
British Library Cataloguing in Publication Data. A CIP record for this book
can be obtained from the British Library.

Designed and typeset in Adobe Jenson Pro by Cinnamon Press.
Cover design by Adam Craig from original artwork by Sophie Erb.
Cinnamon Press is represented by Inpress.

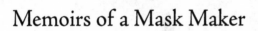

Memoirs of a Mask Maker

Memoirs of a Mask Maker

Part I

Chapter 1

Starting my sewing machine is an act of communion.

The steps are straightforward and firmly etched in my brain. First, lift the loaded bobbin from the winder, open the throat case and tuck the bobbin into place. Next, grab the thread end and pull it through the needle guide, down and under the u-shaped groove, wrap it around the up-take lever and through the needle. Connect that thread with the bobbin thread and pull up the loop. Finally, double-check the tension setting, then lift the pressure foot and slip in the fabric. Lower the pressure foot and step on the pedal.

Invariably, the first stitches are uneven or tangled. The bobbin thread snags. The top thread snaps. Grrrrrr, I say aloud to no one. Inexplicably, this happens even if the last time I sewed the stitches were even and the machine purred perfectly. It's like my machine needs to warm up to me all over again, to recognize it's me, an old friend, who's driving.

Perhaps my Cortina machine acts this way to make me take a moment to visualize all the dresses, skirts, jackets, pillows, curtains, tablecloths and napkins I've made. And to pause for another moment to connect to the women who taught me how to sew. I remember Gram insisting, whether cutting fabric or fixing a hem, that I must measure carefully and aim for perfection. I remember my friend Phyllis; she loved fabrics with bold prints and bright colors. I remember Katsuko, my Japanese host-mother, buying me the most gorgeous cotton to sew my first summer *yukata*. I think of the hours spent sewing together, how productive, creative and fabulously fashionable our sewing made us feel, and then I know I can sort the tangled threads and start again.

I learned from these exquisite sewers but sewing is not my profession. Growing up, sewing saved me from embarrassment at not having a mother to make choir dresses or school play costumes. Sewing connected me to Japanese culture when I had no words. Throughout my life, sewing helped me navigate deep losses and clear the way for new beginnings. Sewing is what I do to fight despair.

Which is why, in early March 2020, as reports of a deadly virus in Asia dominated news, I darted into sewing with purpose and urgency. I woke in the middle of the night, shaken by a dream so vivid, so clear I had to sit up and get my bearings. I dreamed about masks: Kakuta-san, my trusty Japanese high school friend arrived in front of the Maniwa drugstore wearing a white cloth mask over her face. "I have slight cold," she apologized. "No problem," I said, knowing that wearing a mask is what Otōsan and Okaasan, my Japanese host parents, advised their drug store customers to do. That's also what they did at home when they felt a cold coming on.

"*Odaijini*," I heard Okaasan say, in my dream, to Kakuta-san as we walked down the street to school. Feel better. Take care. Stay well. All are fair translations for *Odaijini*.

The sharp contrast between Kakuta-san's black hair and her white face mask were part of my earliest memories of Japan. In Noh plays or Kabuki theater, masks hide actors' faces completely. In everyday Japanese life, cloth masks are worn as a sign of respect, concern for others on crowded subways and buses. During Japan's miraculous postwar growth years, foreigners thought Japanese wore masks to protect themselves from menacing industrial pollutants. Maybe that was true for some. But mostly, Japanese wore masks to prevent passing on their sniffles and coughs to others. As COVID-19 spread from China to South Korea and Japan in early 2020, masks roared back into use in Asia with few, if any, complaints.

I got up thinking: I've got to figure out how to make masks. My dream and its call-to-action message was so clear, so powerful. I emailed a Japanese friend asking if she knew of any homemade mask patterns. The next day, Nahoko emailed me a popular pattern featured recently on an NHK broadcast. The instructions in Japanese included an easy to follow diagram.

Pattern in hand, I rummaged through my fabric stashes, and pulled out suitable cottons, linens, possibly some flannels, and spread them on the floor. I dragged my portable sewing machine out from the closet. I bought the light-weight Cortina from my Tokyo flat mate at her *sayonara* sale almost 35 years ago. For its portability, it has replaced my mother's Elna, which I keep in another closet as a backup.

For elastics, I looked to Gram's pink quilted sewing box. I haven't made anything in a while with an elastic waistband, but surely, I kept some in there from previous projects. The pink box is where I put this and that notions. You never know what you'll need when. In another basket of linens, I found several yards of white linen I must have intended for a table cloth, but never got around to it. This in turn led me to the closet of tablecloths; the ones with the most stains could also be sacrificed for the cause.

I confess I am a bit of a fabric hoarder. One of my greatest pleasures when traveling is to pop into fabric stores. In Thailand, it's easy to go overboard on luscious silks. In Indonesia, the batiks are irresistible. In India, hand-blocked cotton prints are adventurous and thrilling. In England and France, the linens are ever so lovely, wildly botanical. In Scandinavia, the Marimekko designs are just uplifting.

In Japan, well, there is no end to the exquisite textiles found in small towns or in large cities. It's fabric heaven. Over the years, I've developed a passion for *tenugui*, the easily washable, vibrant cotton towels that are a common household item there. Bigger than handkerchiefs at roughly 14 inches by 35 inches, they can be used as hand towels, headbands, or decorations. In a pandemic pinch, when Boston's lockdown made it impossible to go to a fabric store, I reached into my *tenugui* collection and started cutting 9 inch by 6 inch rectangles.

My first few masks were passable but not perfect. It took a few tries before I nailed the exact corner positions for the elastic and evened out the three pleats. But I had to admit the white polka dots on a cobalt blue background, and the thin blue lines on the white background—two of my favorite *tenugui*—made for charming masks. I experimented with crisp white linen lining, and bright red cotton lining. Both worked cheerfully. I moved on to other colors and prints.

Pleased, I posted photos of my home-made masks on social media. I wasn't prepared for the response. A childhood friend in Minneapolis, my father's former

secretary, a graduate school classmate living in Seattle, a Brazilian family in Boston and a host of others praised my colorful masks. Emails poured in from around the country and even Japan. *Could you please make more masks and send?*

It was early on in the pandemic. Several online friends cautioned that the Centers for Disease Control and Prevention did not think masks were a good idea; they could even be harmful. One online post begged me to "STOP SEWING," for all sorts of alleged safety and legal reasons. I acknowledged their concerns, but trusted my instincts. From my Japanese experiences, I knew masks wouldn't hurt and could help.

Many artists who create Kabuki, Noh, or Venetian masquerade masks come from a family tradition of mask making. That's not me. My story is more circuitous. It took a lifetime of developing sewing skills, hunting for fabrics, discovering my artistic self, honing my crafts, and building global connections to be ready. More profoundly, it took digging my way out of a crater of grief and relentless determination to undo old family patterns. Ultimately, the love of three women and my own curious, adventurous spirit helped me imagine a different kind of life. Creating my own family, I found joy again.

So, when the pandemic shut down the world and forced us to stay inside, I had all I needed to push forward with clarity and abandon. I became a mask maker.

Chapter 2

When I was a little girl, I wished I had an invisible mask to hide the scar on my chin. Magically, it would cover the fresh seam that followed the contours of my lower jaw. And just maybe that mask could make everything that happened unhappen.

Waking in the hospital, I heard my sister's voice through the opaque glass wall separating us. I could see her leg, held up by wires at an angle that made it impossible for her to get out of bed. My side of the room had the window, looking out to the middle of nowhere, which, I learned later, was a town in northern Iowa called Mason City. Nurses and doctors came and went: "Try not to move. Stay quiet. Lie still and rest."

And then just when I imagined being still as a frozen lake, another nurse would appear. I was helpless to resist as she rolled me to one side and stuck a thermometer up my butt.

"Where's my mom?" I demanded. "I want my mom. She will make you stop."

No one listened.

Even though I wanted to sit up and yell louder the next time, I couldn't. They said my head was hurt, something about a skull fracture—cracked like Humpty Dumpty. They said my jaw was broken, which is why I couldn't open my mouth wide or chew. What I felt was a strange tightness across my chin where there were stitches. Again, they told me to be still.

But inside my mouth, I couldn't stop my tongue from

exploring a new terrain. With each lap around my uppers and lowers, it discovered chipped teeth. The taste of my blood confirmed the sharpness of the jagged edges. What I couldn't take was the pain in my ears. The unrelenting earaches made me cry. "Make my ears stop hurting. Please make it stop."

The doctors kept talking as if I wasn't there. Maybe it was an ear infection. They couldn't rule out brain fluid leaking. Until they could, they patted my arm and said, "Stay quiet. Lie still and rest." Nurses regularly checked for signs of a fever. That's what annoyed me. After all the emergency room examining, probing, X-rays, stitches and intravenous lines and attention I had received, the one thing that pierced my shocked, heavily sedated haze and loomed like a monster in the room was the dreaded rectal thermometer.

To add further indignity to my broken state, they had me recovering in a crib. I was five, a big girl now, much too big for a crib. No one trusted that I wouldn't try to break out of a bed. I thought Mom should tell them that I don't sleep in a crib any more.

Days and nights blended into an uncountable blur of time. It was my soft-spoken Aunt Mavis who interrupted my fog. She pulled up a chair next to my crib. I was happy to see her, a familiar face. Mavis talked about heaven being filled with loving angels. Why was she talking like my Sunday school teacher about angels? Finally, she said: "God wants your mom to be with him now." That's the only part that stuck. Crying in my hospital crib, I knew, no matter what anyone said—even kind, beautiful Aunt Mavis—I just knew my mother did not want to be with God.

13

I had no idea what dead meant. I didn't know anyone who had died. I still had two sets of grandparents, great-aunts and great-uncles, aunts and uncles on both sides, a brother and a sister, and so many first cousins. I had not lived long enough for our dog, Frisky, or our parakeet, Mr. Poppins, to die. I didn't understand. How could someone go to sleep and never wake up? Does that mean maybe I shouldn't go to sleep? What does heaven look like? What do you eat there? How long do you stay in heaven?

More immediately, how did we get so quickly from the pomp and fluff of Easter, the holiday Mom loved so much, to her going to heaven?

It was late afternoon on Easter Sunday, when we left Greene, Dad's small hometown in northern Iowa, and headed home to Minneapolis. I hugged Grama Helen and Granddad Henry goodbye on the back doorstep. The April air was cold enough for Mom to wear her soft brown mink coat. On the short walk to the driveway, she and my brother argued over who would sit in the front seat. Naturally, Mom prevailed: the three kids and Frisky piled into the back. As I scrambled to my middle spot, I immediately felt small. Being only five years old and the youngest, I was always the one straddling the floor hump on family car trips. It was so unfair; my brother, Mark, and my sister, Kari, got the windows just because they were 12 and 11.

I loved Easter. In the days leading up to it, Mom and I played the Peter Cottontail song over and over on the record player, forever imprinting the bouncy lyrics "hippity-hoppity Easter's on its way" in my brain. Mom bought new matching dresses for me and my sister—

despite our wide age difference. She fussed over my blonde bangs as I tried on a white bonnet with long, trailing ribbons. Unsure what the weather might be, she brought out the snow-white hand muffs from last year, even as she laid out ruffled ankle socks to wear inside shiny new shoes. She outfitted my brother in a grown-up looking suit jacket and necktie. And then on Good Friday, with infectious enthusiasm, she packed us all up for the trip to Greene. She made sure to bring toys and books. At Gram and Granddad's house there was one unbendable rule: absolutely no watching television.

Good Lutherans, we always went to church on Easter morning. With everyone dressed in their Easter best, Mom sat in the pews of St. Peter's Lutheran Church busting with pride for her family. Dad sang the opening hymn "Christ the Lord is Risen Today" with gusto. His bold crescendo on the alleluias made us cringe. He pushed Lutheran propriety by folding the service bulletins into boats and passing them down the pew. But his irreverent flotilla kept us entertained during the interminable sermon and gave Mom a moment of peace.

Back at Gram's house, there were spring baskets full of foiled chocolate eggs, squishy yellow marshmallow chicks and a rainbow of jelly beans. Gram prepared a yummy Easter dinner, built around a baked ham, homemade rolls and green beans canned fresh from her garden. She pulled off large family meals with grace and ease, and an overarching sense of authority earned through her voracious reading and world travels. She set high standards for entertaining. The fully extended dining room table, covered with a neatly pressed table cloth, laid with polished silver and her best china was anything but a casual call to dinner. I knew it meant it was time to buck up and act like a big girl. I eyed the beautiful bright goldfinch salt and pepper shakers that decorated her spring table and fought the temptation to reach and grab. Oh, how Gram loved her birds.

Granddad presided over the meal, just like he presided over his court as a federal judge. He never dumbed down the table conversations for us. You could learn a lot listening to Granddad. But he expected us to do more than listen. He encouraged us to voice our opinions. Whenever we visited, he always had some new books waiting, never mind that overstuffed bookshelves hugged the walls of every room in their otherwise modest house. Granddad was painfully stiff and serious. But I knew one book that would always get him to smile. Sitting in his lap, I'd listen and wait for the part in the story when the little boy stumbled and fell behind his friends. Together we'd say it by heart: "Wait for William! His shoe came untied." Despite Granddad's tall, sturdy Norwegian frame, and the fact everyone else in town called him "Judge," I never felt small reading a book in his arms. I felt big, even a little important.

The inflated sense I was someone special that magically enveloped me on visits to my grandparents quickly evaporated as I sat squished between my brother and sister and Frisky in the car. It would have been nice to have my Chatty Cathy doll to hold, but she didn't travel with us. No one could have survived me pulling the cord and listening to her babble for the three-hour journey each way. Besides, I was getting a bit too old to be dragging her around.

Instead, I held on to my trusty Whee-lo, a cool magnetic space wheel toy. The bright red plastic wheel was propelled along a thin metal track by magnets built into it. I tilted the track up and down to make the wheel roll on a continuous course. In the car, I could work on improving my Whee-lo timing and speed without annoying anyone.

Or at least, I think I held on to my Whee-lo. But then again, maybe I let go. Which was it? I don't know. I'll never know.

There's just a big blank nothing that stares back at me when I try to remember what happened. Followed by flickers of images that may or may not have been real. One minute I'm feeling small and squished, and the next I'm lying on a stretcher, bloody, cold and scared. I think I see my mother lying in her brown mink coat on a stretcher next to me in the hospital emergency room, but I may have just imagined that to have one last snapshot of her in my mind.

Lying in the hospital crib, I was flooded with questions. Most importantly, I needed to know from my Aunt Mavis, "When will Mom come back?"

Neither she nor anyone else had answers for me, at least none that satisfied my five-year-old worldview. They told me it had been eight days since the accident. Mom had lived eight days. I'd been in the crib eight days. Now Dad and the other grownups had a long list of other important things to do, like plan a funeral in Hayward, the small town in Wisconsin where my mom grew up and where Grampa Oscar and Grama Nellie still lived. And they had to figure out how to get around the doctors who were opposed to transferring my sister and me to a hospital in

Minneapolis. And someone needed to be with my brother, who had escaped the accident with a broken arm, and was already back at home. A slew of relatives took turns sitting next to my crib, offering to read me stories. My mom's Aunt Gladys brought me new crayons. But nothing helped. My sister and I still couldn't get out of bed, let alone go to our mother's funeral nearly 300 miles away.

I can't picture my dad spending time with me in the hospital. That doesn't mean he didn't. Initially, he had his own chest injuries to deal with. Or it might have been the shock, or drugs, or my five-year-old mind shutting stuff out. But I saw him at some point, because I remember we compared chins. Strangely, he had stitches across his chin, just like me. He told me not to worry about my face. He said he insisted that the best surgeon sew my chin, while he took whoever was available. I was a little girl with a beautiful face; he could hide his scar under the stubble of a beard. "Over time, it will fade," he said. Fading isn't the same as hiding, I thought.

Mostly, overwhelmed with sadness and loneliness, I simmered in my own worries. Mom was the one who tied the bow just so perfectly on the pretty package I brought to my friend Laura's birthday party. She was the one who hugged me and said, "Now, go and have a good time." Who was going to do that now? Who would defend me against my brother's teasing? Who was going to bake the cupcakes I needed when it was my turn to bring a kindergarten snack? In heart-pounding, terrifying moments, Mom was the one who gave me a reassuring hug. But she was gone. She wasn't going to be there to see me finish kindergarten and march off to first grade and all the other grades after that. Gone. Not coming back.

The grownups, I decided, had twisted the truth. How do they know she is not coming back? My mom turned standing in a boring checkout line at SuperValu into something fun with stickers and coupon books from her purse. She was good at explaining why people did what they did. She got stuff ready for outings. She fixed my messy mistakes. Even if God wanted her, even if heaven was full of singing angels, I bet she could still figure out how to come back. My mom was that kind of mom.

Gone. Not coming back. That's what Dad said again and again in the weeks that followed, when I woke up from a nightmare and ran into his bedroom looking for her. "She's gone. Your mom isn't coming back."

Sometimes, just to try and prove Dad wrong, I would sneak into what had been Mom's closet. Sitting in the dark quiet for what seemed like hours, I breathed in what I imagined must be the lingering smell of her being, my nose searching for a trace of her perfume.

Eventually, I came out.

Chapter 3

Inside our big, red-brick colonial home on Tarrymore Avenue, everything was still the same. Crisp white curtains detailed with a band of yellow daisies hung in the kitchen. Our coats cluttered the hooks near the back door. The black and white television vied with the brown upright piano for our attention in the family room. Upstairs, my bedroom was across the hall from Kari's. I took bubble baths in the avocado green tub and stood on a stool to reach the sink to brush my teeth in the matching-colored pedestal sink. Everything was the same.

No, nothing was.

Mom wasn't there. Everything from now on would be different. Relatives took turns bringing me to the doctor for follow-up appointments, an act of love that I made miserable. After some three weeks in two different hospitals, I had mastered the act of kicking nurses who came near me; I brought my kicking and screaming tactics with me to the pediatrician's office. I was even more snarly in the dentist's chair with the hairy-handed bald guy who was trying to cover my chipped baby teeth with metal caps: I wanted to bite him.

After a time, the doctors said I could go back to kindergarten. But I was under strict orders not to jump rope at recess. That was hard; all my friends were getting really good at jump rope, and I had to watch because my head was still a little cracked and bruised inside—though you couldn't see it. Kids pointed and wondered out loud about my chin. That made my scar feel bigger than my whole face, and therefore beyond the powers of my imaginary mask. My teacher was really kind and said I didn't need to worry about bringing a snack. She and all the kids had made me get-well cards while I was in the hospital. Still, it was awkward. Nobody knew what to say about me not having a mom anymore.

But at least I was in school. My sister was still at home, stuck in a body cast up to her chest, learning to walk with crutches. Her teacher brought her schoolwork to the house so she could finish fifth grade from a hospital bed at home.

Things were really weird, all right. Dad was now in charge—of everything. As a lawyer and a law professor and ambitious politician he was used to standing up and arguing; people admired him for his keen intellect and well-articulated vision. But being a 36-year-old widower with three kids was never part of that vision. He was now flailing in choppy waters, though he didn't want to let on that he was in over his head. He didn't seem to know what to do when I ran to his bed in the middle of the night looking for Mom. My cries called attention to the cold vacant spot next to him. Snuggles and giggles and pile-on jumping were out. Soon enough, instead of seeking comfort, I stayed in my room and cried quietly to myself.

Many times I wondered why Mom wanted to leave us. I overheard grownups talking about blood clots, but I had no idea what made blood clots or the quick carnage they could inflict. I was left thinking it must have been a decision she made. "God wanted your mom to be with him," Aunt Mavis had said. I ran that over and over in my mind. "Why would Mom choose God over me?" It didn't make sense. Do we just choose to die? On the other hand, if it was God's choice, why would God not want me to have a mom? That didn't seem right either. More likely, horrible things just happen, anytime, anywhere.

Chapter 4

Even in June, the fresh waters of Big Round Lake in Hayward, Wisconsin give swimmers goosebumps. But I ignored the cold and focused on the new-found freedom I had in the water. More than anything, the first summer after the accident, I wanted to be a swimmer. I was determined not to be left in shallow waters, to one day swim out to the raft where big kids played. At first, I walked with my hands on the sandy bottom, kicking my legs, putting my face in the water, lifting it up to call to anyone: "I'm swimming." Anyone could see through the crystal clear waters that my hands touched the bottom. But I pretended otherwise. For a few moments, the joy of splashing, the suspension of reality, the vastness of the lake took me far from the heartache that otherwise pervaded my family life on shore.

As fate had it, my parents purchased the lake-front resort property, Wildwood, with nine other couples on Palm Sunday, a week before the accident. Located a few miles outside my mother's childhood hometown of Hayward, Wildwood was a quirky take on the upwardly mobile Minnesotan's dream of owning a "lake place." Mom and Dad and their group of friends envisioned a communal family camp. Families would rotate staying in different rustic cabins, and share a common lodge, canoes and power boat, and the sandy beach. At night, the couples would sip cocktails by the campfire, while the kids roasted hot dogs and marshmallows and disappeared into the trees playing Kick the Can.

Fishermen know Hayward as the "Musky Capital of the World." A billboard with a big mounted fish with ferocious teeth greets every car driving in to town. Every June, Hayward crowns one promising girl "Musky Festival Queen." Mom never made Musky Queen. She wanted to get out of town, go to college, see the world. But now with her husband's steady job as a law professor and their three kids, she imagined going back to Hayward as a "summer person."

Even without Mom, Dad forged ahead with the Wildwood plan. That wasn't a surprise. To me, Dad was exuberant, a just-get-out-there-and-do-things kind of guy. In winter, he put up side boards around the basketball court and flooded it with a hose to create a home-made ice rink. With bunny blades strapped on my boots, I skated while Mom watched from the kitchen window.

Smart and funny, Dad was determined to chart an exemplary course towards all-American happiness. He met my mom, Arlene Lindholm, the love of his life, at St. Olaf College in Northfield, Minnesota, and they married in 1952. He graduated number one in his class from the University of Minnesota Law School; she taught middle school English. He joined the U.S. Army Judge Advocate General's Corps, and they shipped off to Heidelberg, Germany, with my brother in tow, and my sister in her belly. Mom was so excited; she had always wanted to go to Germany.

Two years later, they returned with toddlers babbling in German to Albert Lea, a small, friendly but unremarkable town in the southeast corner of Minnesota. Dad launched a law practice, Olson and Graven, with a law school buddy.

The young couple bought a ranch-style home with a spacious backyard surrounded by Minnesota's nicest neighbors.

Progressive liberals, Mom and Dad eagerly supported John F. Kennedy for President. Mom insisted on voting early on Election Day 1960, in case I decided to be born early. I waited until the following Sunday, giving her a chance to celebrate. I was born into their family political conversation. Kennedy's victory further ignited their shared passion for politics. Two years later, Dad ran for the U.S. Congress. Mom carefully crafted connections to Democratic women's groups using her genuinely warm social skills to host elegant teas. Dad considered her a prize political asset. The campaign slogan "Go Forward, Go Graven," wasn't just a motto. That's how they lived. Even after he lost the election, Dad put on a happy face and said running for office was "great fun." As a next step, "Go Forward, Go Graven" meant Dad accepted a new position as a law professor at the University of Minnesota. We moved to Minneapolis, a city on the Mississippi River flowing with possibilities.

The family slogan took on a different meaning with the accident. Dad suffered a broken sternum, which made it hard to breathe. Doctors watched him for signs of internal bleeding. "I thought if we could all just get to the hospital things would be all right," he said. But eight days after the accident, when a blood clot from her head injuries abruptly ended Mom's life, Dad was devastated. In shock and pain, he stuck with what had worked before: "Go Forward, Go Graven."

The slogan masked the pain and grief Dad couldn't

express. He wanted everyone around him to embrace the motto and put on the "Go Forward" face. At my mother's funeral, he pulled aside his two brothers, Stanley and Lloyd, and their wives, Mavis and Gina, and insisted on no crying inside the church. "Gina and I tried, for his sake," Mavis told me many years later. "But right after the service we ran outside and cried our eyes out. No crying at a funeral for a beautiful 36-year-old woman and mother of three young kids simply wasn't possible," Mavis said.

In June, not even three months after the accident, we drove to Hayward to spend our first summer at Wildwood. Given our sad circumstances, the other families agreed to relax the camp rules. We could stay in Cabin 8, the most modern cabin, for the whole summer rather than switch cabins every two weeks like the other families were required to do.

That made it easier for Ellen, our "summer girl" and daughter of one of my mom's best friends from Albert Lea. She had a big heart to agree to such an impossible summer job: taking care of three grief-stricken kids and their father. My sister, still in a body cast, needed help getting around the camp, so Dad rented a golf cart. Driving from the cabin to the lodge, my sister and brother were the Pied Pipers of Wildwood, as other kids chased the golf cart wanting rides. Of my two siblings, my sister was the more lighthearted and outgoing. She acted more the ring leader, though she was 13 months younger than our brother. She didn't lose that after Mom died. My brother, on the other hand, was quiet and serious, and became more so without Mom.

I'd say Dad managed logistics better than he managed

his and our emotions, which were far more complicated than the Wildwood plan. Our summers by the lake were also supposed to connect us with my mother's side of the family. Gramps and Grama Nellie still lived in Hayward in the light-gray, two-story house at the end of Main Street where they had raised my mother and her two brothers. But after the accident, visiting them was bittersweet. Sometimes my brother, sister and I spent the night, or if we were lucky, at Gramps' fishing shack on another nearby lake. Atypically, Dad dropped us off and did not join us. Not that he wasn't welcome. It was just too hard, too wrenching, too much of everything for him to spend time with Mom's parents now. It didn't help that they were all Scandinavian, which for them translates to: no one says anything directly; stoic facial expressions are preferred.

But as a lawyer, Dad knew facts were facts. He had been behind the steering wheel on Easter. Everyone said our sliding on black ice into the oncoming lane and hitting another car head-on was "an accident." Even so, who could blame my distraught grandparents for thinking what no one could say aloud: my father killed their daughter? Dad never explicitly framed it that way to me, but his body language—uptight and on guard around his in-laws—read that he harbored guilt. Out at Wildwood, after we kids went to bed, his friends took turns visiting our cabin to stay up with him. They were so worried that his grief and guilt would be too unbearable.

I loved Gramps. Just about everybody in town did too. He was nothing like serious Granddad Henry. No, Gramps was always up to something fun. In the mornings, I'd stand on the toilet seat, watching him lather up the shaving cream and paint his face white with a big bristly brush. He dabbed my face with the brush too. Then he cooked us breakfast, the local Sawyer County news blaring on the radio. Hat on his head, cigar in his mouth, he'd walk out the front door, down the street to the "President's" office at the bank. He ran the Lindholm household, as well as the People's National Bank, with lightness, humor and competence. After a full day, he'd come home and whip up dinner. On Sundays, Gramps made a big deal out of the midday dinner, roasting chicken and mashing potatoes. We ate in the dining room, using Grama Nellie's special pink rose dotted china. He baked delicious pies filled with juicy wild Wisconsin blueberries. I thought he made the desserts special for me, but it turns out Gramps generously baked for many friends and neighbors.

While Gramps was out, the lingering grief was impossible to ignore. It felt like somebody forgot to throw open the living room drapes and let in the morning. I knew it was sunny outside, but inside everyone was sad. Mom's childhood bedroom both beckoned and repelled—a reminder of a young woman turned mother who was no longer there. The connective tissue between the three generations was missing: Mom was not there to explain to her mother how much milk I liked on my cereal, or butter on my toast. Grama Nellie didn't know how I liked my hair parted and that I hated fussy bobby pins. She just kept telling me to pin my bangs back, unable to offer comfort or reassurance that I'd be okay without my mom.

I wished Grama Nellie would stop being so sad. Instead, she was parked on her couch, staring vacantly at the black and white television that hummed perpetually in the corner. Monty Hall and "Let's Make a Deal" numbed the pain in the room. To cheer Grama Nellie, to be near her, my sister and I sat on the living room floor in front of the TV and played jacks, countless games of jacks. We became excellent, moving quickly to "tensies," "double bounces" and "around the world." Where was the grandmother who loved to go downtown to Rivkins and shop for dresses? When we became restless, Grama Nellie sent us downtown on our own. Invariably, even without Grama Nellie, the saleswomen in this small-town store knew us. "Arlene's daughters," they whispered to each other. I was proud to be Arlene's daughter. But why did they have to whisper?

Sometimes during the day, I'd wander upstairs to explore Mom's childhood bedroom. The room had become a guest room when she moved out years ago, but it couldn't hurt to open dresser drawers or rummage through the closet for something she might have left. But at night, sleeping in her old room was out of the question. What if her ghost appeared? Gramps understood; he let me sleep in the other bedroom across the hall.

The truth is we all relied on Gramps to make things lighter after Mom died. He never disappointed, though he was just as devastated as anyone at the loss of his darling "Tweeps." At just the right time, he would show up to take us out for ice cream. Or he'd call and say, "Come on down to the bank. I'll give you a dime to blow on fudge or rock candy at Tremblay's," the homemade candy store on Main Street.

Now, more than ever, Grama Nellie counted on Gramps for her every need and whim. He doted on her, despite her constant complaining about her worsening arthritis. He encouraged her to get her hair done, go play bridge with her friends. When I told Dad about Grama Nellie being so sad, he said: "Don't worry. She's always been difficult. Even your Mom thought she was difficult." I worried anyway. I grew up thinking I never wanted to be like Grama Nellie, broken by grief and in constant pain. I couldn't know, or even begin to imagine then, what it would be like to have your only daughter stolen so young, so quickly. She may not have been likable, but she was honest, perhaps brave. She never covered her face; she let her pain and tears show.

When Dad picked us up to go back out to Wildwood, Gramps would not let us leave until we joined him in his favorite cheer: "Minny, skinny a-po-lis, fat St. Paul, Hayward Wisconsin beats them all." He was right in many ways. Wildwood was where we as a family began our healing. Surrounded by families with kids of all ages, we were thrust back into childhood. We played ping pong, pool and board games in the lodge. I learned to read that summer, beginning with the proverbial Dick and Jane see Spot run. By the end of August, thanks to Ellen, I was a real swimmer.

Yet when I stopped kicking and splashing and plopped on the beach, sadness and loneliness returned. I couldn't just play. Other moms sat in their bathing suits on lawn chairs watching their kids splash in the lake, or play in the sand. Occasionally one yelled "cut it out" at the kids who got too rowdy. I held my shovel and unenthusiastically dug sand. I could take all day to fill one bucket and no one would notice. If I built an amazing sand castle and then stomped it back to nothing, who would care? Part of me stopped playing that summer.

For all the healing at Wildwood, we never established a family ritual of tending Mom's grave at Greenwood Cemetery, bringing her flowers or offering a prayer. There she was, buried just a few miles from Wildwood, but Dad didn't take us. He made it clear he did not believe in sitting around and crying about things. Even before Mom died, Dad answered my tantrum moments with "I'll give you a count of three to stop crying. Or, on three, I'll give you something to cry about." I had something important to cry about, but I knew what he would say if I started. I learned to shut down the tears—and quickly. Close your eyes, shut your mouth, grit your teeth and push the welling up in your throat right back down where it came from. Swallow. Repeat.

"Go Forward, Go Graven."

Before summer ended, Dad had found a new housekeeper to help us at home in Minneapolis. Now an eager reader, I was excited to start first grade and jump rope at recess.

Chapter 5

Just after we returned home from Wildwood, Marge blew in from Dawson, a farm town 150 miles due west of Minneapolis, thanks to an ad my dad placed in a Lutheran magazine. Dad had the basement fixed up into an efficiency apartment. Marge, a divorced mother of two grown girls, would cook, clean and get us off to school, but live in her own space downstairs. Heavy set, wearing no makeup and plain house dresses, Marge wasn't polished and "spit spot" like Mary Poppins. She couldn't sing, or play guitar like Maria in *The Sound of Music*. But Marge was perfect: warm and practical.

I hesitated to open the door to the basement stairs. I wasn't sure of the new rules about going down with Marge living there. But I was curious, so I'd sometimes tiptoe down on Saturday mornings. Once, I found Marge giving herself a home perm. Her head was covered in prickly rollers and the room smelled of stinky goo. Luckily, Marge wasn't much of a stickler for rules and she didn't mind me watching. In time, I'd head to the basement without fear, climb into Marge's lap, lay against her soft, abundant chest and fall asleep watching television with her.

Like most farm women, Marge cooked and baked like nobody's business, happy to be feeding love to those who needed it. She got me ready for my first day of first grade, was waiting when I came home for lunch, and then again after school. Marge's positive steadiness got us through the next months.

But Marge couldn't possibly replace Mom when it came

to decorating and organizing for Christmas. The lovely blue velvet dress I wore last Christmas and in the family holiday card surely wouldn't fit now. Anyway, Dad said he wasn't doing Christmas cards anymore. The thought of the holidays coming up without Mom sent Dad into planning mode. Stay at home and feel the agonizing loneliness and ineptitude of pulling off a joyous Christmas morning without the person who did all the decorating, baking, shopping and wrapping? Or get out of town? Dad decided we should spend Christmas with Gram and Granddad in San Antonio, Texas, where Granddad held court. Then we'd fly to Mexico for a vacation.

The first Christmas without Mom would have been heavy, sad, no matter where we were. But there seemed no escaping the gaping hole when my brother got his hand slammed in the car door on the way to the church nativity pageant. Instead of us singing "Away in the Manger" together, Dad and my brother spent Christmas Eve in a San Antonio hospital emergency room getting Mark's finger stitched up. Gram said she was sure everything would be fine. But given what happened at Easter, I wasn't reassured. I was afraid to go to sleep until they came home. The next morning, Dad said we were still on schedule, still good to go to Mexico.

On landing in Mexico City, my sister developed an ear ache. In the hotel, she complained again that her ears hurt. Dad said it was probably from the altitude change. It would go away. "Take a bath," he instructed. She bathed, but it didn't help. "You didn't stay in long enough," he replied. Being eleven and now the oldest female in the family, she tried to be the mom in the family in many ways.

She took it on herself to watch out for me. But when her ears hurt and Dad's remedy was "take a bath," I guessed she missed Mom too.

The next day, Dad was keen to take us sightseeing. A history buff, he was dying to see the newly opened National Museum of Archeology in Mexico City that had been highly reviewed. On entering the museum, I stomped my feet and refused to walk beyond the lobby. My wailing, crying, not budging, embarrassed my father and siblings. But what sent them over the edge was my explanation: "Everything is cracked."

Dad got mad. It was an *archeology* museum, he said. Things were supposed to be cracked. He told me to stay put in the lobby. Off they went to take in fascinating Mexican artifacts. I sat there, overwhelmed by the hugeness of the place. Mostly, I was profoundly sad. Why did we need to look at old, broken things?

Our family was cracked, more than cracked. It was broken with grief. A grief so profound nobody could talk about it. This was no way to live, I pouted.

Sunnier days at the beach in Puerto Vallarta would no doubt lift everyone's spirits. I was excited to swim in warmer waters, expecting to taste the freedom I had at the lake last summer. But it was different. The water was salty. The waves rolled in but then pulled me out deeper, further than I was prepared to go. The water was scary; my heart pounded.

My siblings laughed at my stricken face. Oceans have salt water, they teased. I just knew that Mom would have prepared me. She would make sure I didn't get sucked out too far. What else were they not telling me? Dad tried to explain about tides, how they ebb and flow with the moon. What else was he not telling me?

After ringing in the new year, 1967, in Mexico, it was time to return home to hug Marge and face the rest of the bitter cold Minnesota winter. I was excited to show off my new floppy pink beach hat and multicolored serape. Forever after, however, my family never missed a chance to tease me about my first international meltdown. Perhaps I shouldn't have been quite so loud. But once you've screamed for all of Mexico to hear, you can't take it back. Once you say your truth, there is no going back. Cracked artifacts and scary tides left indelible marks on me.

My dramatic moments put me on a slow but assured collision course with my dad. "You'll win an Oscar someday," he predicted. He, by contrast, did not stomp and cry. He pushed on, wishing uncomfortable moments away or behind him. He put his face into the wind. That's what ice sailors do. Dad discovered the thrill of ice sailing as a teenager in Clear Lake, Iowa. Skippering a sailboat on metal runners, bundled up head to toe, whipping across a frozen lake at 50 to 60 miles an hour requires fortitude, courage, and a little stupidity; there's no time to process emotions. Defying frigid windchill factors and frostbite is part of the fun. For years, he dared his two younger brothers to ride along. Later, in Albert Lea, he dragged my brother along. None of them came to share his enthusiasm for the sport, so he gave it up before he had a chance to cajole me.

But he never let his passion for messing around in boats in other seasons slip. He paddled canoes down the Shell Rock, Saint Croix and Namekagon Rivers. He sailed small

Sunfish on the lakes in Minneapolis and up at Wildwood. On boats, he found a curious mix of emotional balance and new energy. So while it was easy for me to fault Dad for failing to deal with our collective and individual grief, I know his fun-loving side also contributed to our survival. During our many summers at Wildwood, Dad jumped off the raft with us kids, producing a whale-like splash. He taught me how to paddle the green canoe, a gift from Granddad, with a J stroke. His bulky six-foot-plus frame barely left enough room for another crew member on the little red Sunfish, unless that passenger was me. He was grinningly satisfied, wind at his face, driving a speedboat, pulling up water skiers. He elevated pontoon boat rides to new excitement levels, cutting the motor to fish for walleye at just the right (self-proclaimed!) fishing spot.

Dad's favorite song, one he learned as a boy scout and sang in the wee hours of the morning in the newsroom at St. Olaf College, involved a famous ship: The Titanic. He sang it so much, I learned it by heart. The camp song version we sang in the car on trips to visit relatives went like this:

Oh, they built the ship Titanic
To sail the ocean blue.
And they thought they'd built a ship
That the water could never go through.
It was on its maiden trip
That an iceberg hit the ship.
It was sad when the great ship went down.

Chorus:
It was sad, oh so sad.
It was sad, oh so sad.
It was sad when the great ship went down
To the bottom of the sea ea ea ea...
Husband and wives, little children lost their lives
It was sad when the great ship went down.

The builders of the luxurious ocean liner said the Titanic could never sink. But it did. My dad may have been tough, but in truth, he was sinking. His friends warned him. They pleaded with him. "Don't do it. It's too soon," they said. But adrift without a partner, adrift with three kids, awash in unrelenting grief, my father, the ship that the water would never get through, went and did it anyway. He grabbed the first life raft.

One year, three months and twenty days after Mom died, Dad remarried.

Chapter 6

Just like I didn't know about tides, I didn't know my Dad was dating. Actually, I didn't know what dating was. I thought he just went to join friends for dinner like he and Mom used to do. Dad's friends invited him to small gatherings to keep up his spirits. But one couple from our church took it up a notch and decided to play matchmaker. They asked Dad to dinner and introduced him to Joan, a widow in her mid-thirties who also had three kids, who had just moved back to Minneapolis from New Jersey. She was attractive, energetic, and a graduate of St. Olaf College. He was a widower, and also a graduate of St. Olaf. On the surface, all of Norway's kings and patron saints couldn't have put together a better match of Norwegian traditions and Lutheran faith. After knowing Joan for only ten days, Dad proposed.

Friends and family were not on board with Dad's plan or choice of second wife. Not long after he proposed, Dad introduced Joan to Lillian and Howard, dear friends from his St. Olaf days. Lil, a close friend of my mother, thought Joan was cold and uncaring and not a good match for him —or for us kids. Lil was so upset after Dad and Joan left that she went to bed and cried through the night.

My sister pleaded with Dad not to marry Joan. She tried to convince him that we didn't need a new mother, that we could get along fine without one. After all, we had Marge. But Dad wasn't listening or thinking clearly. Which may explain why he and my brother went shopping for boats. While ultimately Dad decided against buying a new boat, he did choose a new wife for himself and a mother for us.

Only six then, I don't remember the wedding, or Dad and Joan leaving for a honeymoon. But their return felt like one of those tornadoes that comes up and sends people scrambling to the basement, only it wasn't a school drill. All at once, this woman and her three kids, ages 6, 4, and 2, moved into our house.

She wanted us to call her Mom. Dad said we could call her Joan or Mom. My brother and sister refused to call her Mom. I didn't know what to do. What I called her failed to address the questions that raced through my head. If we called Joan "Mom," what did that mean about our real Mom? For sure, she wouldn't come back if I was calling somebody else "Mom," which was still my deepest secret wish. And what if we didn't like Joan, or she didn't act like a mom?

New Mom did not want a live-in housekeeper. Joan let Marge go. Marge translated that gently for me. She said she was moving on to care for another family who needed her. She would still care about me, and I could even visit sometimes. She was leaving, not dying. I wasn't sure that was possible. In a jiffy, the basement apartment was emptied. That made me mad at my dad. How could he have agreed to send Marge away? I still needed Marge. We all needed her love and talents in the kitchen. I missed her making homemade bread and donuts, the delicious smells soothed and calmed me. Marge made me feel special: she always gave me the first sugary donut ball to taste test.

In addition to her three kids, Joan brought in an interior decorator and enough money to make over our five-bedroom house in *her* style. My mom's touches disappeared. Ditto for anything introduced by Marge. On the bright side, I lucked into a beautiful new bedroom suite. The twin beds and two new dressers were painted bright yellow with popping lime green and orange trim lines. Add in the new drapes and matching lamps, and I could boast of a perfectly decorated, slightly groovy girl's room. On the downside, I had to share it with a new younger stepsister who arrived with the furniture.

"Peanut" was not the little girl's real name, but that's what everyone called her. She was four, two years younger than me, but she seemed even smaller than her age. She was shy, quiet and still a thumb sucker when we became roommates. Peanut and I had nothing in common. She was born in New Jersey. I had never been to New Jersey. I probably wasn't very nice to her, though I don't remember being particularly mean either. Peanut cried in her bed at night, probably because her whole life had just been upended: new city, new house, new dad, new siblings. I used to cry a lot in my bed, too. But now that I was the "older sister," I was outwardly unsympathetic. When the lights were turned off and Peanut lay sniffling, I told her to go to sleep. I wanted Peanut to cover herself in a blanket, to become invisible.

But I couldn't make Peanut's older brother invisible. He was only two months older than me, so we were assigned the same second-grade classroom at Walter Hines Page Elementary School. All three of Joan's kids used the Graven last name at school, though legally my father never adopted them and they never officially changed their last names. Suddenly, at school I had a "twin." How else could

40

there be two Graven kids in the same grade? Only I never developed a twin kinship with him. We did not look alike, talk alike, or share any friends. He was from New Jersey; I was from Minnesota. We didn't even share a birthday. I never wanted to be on his dodgeball team at recess. My "twin" shared a room with his blonde baby brother, who was barely two years old when our two families merged. This youngest addition to our mixed family was cute, somewhat mischievous, but basically not a factor in my day-to-day world.

Mark and Kari kept their same bedrooms, much as Mom had left them. Somehow becoming teenagers gave them a pass to slip off into their own worlds at junior high school and shut their bedroom doors at home. Before long, without anyone being aware of the implications, the family configuration shifted. Instead of three kids, I was lumped with the younger step-siblings in an awkward foursome. I was no longer the baby, or the youngest. I ranked in the murky middle, which was just the worst position of all.

The little kids were always getting stuck with a string of babysitters, or shuttled off to stay with Joan's many aunts. One of those aunts taught Norwegian language lessons, so once a week after school, I went to Tante's house. I liked the new great-aunt, reading Norwegian stories, practicing saying grace in Norwegian: "*I Jesus navn gaar vi til bords, aa spise, drikke par ditt ord.*" I felt proud that at Christmas, I could handle the classic carol in Norwegian: "*Jeg er saa glad hver julekveld.*" And I liked the homemade treats Tante prepared. Sometimes, I felt a little guilty that I liked this new after-school activity, which was becoming another thing differentiating me from my brother and sister, who never took Norwegian lessons.

At school, kids often made fun of us; we were the local "Brady Bunch," a popular TV series. The sitcom, starring Robert Reed and Florence Henderson, portrayed two families, joined through marriage, on a complicated but happy adventure of learning to get along. I watched the show, and wished we had an "Alice," the wise, funny housekeeper who smoothed the merger's rough edges. It made me really miss my Marge.

Being modern, and oh so busy with six kids, New Mom had no time to bake bread or make donuts. Worse, she loved the convenience of TV dinners. She packed the second freezer in the basement with those time-saving, tinfoil-covered wonders. New Mom must have cooked, but nothing she made came close to comfort food. Dad didn't seem to notice. A new wife and six kids under one roof called for a shift in perspective on what was an acceptable daily routine, he said. Moving forward, he argued, wasn't always easy: "Give it time. Wait and see." Yes, my brother and sister were acting like rebellious teenagers under New Mom's rule. No, he wasn't going to do anything about her rules or their behavior. "Give it time."

Meanwhile, a rare opening in the Minnesota political landscape reignited Dad's political ambitions. Politically, it was now or never for him to run for the Democratic nomination for Governor of Minnesota. Just days after my ninth birthday, in November 1969, he announced his candidacy. A family campaign photo shows me with Joan's kids in the front row, with Mark and Kari next to Dad in the back and Joan beside him. Everyone is trying so hard to smile.

And then, for all practical purposes, Dad disappeared, swept into the excitement of the campaign trail. He canvassed the state, delivered speeches, pleaded for endorsements, raised money. He looked so smart, so confident in his black and white photo on the campaign poster that boldly proclaimed: "Graven's Got It."

At first, I thought it was exciting to see our last name on yard signs popping up on lawns throughout the neighborhood. But then some pranksters piled the signs back on our front doorstep, and it didn't seem so great having Dad as a candidate. I thought I played the piano well in the few solo seconds I had during the commercial featuring the candidate at home with the family. That is until kids at school mocked me after it ran on TV. They tortured me by humming "Raindrops Keep Falling on My Head" over and over until my face turned apple red. That kind of local fame stunk. Worse, there was no place to hide.

The campaign acknowledged that Joan was Dad's second wife, and made it sound like our newly combined family was a happy coming together of two people who had lost their first spouses, one in a tragic car accident and the other from a sudden heart attack, and were on their way to sunnier days ahead.

When Dad was home, the house was even crazier. I thought we could have really used Marge; maybe Dad could bring her back. But it might have been too much even for her—people coming in and out at all hours for staff meetings or heated strategy sessions. Sometimes I hung out with the campaign staff in the kitchen, playing a quick game or two of cribbage, while they waited for Dad to prepare for the next campaign event. Always, the phone rang off the hook. Eventually, it became so chaotic the campaign installed a second home phone line, unheard of in most households then, so the six kids could call friends from a different line, and not mix our lives with the campaign.

In the midst of it all, in early February 1970, Granddad Henry died of a brain aneurysm. That was after he had had one lung removed that was full of cancer. Granddad had smoked two packs of Camels a day for decades, ignoring Gram's warnings, so in a way, it was a miracle he made it to 76. There was a big funeral in Greene. Dad quit smoking cigarettes then and there. He switched to a pipe, saying it wasn't bad for you because pipe smokers don't inhale.

Granddad left me, nine years old, with many books with my name and the date scribbled on the first page, and a love of reading. I looked at all the books in their house and tried to grasp how one man absorbed so much knowledge. I hoped there was a big library for him in heaven. But once again, as a family, we didn't sit with the loss, or ponder what it meant that he took so much wisdom with him. There was a campaign to catch. The Graven for Governor campaign moved towards the convention—just a few short months away.

I didn't get to the Democratic convention held in Duluth in August. Six kids were too much to handle, so, as usual, I got stuck with the younger bunch with a babysitter at Wildwood. Maybe it was for the best. I didn't have to see the look on my Dad's face when after all his time and effort he lost the nomination to Wendell Anderson. Two Minnesota political legends, Hubert Humphrey and Walter Mondale, tried to persuade Dad to accept the number two spot on the ticket. He thought hard about it, but decided no. The decision ended his political career. Anderson rode on to a general election victory in November, which had lots of friends and supporters wondering if Dad had made the right call. But Dad insisted that he hadn't been excited about being number two.

But once again, there was more going on than Dad let on. At home, his second marriage was unraveling. Dad had told his brother Stan before the campaign that he had doubts whether his marriage to Joan would last. She was erratic, irrational at times, even manipulative, Dad confided to his brother. But both Dad and Joan were politically ambitious, so they put their problems aside for Dad to pursue elected office.

After the convention, they tried to return to a normal family routine. But too much had happened between them during the campaign. There were stories of Joan's multiple flirtations, quite possibly affairs, that hurt my dad and put staffers in an awkward position. Were the stories true? I had no idea what to believe. Outwardly, Joan played the candidate's wife role well, appearing confident and cheerful. But if there are any cracks in a relationship, a full-on political campaign will expose them. Dad might have compromised and stayed with Joan to become governor, but not lieutenant governor. Politically defeated, Dad turned to getting out of an unhappy marriage.

Dad hid his political and marital problems from me. I did not know the end of our Brady Bunch days was near. Sure, Dad and Joan disagreed over how to discipline my brother and sister, who were teenagers exerting "don't tell me what to do" rights. I thought that was normal family

45

stuff. To me, the house seemed so much less hectic now that it wasn't campaign central.

And I had other big, exciting news to report. A new family moved in across the alley behind us. Their oldest daughter, Kristi, was smart and fun. She quickly became my new best friend; we were inseparable in and out of fifth grade. I liked my teacher. He had been my sister's teacher at the time of the car accident, the one who brought her homework to the house, so he knew our family's messed up history. At school, he started the morning meeting off with a news broadcast, using a new and wildly expensive "video" camera to tape us reading stories plucked from the *Minneapolis Tribune*. Ambitious, I aimed to become the class' top news broadcaster. Before bed, I practiced my news voice over and over until I sounded professional. So, wrapped up in having a new best friend and becoming a rising news star, I didn't see the marriage crash coming.

When it did, it wasn't pretty. Though nobody died this time, I was scared to see my family ripped apart on biological lines. I knew Joan's kids weren't my *real* siblings, but I had spent more time lately with them than with my biological siblings, so going back to the original boundaries was confusing. What makes someone your brother or sister?

At the other end of the upstairs hall, Dad's voice grew louder and louder. Joan was arguing and crying and screaming like crazy. At around midnight, my brother burst into my bedroom and shook me. "Grab some clothes; we're leaving," he whispered. No, Peanut was definitely not coming. My brother hurried me downstairs. As we headed out the backdoor to the car, Joan grabbed my arm and pulled me toward her crying: "Don't take Kathy. Don't take Kathy."

Why does she want me? In that moment of her hysteria and my racing heart, I knew I had to follow my brother, to my *real* family waiting in the car. I didn't love Joan or her kids enough to think—even for a second—that I wouldn't go. It felt weird that she even thought to try to separate us. Why want me and not my brother and sister? What did I do?

Chapter 7

It was after midnight when Pastor Bill opened the door and invited us in—three shaking kids and a desperate father. Dad must have called ahead, as Pastor Bill seemed to be expecting us. Inside his living room, I couldn't stop trembling. Losing two mothers in less than five years, both in April, was beyond my imagination. And now we were fleeing to the minister's house in the middle of the night, and there was no way I was going with my class to the Minnesota Twin's game on Saturday. Pastor Bill offered me a small glass of red wine. I drank it. My throat burned. His wife and four kids were asleep upstairs, so Pastor Bill quietly rounded up extra blankets and pillows and laid me down to sleep on the couch.

That we landed at his house was not because my Dad was deeply religious or anything. Pastor Bill had been there for Dad after Mom died. He was the closest person to a counselor or therapist Dad ever had. They became friends; Bill turned to Dad for career advice. To me, Pastor Bill was warm and kind, never pushy or dogmatic. You could tell he cared about people, the way he stayed with them, sitting, listening, praying with them and for them. Soft spoken, he boiled down all the religious jargon to the plausible proposition that God's grace was a gift available for anyone at any time. Pastor Bill's presence that night did more to reassure my soul than Luther's small blue catechism book, years of Sunday school and confirmation classes combined ever did.

More practically, Pastor Bill calmed my father down.

Together they worked out a plan. The next afternoon, we moved over to another family friend's house near downtown Minneapolis. We would stay there until Dad could find us a temporary apartment. Displaced from our house, distanced from our neighborhood and friends, Dad patched together arrangements. He leased an apartment in a suburb called Edina, which wasn't convenient to our school, but it would have to do. Things, he finally admitted, just got complicated.

With only a few clothes that we are able to stuff into bags during a negotiated time when *they* were out of the house, life in "the apartment" was stark. Showing new fortitude and determination, or perhaps tapping into his espoused "Go Forward Go Graven" spirit, Dad devised logistics for getting us to our schools, kept his teaching at the University of Minnesota going, all while he navigated legal and financial hurdles. Dad wasn't easily embarrassed, but running out of options, he no doubt tasted humility when he phoned his mother in Iowa and asked if she could come up and help us set up our temporary living space.

Gram, recently widowed, arrived on a mission and stuck to business. In the years after Granddad retired as a federal judge, they had traveled to new cities, from New York to San Juan, Puerto Rico, to San Antonio where he held temporary court assignments. Gram was a pro at setting up an apartment and running a household anywhere. She came in with a steady confidence that I was hungry for. We shopped together at the Southdale Mall for sheets and towels, and basic pots and pans and dishes for the kitchen. Nothing fancy: enough to get by, to get through, until we moved back into our house. I knew we were making it up as we went. But at least Gram was there.

In the beige, bare-bones apartment kitchen, I learned that while the living quarters might be temporary, the new roles we were about to assume were not. "Girls," Gram said matter-of-factly, "you are now going to have to learn to cook." My sister and I accepted our duties—without a whimper. Gram showed us how to brown pork chops in the skillet before baking them in the oven at 375 degrees Fahrenheit for an hour. She demonstrated dipping chicken in buttermilk, then rolling the pieces in bread crumbs for another easy-to-bake success. The key, she said, was to "always keep some buttermilk in the refrigerator," to make biscuits, or pancakes or salad dressing. She liked to drink buttermilk straight, but I couldn't handle that. We went on to wrapping potatoes in tinfoil and having a bit of fun stabbing them with a fork so that the steam could escape. When in doubt, Gram said, look it up in *The Joy of Cooking*. Oh, and always set the table with placemats and napkins; family upheaval was no reason not to set a nice table. Diligently, we filled the void of no-mother-in-the-kitchen. My sister was 16 years old; I was 11.

Any chance of salvaging a steadier childhood slipped away in those few months at the apartment. Driving to school, the radio blared: "Our house is a very very very fine house," the hit song by Crosby, Stills, Nash and Young. Hearing the song over and over made me long for my old room. Kenny Loggins' song "House at Pooh Corner," an homage to my childhood literary hero Winnie the Pooh, also pushed me to tears. There was something about a lost bear needing help to find his way back home that resonated deeply.

Sometimes my wanderings were scarier than being lost in a creepy forest. Like the time I went to Kristi's house after school to wait for my sister to pick me up. As we walked in through the front door, Kristi's mom, Phyllis, met us with her hands in the air, and pushed us back outside on to the steps. "I am so sorry. But it's not a good time for you to come in," she said softly. "Joan is here. She's crying and very upset." Kristi and I agreed it was lucky we hadn't gone to the back door like we normally did. Seeing Joan—that would have been beyond awkward. Would she have grabbed me again, like she did when we left, maybe even try to kidnap me? What would I say to her? I had to avoid her. Kristi and I ran back up the street to wait for my sister at the school.

During the separation, Dad said besides a divorce, the only thing non-negotiable for him was returning to our brick house on Tarrymore. He wanted the neighborhood, the house, the life he had started with Mom. To get it back, he would have to buy Joan out. He plunged into debt for this, a debt that would take him years to dig out from under.

When we finally moved home some six months later, I was surprised that my groovy yellow bedroom furniture was still there. Miraculously, my bedroom was completely intact. I say miraculously, because while we lived in the apartment, I was privy to the inner family circle talk. Or maybe I just started listening and heard what the others had been experiencing all along: Joan was the evil stepmother. She was the manipulative, crazy, out-of-control woman who had brought us to the brink. She was, by my dad's admission, his life's "biggest failure." With those images swirling, I expected to return to a room pillaged and burned. But instead, it was all there. Except Peanut.

Dad, the sole captain of our family ship, felt relieved to be home again. He adopted a new mantra: "Upward and Onward," with his unconventional choice of starting the phrase with upward, instead of onward. I never doubted that he loved us three kids deeply. He proclaimed it loudly and often. He said it even better with big, embracing bear hugs. Still, as a single dad, he had a full plate of heavy responsibilities. When it came to processing our mounting losses, to understanding our emotional wounds and needs, our ship was rudderless. I was on my own for my emotional needs, a scary and lonely place. No one helped me sort through what was going on, so I had no way to judge whether my feelings were normal, weird or extreme.

For Dad, it was a matter of picking up where we had left off. Outside on the basketball court, we played endless family games of HORSE, where each person has to shoot the ball from the prior person's spot. If you miss, you get a letter. You are out of the game when you spell HORSE. My granny shot, two-handed lifting the ball between my legs, was my only shot, so I never tasted basketball victory. Inside, we played four-handed Pinochle or Hearts, with me winning more than losing. He invited uncles, aunts and cousins to our house for Thanksgiving and Christmas dinners. My sister and I cooked.

In a short time, I became the master of the kitchen. Just after my 13th birthday, I cooked my first full Thanksgiving dinner for the extended family. I got up at 6:00 a.m. and stuffed the 20-pound bird. I woke my father an hour later to help me lift it into the oven above the stove; I couldn't reach it by myself. Keeping up my grandmother's and mother's standards, I set the table with a turquoise linen tablecloth, Mom's Lenox dishes and sterling silver. I placed the bread and butter plate above the fork, and the salad fork to the left of the dinner fork. I never dared wonder out loud whether this role was reasonable or not. Instead, I fumed inside when the relatives showed up with a store-bought pumpkin pie.

My brother graduated from high school and flew east to college in Massachusetts. At the time, Amherst seemed very far away, and indeed it was far enough that he would only come home once between semesters at Christmas. He called and talked to my Dad regularly, but I didn't have much direct contact with him. A year later, I cried when my sister graduated and headed to St. Olaf College. But Northfield wasn't too far away, I consoled myself, and she could come home more often than my brother.

With their departures, I was now in charge of all the cooking and household chores. As a 13-year-old eighth grader, I came home from school, did my homework, and prepared supper. On Monday nights, Dad and I had a standing tennis match with family friends. On weekends, we went grocery shopping—the timing of which depended on whether the Minnesota Gophers or the Minnesota Vikings were playing football at home or away. If I was sick, I stayed home alone from school. It was lonely and scary, but doable. It wasn't what other kids I knew did, but then again, most of the time I had my father, all to myself.

Financially, these were tough times, and they left an indelible mark on me. I hated seeing my father stress about making interest payments, living on the edge of the possible one minute, but inexplicably it seemed, splurging at other times. When he had to travel for work, he often took me, sometimes to fun places like Los Angeles and Puerto Rico and even Vail, Colorado where he was "of counsel" to developers. I loved traveling with him, and skiing together in Vail is one of my favorite memories. Maybe those weren't exactly splurges; maybe he didn't know what else to do with me.

Nevertheless, when it came to money, I vowed never to become vulnerable to such volatility. I had a savings account at Farmers and Mechanics Savings Bank which I made regular deposits to through a school program. I once put a check from Gramps into my piggy bank so I could have it—for emergency purposes. Months later, Gramps called my dad to ask why the check hadn't cleared. I retrieved the crumpled check and got a lesson in the differences between checks and cash.

Dad calculated the only way he could get out from under the divorce debt and manage college tuition payments was to leave law school teaching and return to private law practice. In the meantime, needing cash right away, Dad decided that it was time to sell his share of Wildwood. I needed and wanted Wildwood more than our big five-bedroom house. But Dad clung to the house and let Wildwood and our summers in Hayward go.

The failed second marriage shook Dad's confidence—especially when it came to women. As if to atone, Dad pledged: "I will not remarry as long as Kathy is still in the house." It was too soon for me to be thinking about specific colleges. But not too soon for me to begin dreaming about where else I might live someday. Somewhere far away sounded nice; I liked studying history and foreign languages. Dad kept his pledge, but he never said anything about not dating.

He waited until after launching my siblings off to college, and then slowly waded back into the dating world, creating some bewildering, awkward moments for me. Sometimes on weekend nights, he wouldn't return home until the early hours of the morning, leaving me alone all night in the house with our dog for security. At breakfast, he would skirt the issue of why he came home at 6:00 a.m. by muttering "I fell asleep on her couch." I believed him. Until once I got invited to his date's house for dinner. I walked into her living room, saw her very small, barely-a-love-seat of a couch, and my jaw dropped. There was no way my towering father slept there.

Even as he moved on, Dad only talked about his second wife in the context of his biggest failure. "Everyone's entitled to fail," he professed. "Never trust anyone who has never failed." But that was as far as he would go emotionally. There was never a real apology, a taking responsibility for bad decisions, or an emotional debrief on what the fiasco had meant to us kids.

We three kids took our cues from him. Second wife came and went. Completely different circumstances from my own mother's death, but with the same outcome for me: another mother gone. She shared one thing in common with my biological mother: There was never an open window to talk about her with Dad.

I never saw his second wife or her kids again. Friends reported that soon after the divorce, in a matter of weeks, she remarried and moved to Ohio. Not wanting to upset my dad further, I never told him about the rumors swirling at school; kids wondering out loud on the playground what happened to my "twin" and the other two kids. My brother, sister and I all learned to shut up about the ordeal, even amongst ourselves. For my dad, that marriage was a four-year period best erased from the family story and memory.

But that experience marked us all, and the truth is that erasing is not the same as deleting. Erase a sentence written in pencil, and later you can still find the contours of the words, the imprint of the force of the pencil on the paper. The words, like memories, may be faint, but if you look closely they are still there. Joan left deep emotional scars on my older siblings. They knew our mother better than I did; they had more memories of her with which to compare Joan. They were teenagers with untreated grief, locked in a battle with a stepmother who saw them as problems. She wished they would go away. For whatever reason, I never experienced Joan wishing I would go away. I complained about her terrible TV dinners, but that didn't get under her skin enough for her not to like me. The emotional damage she inflicted on my family was not inflicted evenly. Joan never gave me reason to hate her, but I did hate the divisions she left us with.

After the divorce, I was complicit in the code of silence that enveloped us. I cringed when Joan's name was mentioned. I could not bring myself to even refer to her as a stepmother. In time, I told a few close friends this part of my family's story. When I did, I simply called her my father's second wife. I learned from Dad's failed second marriage that quick fixes can be expensive, financially and emotionally. By marrying Joan, Dad denied us the time and room to grieve our biological mom. After the divorce, there was no way to go back and reclaim that crucial emotional piece. We all had new urgent circumstances to navigate, new challenges to get through.

This is how layers form.

Chapter 8

A single working parent again, Dad needed somewhere to park me during summers. I tried a Camp Fire Girl's camp in northern Minnesota the first summer. It was a fiasco. For starters, Dad overslept on departure day, so I missed the camp bus. After being scolded by my friend's mother for being late, we sped north to catch the ride. Just as we flagged the bus down on the highway, our car ran out of gas. Simultaneously relieved and anxious, I hopped on the bus, leaving my Dad on the side of the road. While my siblings loved summer camp, I couldn't wait to put frigid Lake Trelipe, the giant mosquitos, dank cabins and whiny fellow campers behind me.

Camp arts and crafts paled to what my Gram offered in Iowa. I much preferred the adventure of heading south on a Greyhound bus bound for Mason City. Gram would meet me there with a picnic lunch and together we'd drive to Greene. Sometimes, I had Gram to myself; other times, a heap of cousins were there too. Gram had a limit of six grandkids at one time. That was a firm six.

Regardless of who and how many were there, Gram packed each day with purposeful activities: We made trips downtown to Dralle's Department Store for groceries and fabric, and always stopped at the Greene Public Library. Back at the house, we baked bread and pies, or hammered together new creations in the garage. She sent us outside to her vegetable garden to pick tomatoes and beans for supper. Then every afternoon, around 4.00 p.m., we drove to the Greene swimming pool so Gram could get in her daily swim. For the ride home, Gram laid out a plastic sheet so our wet bums wouldn't spoil the car seats. Intent on avoiding "musses," and devoted to teaching life skills, Gram posted our chore schedule on the refrigerator: dish wash and dry, table set and clear, garbage takeout. No one shrugged chores.

Gram approached sewing in the same orderly way. She had been sewing her whole life. She learned from her mother, Elizabeth Davis, who had five daughters and one son and sewed to keep her children clothed. They loved discussing fabrics and colors and whipping up a new dress for a special occasion, if the tight family budget permitted. For Gram, sewing could be both practical and dreamy.

So it was in Greene, in the unlikeliest of nothing-fancy-or-extraordinary places in small-town Iowa, I learned to thread a sewing machine, cut out a dress pattern, put in zippers and finish seams. Helen Ticknor Davis Graven demanded things be done well, with intention and precision. Whether a straight seam, or a zipper, Gram's intonations were always the same: "Absolutely, absolutely, you have to line things up so they match perfectly, otherwise you must rip it out and start again." She inspected my seams with a ruler to make sure they were five-eighths of an inch wide. She pressed them open flat before allowing me to go on to the next side seam. Unflinchingly steady to the end of the project, she insisted that the hem stitch be uniform and unnoticeable. When it was, she clapped her hands and exclaimed: "Beautiful!"

And if Gram wasn't demanding enough, her sewing machine added to the challenge. To get her pedal-foot Singer machine humming, you had to rock your feet back and forth. Keeping the motion steady required patience and practice. And those old Singers sang by producing only one single chain stitch. When it came to sewing and life, there did not appear to be a wishy-washy bone in Gram's body.

My father knew this about his mother. And while he might have rebuked her for being too strict while he was growing up, he had now turned to her to help raise and teach me what he could not. When my parents were living in Germany in the mid-1950s, my Dad bought Mom an Elna, a Swiss-made, avocado green sewing machine. "Top of the line at the time," Dad loved to say. After Mom died, Dad gave away most of her clothes. He saved her jewelry to give to us when we got older. He stored her mink coat. But he didn't give away the Elna, or shove it in an attic corner. Instead, he entrusted it to Gram to make sure that I learned to sew.

Compared to Gram's Singer, the Elna at home was a modern wonder machine. It had "cams," or various black discs that could be interchanged to produce different stitches, from zigzags to button holes. It even had a bobbin, which meant there were two threads, not a single easy-to-unravel chain stitch. When Gram came to Minneapolis, we sewed using the Elna.

Under Gram's tutelage, I was making my own dresses by the time I showed up for seventh grade home economics class. I remember the sewing teacher praising my 16-inch square pillow, finished way before the others, and thinking, "Well, that only involved four straight seams." When our eighth grade Madrigal choir group needed costumes for a concert, the mothers went into action. I sewed my own long dress, complete with high collar and contrasting front panels, thereby saving me the embarrassment of having to tell the teacher I didn't have a mother to sew for me.

For my thirteenth birthday, I begged my dad for a new down winter jacket. He countered that he would buy me the materials, thereby challenging me to make my own. At the fabric store, I found a kit that came with bags of down, nylon material and a heavy-duty black zipper. Outwardly triumphant in my sewing accomplishments, I wore that sky-blue down jacket for several winters. Inwardly, the flaws nagged at me. The stitching along the zipper clumped in a few spots, probably only noticeable to me (and Gram if she had looked). I didn't rip it out because that would have left needle marks in the nylon. Caught in a sewing dilemma, I lived with the mistake, but never forgot it.

Needle sharp is one way to describe Gram. The way she acted, authoritative, opinionated and educated, earned her that description. And the way she dressed confirmed it. She pulled her long gray hair up into a neat bun and held it place with giant bobby pins. She wore serious glasses, neatly pressed dresses belted at the waist—never slacks— nylons not panty hose, and sensible, thick-heeled shoes. She lightly powdered her face but eschewed eye makeup. But I didn't see Gram as too prickly. To me she was sharp, as in smart sharp, the kind of person I wanted to be around because she was always learning, trying new things and willing to teach me.

Beyond our baking, sewing, knitting and crochet lessons, Gram liked to talk about how she studied math and science at the University of Minnesota. She wanted to become a doctor, but by the time she graduated, she was desperate to get out of Minneapolis to escape the burdens of her perpetually absent traveling salesman father, her fragile mother and five demanding younger siblings. Ditching medicine, she found an acceptable exit through her Methodist church: a job teaching at a girls' school in Madras, India. Not too many women would have leapt at that opportunity in 1923, but Gram saw a chance to travel and teach Indian girls how to read as her golden moment.

At university, she met Henry Graven. He was smart and a serious suitor. She took a big chance and left him behind to go to India. She hoped it would all work out for her in the end. Henry accepted that Helen needed to get away to see the world, just as he had hungered for some adventure and signed up to fight in France during World War I. He could use the time to set up a law practice with his brother in Greene. He waited for Helen's return.

Gram said she was always glad she took the chance. Sometimes when we were laying out a pattern on colorful fabric for a new dress, she would tell stories about being a teacher in India "There is nothing more important than learning to read," she said. "I wanted those girls to read." But half the time, before she could get to the lesson, she had to first nurse a girl's cold, change a bandage, or make sure the girls had some food. Sometimes, she worried that her work wasn't making much of a difference. But then the little girls would smile at her, or write her sweet notes saying "Thank you Miss Davis," and she felt it was all worth it.

Looking at the fabrics often reminded her of the beautiful saris the women wore in India. She brought an orange silk one back and kept it in her special cedar chest.

Gram went to India to escape; she returned with stories, lace and fabric for her wedding dress and veil. She learned how to survive and thrive on her own in a foreign country. She wished everyone could travel and experience other cultures. She hoped I would travel far and wide, maybe even to India.

Gram may have kept her warm, tender side out of everyday view, but I saw it at bedtime. A day at Gram's always ended with a song. She tucked me under the blankets, kissed my forehead and sang:

> Skinnamarinky dinky dink
> Skinnamarinky do,
> I love you.

> Skinnamarinky dinky dink,
> Skinnamarinky do,
> I love you.

> I love you in the morning,
> And in the afternoon
> I love you in the evening,
> underneath the moon,

> Oh Skinnamarinky dinky dink
> Skinnamarinky do,
> I love you.

Near the end of the song, as she sang the final "I love you," Gram's voice quivered—every time. In that uncontrollable vacillation of a second or two, I knew that she, too, felt sad. Gram knew that she could never replace my mother, but she was resolved to love me and teach me as if she was. Like any mother, she wanted to make sure I never slid into despair. So on her watch, she was always pushing me to think beyond my immediate circumstances. There was a bigger broader world out there that called— even and especially to young girls. "You can go anywhere," she said. Over and over again. Gram nurtured roots and cherished wings.

To make her point, one day Gram gave me a special gift in a small white jewelry box. Inside was a tiny sterling silver thimble, cozily housed in its own orange and yellow case shaped like a miniature sombrero. A tiny snap opened to reveal a tarnished thimble and three sharp needles. She put in a little handwritten note so I would always know the thimble's provenance.

"This thimble was my mother's—Elizabeth Blew Davis (EBD). It's sterling silver, she crocheted the case for it. You sew—maybe you don't use a thimble. I do, for sewing hem stitches. Thought you would like your great-grandmother's pride and joy!
"Love, Grama Helen"

Sewing with Gram, I glimpsed how piecing things together could lead to a bigger, more exciting world. Needle and thread, only a thimble as protection, one stitch at a time. That's how a family story starts; that's how its fabric is stitched together. The threads become the text, and the context, for how one lives deeply in this world. Put another way, my great-grandmother's feebleness lead to my grandmother's adventure, which in turn grew into wisdom that she used to shape me, and generations to come.

Chapter 9

In Minneapolis, two minutes from my house, up some brick stairs, through our unswept, disorganized garage, across the back alley, through a gate, and a short run on a sidewalk that divided the yard into two, a different emotional world beckoned. Without hesitation, Phyllis would open her back door and gush warmth and welcoming. "Ka-thy, come on in."

Phyllis invited me in, whether my best friend Kristi, her oldest daughter, was home or not. She invited me in, even if I showed up at the most inopportune times, which was probably most times. Standing outside, I could hear the giggling voices of younger kids running up and down the stairs inside. I could smell warm chocolate brownies, fresh-baked bread coming from the kitchen. I could see the lime-green shag carpet running down the hall, spreading wall to wall through the living room and dining room, as inviting as a field of spring grass. I walked through the door Phyllis held open into a tiny, crammed entryway. I took off my shoes and hung up my coat.

The Sorteberg family moved into the compact two-story gray house with white shutters on Luverne Avenue, across the alley behind our house, in the fall of 1970, just after Dad's gubernatorial defeat. Kristi and I were in the same grade, and though she was only five months older than me, she was a full head taller, with long, reddish hair and dark-rimmed glasses. Kristi's thoughtful, more cautious nature complemented my bossy, sassy, impetuous personality, and we formed an impermeable bond.

Kristi and I walked to and from school together every day until we graduated high school, enduring definite highs and lows. We learned to knit together, and on the first day of sixth grade, we proudly strutted the ponchos we had knit over the summer. The next year, we wore dresses and carried purses to the first day of junior high, only to arrive at our new lockers and find everyone else wearing jeans and carrying backpacks. That shared embarrassment sealed our friendship. Kristi and I sang duets in school chorus and musicals, and I sounded better than I was because I was singing with her. At slumber parties, Kristi correctly predicted I'd be the first one to fall asleep. She forgave me for bailing on the late night fun. One Halloween, we cut two holes out of a big box, painted our cheeks red, tied our hair into pig tails, and voilà: we went as a two-headed birthday present. Whatever else was going on in the world, I had the best, best friend.

And she came with a big happy family: Two parents, Warren and Phyllis, and three younger siblings, David, Karin and Mary, and a black terrier mutt named Snoopy. They sometimes complained that they suffered from being "PK's" or preacher's kids, because that meant they had to behave like perfect angels in public. From where I stood, they had no idea how good they had it. A Lutheran pastor, Warren was devoted to shoring up poor, inner-city neighborhoods. He lived and preached racial and economic diversity before they became liberal buzz words. He recycled before recycling bins. In the winter, he'd call us outside and brag about rescuing a perfectly good pair of skis from someone's trash. In the summer, he'd summon everyone to the garage to show off a bike he'd just repurposed, claiming it "better than new." And, to my father's delight, he was a die-hard Minnesota Vikings football fan. "Keep your sermon short," Dad advised Warren on home game Sundays (when they drove to the game together). "We don't want to miss the opening kickoff!"

Kristi's mom, Phyllis, complemented Warren's do-good zeal with artistic flare and genuine love and caring. She grew up on a farm but was determined to leave, become a nurse, and carve out a more colorful life in the city. What she kept from her farmer father, who died just before she married Warren, was a love for anything Danish. By the time I met Phyllis, she had adopted a contemporary, urban style that was so far from practical Minnesota farm you would have never known she was from rural Fairmont. She wore colorful clothes, not too much makeup, happy lipsticks, and big, bold Jackie O-style sun glasses. She adored her modern Danish furniture, dishes, flatware and candles.

Like her mother, and so many farm women in those days, Phyllis was an accomplished sewer. But she took things up a notch, even by Minneapolis standards. She bought bold Marimekko fabrics and designed her own dresses. She sewed Warren neckties that were shockingly bright with dizzying patterns—out there even for the 1970s. She sewed blazers with collars and puffy shoulders for her girls, sport coats for her son. Once she fell in love with a certain abstract orange fabric and decided to make a bedspread out of it. She loved the fabric so much she framed a piece to keep, long after the bedspread had worn thin.

When we first became friends, Kristi had no reason to think I did not come with a big happy family, too. Her younger siblings and my step-siblings all knew each other at school, from running around and riding bikes together. Probably all the neighbors were in shock when they learned we fled without warning and moved to an apartment. I couldn't explain it to myself, let alone to friends, so I'm not sure what I said. Every day, I couldn't wait to get to school to see Kristi. In the midst of my family turmoil, she remained steadfast. Some girls might have moved on to find a new, easier-to-be-around, more reliable best friend, but she didn't.

Living at the apartment, waiting for Dad's divorce, I missed the freedom of just running back and forth across the alley between our houses; everything had to be scheduled, coordinated. Our suburban existence was a different galaxy with my life spinning in a different orbit. The best thing about moving home after the divorce was finalized, was not our house itself, but its location next to Kristi's.

With no Mom, Marge or Dad's second wife at home, I hung out with Kristi in her room most days after school. For sure, I was never in a hurry to get home. I lingered. A bit awkwardly. Too long.

"Would you like to stay for dinner tonight," Phyllis would ask, just as I had hoped.

"Oh, yes." I nearly always accepted.

Kristi was thrilled. None of her siblings got to have friends over for dinner all the time. Phyllis had strict rules about no school night sleepovers. She bent them for me, and by extension Kristi, but not for her other kids.

Together, Kristi and I could get away with a lot more than either of us could alone. My unusual situation gave Kristi special privileges.

Without me saying much, Phyllis seemed to know that, emotionally, things were complicated at my house. With Dad back to winging it as a single dad, each of us was trying to find a new footing. My brother ducked out of the family into sports or into his room to study; my sister escaped with her friends and into the embrace of a new boyfriend, whom Dad disapproved of; I needed a safe haven. Ever since the day Phyllis shielded me from Joan, I had a sense that I could trust her. Phyllis had known Joan since college, though they weren't close friends. Distraught over the turn of events after our half of the family left the house, Joan would wander across the alley in the morning and cry at Phyllis' kitchen table. Phyllis being Phyllis, she listened. It was unusual that Joan was still there sobbing in the afternoon, which is why Phyllis had to act quickly the day she turned me away. When I got over the what ifs of accidentally running into Joan, I realized Phyllis had not been dismissive, she had been incredibly loving. She had looked out for me. That evolved into a quiet understanding. I knew that she knew my family was not like hers.

That was just the beginning.

Phyllis hugged her kids going out the door to school. She hugged her friends when they dropped by for coffee. When I came over looking for Kristi, Phyllis hugged me too. At first, for a little while, I held back, unsure what to make of her affections. After Joan, I wasn't going to trust just anybody. Phyllis understood. But she offered her hugs anyway. They were never empty, going-through-the-motion hugs. No, they were powerful signs that she held me close—emotionally and physically. Her arms, wide and warm and adorned with chunky silver jewelry conveyed a message of abundant love. In time, as she held me longer and tighter, she soothed me. I went from pulling back to wanting more, and I wasn't the only one. On Sunday mornings, parishioners at Our Saviour's Lutheran Church waited in line for a Phyllis hug. More than any other pastor's wife I've ever seen, she extended hugs to old people, little kids, church staff and fellow choir members before and after Sunday services. She melted them too and loved doing it. How did one woman have so many hugs to give?

Kristi had no way of knowing our friendship would balloon into a full-fledged family thing, that I would basically adopt her parents and they me. Neither of us grasped at the time how my becoming a two-time motherless daughter effectively ripped the pages from the script and replaced it with a new plot. Truly, I wanted to be her friend, but now unlike her, I also needed to figure out how to survive. Actually, I wanted to do more than just survive.

"If you want to have an excuse for your problems in life, you have one," was one of my father's well-meaning, but overly blunt proclamations after "the accident." But I didn't want to live with an excuse. I wanted to be enveloped in grace and beauty, the way I imagined things would be had my mother lived. In addition to being Kristi's friend, I was also on an urgent, serious, all-out reconnaissance mission. I watched how other women did things: How they talked and cooked and listened and hugged. Kristi did not need to watch so keenly, intently. She had years to absorb how to love a family and run a household. I needed to know how to do it—now.

Phyllis was already cooking for six, so one more never fazed her. But when I stayed for dinner their family seating arrangement needed tweaking. I sat next to Kristi, which meant the youngest daughter Mary had to shift and squeeze around the corner to the table end next to Phyllis. I wanted to fit in without causing disruption, so I watched and mimicked what everyone else did. The family held hands while Warren said grace. I held Kristi's and Mary's hands. "*Gesegnete Mahlzeit!*" or "blessed mealtime" in German was Warren's way of giving everyone the go-ahead to dig in. "*Gesegnete Mahlzeit,*" I said too. At the end of the meal, Phyllis looked at the small amounts left in the serving dish and said, "Clean it up, Lyle." That was an inside teasing reference to the kids' Uncle Lyle who disliked being urged to clean up tidbits not sufficient to add up to leftovers. I met their Uncle Lyle several times, so I knew what Phyllis meant. If I was still hungry, I helped myself to the tidbits. Over time, my presence at the Sorteberg dinner table seemed unremarkable, no big deal. If my dad was working late, and I did not have to cook, I knew I would be welcome for dinner—no questions. There was always a place for me.

"This is Kathy, our other daughter," is how Phyllis started introducing me to her friends and relatives. Every time she said it, I softened a bit more. She said I should call her Phyllis, not Mrs. Sorteberg as I did in the beginning. I never called her Mom, and yet practically and emotionally,

I had found another mother.

Like any mother devoted to her child, Phyllis paid attention to me. Amidst the clamor of her own family's pressing needs, she noticed and affirmed my likes and dislikes. She warned me ahead when she was serving *torsk*. I was not a big fan of Norwegian cod then, so the heads up gave me time to conjure a polite excuse for not staying. When she made brownies, she made sure I got one without nuts. When I went crazy for her vanilla pudding Bundt cake, she surprised me with it again on my birthday. It was our "special cake," the one she made to celebrate me, until somehow, she knew it was time to switch to chocolate. In the mixing of the cakes, and in the noticing of my shifting tastes, Phyllis' message was clear: She cared. I mattered. To be Phyllis' daughter, now, that was something unexpected, profoundly lucky.

Kristi didn't object to her mom reaching out to me. Well before me, Phyllis had welcomed strays and extras from their church life into the family fold. As the oldest of four kids, Kristi was also already used to a certain independence and a level of divided parental attention. She never really probed into what it was like for me to not have a mom or go through a divorce. Whenever she felt a little jealous, she later told me, she talked herself out of it, and even felt a tinge of guilt. She had a mom. I didn't. Generously, Kristi shared hers.

Phyllis' tiny kitchen was another matter. Literally, there was not enough room for the whole family to stand in the kitchen at once. They ate breakfast in shifts there and ate all dinners in the dining room. Somehow, Phyllis made it work. With barely enough counter space to cool the five loaves of bread she kneaded every week, she cooked, baked and fed her husband and four kids plus one. The kitchen may have been small, but it was in Minneapolis, not on the farm in southern Minnesota. City living required different routines. Phyllis invented them. She pulled the toaster out of its spot under the counter for breakfast and then hid it for the rest of the day. She whirred frozen orange juice concentrate into a bubbly mix every morning, which is why her trusty blender earned the prime spot to the right of the sink. Curlers still in her hair, she perfected her sandwich production line. Ten pieces of bread, two rows of five, slapped with sliced ham, lettuce and mustard. Effortlessly, it seemed, she filled the brown paper lunch sacks with the sandwiches, a piece of fruit and a homemade cookie or brownie and sent the gang off to school.

I watched.

In the 1970s, foodies were hard to find in my neighborhood. Standard fare included a tuna hot dish made with frozen peas, egg noodles, and garnished with crushed potato chips. Every church fundraising cookbook prided itself on its own special version of this. Not Phyllis. She served tuna sandwiches, but never tuna casserole. She never cut corners with cake mixes or hot dish helpers. She simmered homemade soups, stews, sauces. She shunned Wonder Bread and Campbell's canned soup. She turned the Sunday morning pre-church rush at their house into something sweet with her specialty: homemade pecan-studded caramel rolls. Even as Phyllis elevated the day-to-day family meals, she liked to experiment for friends. I walked into her kitchen one Saturday afternoon as she was pounding chicken breasts for Chicken Kiev for a dinner party that night. Like an artist in her studio, she filled the deboned and pounded breast with herb-spiked butter, rolled and sealed them tight, before dipping the perfect bundles in homemade breadcrumbs.

Rarely, only rarely, did Phyllis lose her cool in the kitchen. Once, when someone dropped a bottle of soda on her freshly mopped floors, she yelled "oh shit." We scrambled the heck out of there and hid in the basement.

Curious, I studied Phyllis' moves.

Phyllis presented elegant meals every day. She made it seem effortless, but in fact, her presentation was based on a couple of unbendable rules: No green parmesan cheese shakers, or red ketchup bottles, or white drippy ranch salad dressing bottles were ever allowed on the table. Condiments had their own serving dishes. Without fail, she served salad in separate salad bowls, which, by local standards then was exotic. Phyllis slipped in fresh avocados and garnished with fresh pomegranate seeds, while the rest of Minnesota was grateful for a wedge of iceberg lettuce and artificial bacon bits, or worse, canned spinach. At Phyllis' table, I learned what to look for in the grocery store to make salads sing.

Then I wanted to go beyond watching. I wanted to work alongside her.

So, in addition to my good fortune to have a seat at Phyllis' table, I was also lucky to call Phyllis my cooking teacher. She taught me how to scald the milk, and then let it cool just so before adding it to the yeast to make the dough for the caramel rolls. She showed me how to knead the dough until it had just the right give. She taught me how to follow recipes and adjust according to what I had in the cupboard, to face those culinary turning points with confidence not fear. She taught me to use the tired veggies in the refrigerator drawers to make soup stock. I treasured beyond measure the first cookbook she gave me for my birthday: *Dish Up the Love*, the Our Savior's Lutheran Church cookbook from the late 1970s.

Phyllis became my role model. I watched how she made a house a home, how she tended her children and supported her husband. Those efforts did not diminish her, but fueled her to be even more loving, competent and artistic. If Phyllis had not held the door open, and I had not walked through again and again, I would have remained a motherless child. My life would never have been so rich. Her open door opened the next door, and so many others after. And importantly, I learned the lesson of a lifetime: if there is an open door, it's good to walk on in. Amazing, wonderful and happy things can happen. But you have to step up and chance the threshold.

I liked Warren too. But since I had a dad and didn't particularly need another, I watched him less closely, and never took him too seriously. In contrast to my dad, he had a low threshold for boisterous kids messing around inside the house. "Go to the basement," he'd yell, displaying a feisty temper. I found his bellowing more amusing than threatening, but I still ran to the basement with the others.

I took what I learned at Phyllis' and carried it back across the alley to my home. But it wasn't a simple skills transfer. After my sister left for college, Dad and I eased into our own routines. I was too young to drive, so we grocery shopped together. We were an unusual pair at the nearby SuperValu. Not too many fathers pushed grocery carts in those days. The checkout girls sneered. Slowly, I worked Phyllis' ideas into the shopping cart. But not too many. I did not want to upset our own sweet culinary traditions. Dad and I religiously ate grilled cheese sandwiches and tomato soup for lunch on Sundays after church. We bought the bread, and the cans of soup. I never let on that I knew homemade tasted different.

I relished the one-on-one time, without the tensions of having my older siblings at home. After we finished eating, we'd push aside the plates and play a cribbage match at the table, best of three games, before tackling the dishes. We kept score on a white poster sheet taped to the wall: hundreds of games of cribbage. Over the years, we invented titles for our tournaments, culminating in the "Father-Daughter Cribbage Championship for the Free World." No one ever played cards at the table across the alley. Wanting both a connection with my dad, and the safe haven of a "normal family," I straddled two worlds.

That my father was friends with both Phyllis and Warren made it easier. Dad never objected to my spending time at their house, indeed he was grateful I had Kristi as a best friend and a second home away from home. Sometimes he would wander across the alley to find me and stay for coffee or a drink. Dad understood reciprocity, so once in a while he would invite the Sortebergs for a backyard cookout and basketball game.

Never expressing resentment or jealousy, he knew I loved the Sorteberg family and let me vacation with them. One summer, I joined the four kids in the back of their station wagon for a road trip to Estes Park in the Colorado Rocky Mountains. Kristi and I were excited about the extended time together. No one else got to bring a friend on vacation. "Is everybody happy?" Warren would ask every few hours from behind the steering wheel when he sensed our squished-in squirming was about to get out of hand. We all knew he meant "cool it."

Dad also came to rely on Phyllis' judgment, caring and counsel. I let Phyllis be the one to tell him I had started my period and needed to buy sanitary supplies. When I badly injured my neck in a trampoline accident during gymnastics practice, the high school reached Phyllis to take me to the hospital before my father's office could pull him from a trial. I spent a week recovering from torn neck ligaments in Kristi's bed, Phyllis watching over me, lifting the straw to my lips. Dad visited my bedside before and after work, grateful Phyllis was there to take care of me.

Even Gram approved of my second family. On visits to Minneapolis, she wandered over to have coffee with Phyllis; they became good friends. In turn, Gram invited Kristi to come to Greene, to join our sewing and knitting circle, to pick beans in the garden.

Phyllis offered me nourishment beyond meals and after-school sweets. Sitting at her Danish teak dining table, surrounded by the family, I belonged to something normal, something good. Not everyone had a mother who died; some mothers lived. Not all households were unbalanced, weighted heavily to the needs of a struggling father. Not all houses smelled of pipe tobacco and pre-dinner Scotch. Not all houses had portraits of a dead mother hanging above the fireplace.

Sometimes to imagine something as profound as a stable family life, you have to smell it, see it, feel it, taste it.

At Phyllis' table, I felt the *ahhh* of "I am safe," which carried me through life's turmoil. There, in all the deliciousness, I tasted that *ahhh* of "things will be okay." There, in the moments of being noticed, was the mothering I craved. Phyllis' mothering felt beyond good. I held it close. Her mothering filled the void of my no-motherness at a crucial time. It gave me hope.

Chapter 10

Every morning, Kristi picked me up to walk to Washburn High School. She let herself in our back door and patiently waited for me to pack my lunch and pull my homework together. I was always a bit late, a bit scattered getting going. One morning, when she didn't find me in the kitchen she walked upstairs and discovered me sleeping in the bath tub. "Get up! We're going to be late," she yelled.

Even on dark winter mornings, we hardly noticed the bitter cold or the 15-minute walk, which took us across Minnehaha Creek, to the 35W interstate overpass, and up towards 50th and Nicollet Avenue. We were so engrossed in analyzing the social scene at school. Mostly we'd figured it out already, but there were always developments worth dissecting. We were not in the cool cheerleader clique. But then, we were no longer complete losers scraping the bottom of the social heap. Definitely, we were too smart and talented for that, and besides we both made the girls' tennis team. We shared a common desire to rise above the sorry state of "no-boys-will-even-look-at-us." We had things to do.

In the fall of my junior year, somewhere between conjugating French verbs and memorizing definite articles for German nouns, I realized I was good at foreign languages. Monsieur Dunn and Herr Dills both gave me high marks. They said I had a "natural ear." I wasn't sure what that meant, but I soaked up their praise. Because I was taking two foreign languages, I caught the attention of a counselor who thought I might be a good candidate for an exchange program. She invited me and my dad to a pot luck dinner to learn about the American Field Service, or AFS. Dad had a schedule conflict and couldn't attend, but I didn't let that stop me from showing up. An exuberant woman named Marilyn extolled the benefits of studying abroad, but I didn't need her fancy slide show to convince me. I left the dinner knowing I had found a way to break away from my life in Minneapolis. My father agreed, but on the condition I come up with the funding—$2,000— on my own. With my brother and sister in private colleges at the same time, his finances were already stretched tight. If Dad meant his condition as a deterrent, it didn't work.

I went to bed dreaming of a year in France, or Germany, maybe Switzerland or Austria. If Gram could go to India in the 1920s, surely I could handle Europe. Once I allowed myself to think about getting away, there was no turning my brain back. There were other possible outs—drinking, drugs, sex—but being naive, nerdy and heavily influenced by Gram who believed in books and travel, those didn't appeal. Gram thought AFS was a great idea, and told my father. Phyllis told me to "go for it." That I had the confidence to consider such a move was testimony to all the love and care I'd gotten from them. Instead of being defined by my circumstances, I thought of ways to look out for myself. On my application form, my determination knew no bounds. Country preferences? I checked the last box: Send me anywhere.

To help pay for all this, I told the next door neighbor I was available for more babysitting hours. I didn't like babysitting much, her four kids were a handful, but I needed the money. Over the next several months, I brought homemade cookies and banana bread to bake sales. Like the Boy Scouts used to, I stacked newspapers in bundles and tied them with twine to bring to the collection point for cash. "Paper Drives" were early recycling efforts and a way kids earned money. Occasionally, I'd join a group doing Saturday car washes. Whatever it took. It never amounted to much, a few hundred dollars—maybe. But I wanted to show Dad I was trying.

In early February, I learned that the anywhere box I had checked would be Japan, which hadn't even crossed my mind as being somewhere. Or at least somewhere on the map where a 16-year-old girl from Minnesota might land. I didn't know anyone from Japan. There was only one Japanese-American student at my high school. My piano teacher's husband had been to Japan in the 1960s to teach English, but that was as close a connection as I could muster.

"I'm going to Japan. Ja-pan, Japan," I screamed, running across the alley to deliver the news to Kristi and Phyllis, and everyone else in the neighborhood.

And then I called Gramps. Being a generous and smart banker, Gramps told me he had a way for me to cover the costs of my AFS year. With Grama gone, he was now planning to divide what would have been my mother's share of his estate between me and my two siblings. He could give me a $2,000 advance on that inheritance to save on taxes. Gramps' advance proved to be the gift that kept on giving.

I don't think Dad expected me to pull off my year abroad plan, but once I secured a spot in Japan and the financing, he gave me his unqualified approval.

My departure was sooner than anyone anticipated. To catch the start of the new Japanese school calendar, students had to leave in mid-March, not summer, as I had originally imagined. That left me barely enough time to obtain a passport and visa, and no time to second-guess my decision. It also meant I had to set up an urgent meeting with the guidance counselor for college planning. I'd have to apply while I was in Japan, take the SAT in Tokyo, and line up letters of recommendation from afar. I went into the meeting with a short, vague list of possible colleges to run by him: Middlebury College in Vermont was known for its foreign language programs; my piano teacher's neighbor was at Lewis and Clarke College in Oregon; my dad said Stanford and UC Berkeley were good schools on the west coast.

The guidance counselor was not much help. No, he was worse, he was disparaging. He told me I shouldn't even consider Stanford. Only one student a year from Washburn got in there, and Mr. Varsity, top in our class, star football player and yearbook editor, was already considering applying. "You don't stand a chance next to him." His blatant sexism made me so mad I stomped out.

My walks to high school with Kristi became more precious as my departure grew closer. I would miss her terribly, but admittedly not enough to consider staying. We talked about how the kids at school didn't get how I could possibly give up a year of pep rallies, football games, school dances and most of my senior year for an all-girls high school in Japan. Those high school rites of passage seemed stupid compared to traveling across the world, but I didn't want to be too dismissive. I was leaving; Kristi was staying.

The idea must have been hard on Kristi. How did we go from studying French together to me going to Japan for a year? It was happening so quickly. She would notice my absence more acutely than anyone. She understood I had this undeniable need to get away, but didn't share it; she loved her close family. At high school, she was going to have to make new friends and navigate the social scene without a sidekick. From the nervous look on her face and the fragile sound in her voice, I sensed she hated being left.

You'd think my dad might have been a little concerned about sending his youngest daughter off to Japan not speaking Japanese or knowing much about the country. But no. It was odd, neither he nor anybody else seemed concerned about how I would survive. Instead, they asked openly and often, "So, what's *he* going to do without Kathy?" That bugged me. But it was probably the right question.

Phyllis told me not to worry about my dad. She said a year abroad was "something to celebrate." So that's what we did. Phyllis hosted a goodbye dinner party. She invited my closest high school friends, Kristi, Tom, Andy, Dan, Mark, Peggy and Beth. No one was better than Phyllis at marking big life moments with little loving touches, thereby turning them into lasting memories. She set the dining room table with teal colored placemats, wooden salad bowls, four teal candles, and two porcelain white bunnies for a spring centerpiece. She pinned a red rose corsage on my light green sweater, and directed me to Warren's seat at the head of the table. We feasted on salad, lasagna and garlicky French bread. For dessert, she unveiled a homemade chocolate sheet cake, decorated with Japanese lettering:

"良い　旅行　を　キャシー." She came up with "Bon Voyage! Kathy" in Japanese in 1977.

Chapter 11

Makoto Maniwa greeted me at the small, uncrowded Nishinasuno station. He walked with a vigorous, victorious bounce. "Hi, very nice to meet you," he said in over-enunciated English. "Welcome to Japan."

His friendly manner lightened the spring air, but didn't eliminate my unexpected angst. Since my mother died when I was five, after a car accident on an April Easter Sunday, my life had taken unusual turns. I was clever and successful at finding alternatives to my motherless home life. So at 16, going to Japan for a year in 1977 didn't seem too far-fetched. I definitely needed to get away from cooking and running a household for my dad. But now, awkwardly shaking Mr. Maniwa's hand, I worried I might have been a bit too clever.

"*Watashi wa Kyasarin Gureiben desu. Amerika no Minnesota shu kara kimashita.*" "My name is Kathryn Graven. I am from the state of Minnesota in America." That's what they taught us to say in the ten-day crash course in Japanese in Tokyo. It took hours of practicing new syllables to get that to flow smoothly, and only seconds to utter it and drain my vocabulary bank. "*Hajimemashite.*" "Nice to meet you."

It's a good thing Muto-san, my AFS chaperone, accompanied me. She filled in the uneasy silence by chatting with Mr. Maniwa in Japanese. Muto-san grew up in Tochigi prefecture and spoke the same dialect. I was too nervous to make out a word of the conversation. Muto-san translated: "Please call me Otōsan. That means father."

Otōsan lifted my two brand-new, sky-blue soft suitcases containing my entire belongings for the year into the trunk of his white Toyota. For the twenty-minute drive, past rice fields and clusters of tiny houses, to the Maniwa home, Muto-san was my lifeline. "Please don't leave, ever," I thought. I could not imagine how I was going to survive after she returned to Tokyo later that evening, abandoning me to a strange family in a small town in Japan.

I was still stunned from learning on my arrival at the orientation in Tokyo that I was not living in Odawara. The AFS acceptance form listed my host family's location as Ohtawara-shi. But the closest thing my father and I could find to that on the atlas was Odawara-shi, southwest of Tokyo. We assumed the match was close enough. "You'll have great views of Mt. Fuji," Dad predicted. But t's and d's are not interchangeable in Japanese. Odawara, 小田原 or "Small Rice Field City," was not the same as Ohtawara, which is written 大田原. "Big Rice Field City" was a small town of about 65,000 people, nestled in the rice fields about two and a half hours *north* of Tokyo's Ueno Station by train. Even Japanese people needed help locating Ohtawara. The town didn't merit its own train station. The closest connection to big city life by the Japan Railways network was the next town over, Nishinasuno. It seemed quite possible I was the only foreigner in the prefecture. Mt. Fuji was nowhere in sight.

Otōsan deftly maneuvered the car down the narrow main street of Ohtawara, past restaurants, bars, and vegetable stands, pulling over to let oncoming cars squeeze by. My heart pounded as fast as a taiko drummer. When we came to a full stop, a small woman, dressed in a kimono, waited in front of a store with bold letters that I struggled to make out: まにわ薬局.

"*Irasshaimase*," she said, with a big smile on her face, as we got out of the car. "Welcome."

"*Hajimemashite*," I replied. "Nice to meet you."

She looked me in the eyes and continued speaking Japanese, as if she was talking to another Japanese person, not a 16-year-old, blond, blue-eyed American girl. Did she realize I had no idea what she was saying? She kept talking anyway. That was my first clue that there was something special about her. She smiled right through the confused look on my face, and offered a non-hug, hug-equivalent moment of "it's going to be okay." Muto-san introduced her as Katsuko Maniwa but said I could call this warm and intriguing woman "Okaasan," or mother.

Nothing in Okaasan's voice or actions suggested that she harbored doubts about my being there, or was irked with her husband for signing up for this added responsibility of hosting a student for a year. She showed me the way through the drugstore to the entryway. We slipped off our shoes and stepped up into the kitchen.

"*Douzo. Douzo*," she said brightly. "Please come in."

Obaachan, or Grandma, had prepared a special welcome meal of sukiyaki. On their host family application, the Maniwa family described the grandmother who lived with them as "not very cheerful." First impression: they were honest. Barely speaking, Obaachan laid out the meal on the low table in the living room. The five of us sat on the tatami floor, our feet scrunched under the low table, warmed by the electric *kotatsu* heater under the blanket, and sipped green tea.

Muto-san translated the essentials of my new daily life: the Maniwas' drug store opened at 10:00 a.m. and closed at 7:30 p.m. The family ate dinner after that. The Maniwa daughters, Rie, 24, Toshie, 22, and Masae, 20, were all living in Tokyo, but would be coming and going throughout the year. As the sukiyaki simmered in a black pot on the table, I followed Muto-san's every movement: crack the raw egg into a bowl, stir it with chopsticks, dip the cooked meat into the yellowy froth. After dinner, Muto-san left for the train station. I climbed the stairs to my new four tatami mat room, buried my face in my futon and cried my blue eyes out. The pillow was small and hard, filled with some kind of rustling husks, not feathers. I made a hasty but lasting decision: I hated Japanese pillows.

The next morning, my tears gave way to a new urgency to figure things out. Try to smile, I reminded myself. At breakfast, we sat on chairs at the kitchen table. Everyone had their own designated rice and miso soup bowls, and chopsticks. All the chopsticks went into the same bamboo cup holder. Finding mine, without touching everyone else's, was like a real-life pick-up sticks game.

Okaasan went over basic household rules and quirks, pointing as she spoke to help me understand: Come in and out through the drugstore, not the side entrance which, by virtue of the flower arrangement on top of the shoe storage box, was reserved for formal occasions. Please wear house slippers inside, but never into the separate men and women's toilet stalls. There were toilet slippers inside the stall. And, oh, the toilets don't flush. For lack of a better toilet vocabulary, they were essentially outhouses in the house. They were also the old-fashioned squat type toilets.

You did actually have to squat, not just pretend to. The smell? Well, that depended on how recently the truck had come with the long hose to pump the stalls.

"You'll get used to it soon enough," Otōsan said.

Overwhelmed by everything, I hadn't fully grasped what Okaasan meant when she mentioned to Muto-san that they had made plans for a short spring break trip before the school year started. A week later, Okaasan, Toshie, Masae and I were off on my first Japanese family adventure. Leaving Otōsan to mind the drugstore, we boarded the local train to Tokyo, then changed to the *shinkansen*, bullet train, bound for Kyoto.

There, I walked proudly with my new family to famous temples and shrines, mimicking their bowing, clapping hands and ringing bells, lighting incense. At each site, school children crudely yelled "*gaijin da*," pointing out "she's a foreigner." As if we were not already, that made us all keenly aware of our unusual family combination. Taking a cue from the light-hearted cherry blossoms, we quickly learned to laugh.

For Okaasan, the main purpose of the trip was to visit Yakushiji, a sacred famous eighth-century temple in Nara. The iconic six-story East Pagoda is the only original building remaining in a large complex that venerates Yakushi Nyorai, or the Medicine Buddha. Okaasan had called ahead to arrange to meet a Buddhist priest who lived at the temple; he kindly gave us a private tour and introduced me to Buddhism. Still unclear on specifics, I came away appreciating how spiritually important pilgrimages were to Okaasan. She cared about healing—her mission was to tend the sick in Ohtawara, and she earned her livelihood that way. At the same time, pilgrimages might create good karma for the drugstore business.

The *ryokan*, or Japanese style inn, where we stayed, made me feel like I was part of a long line of cherry-blossom-viewing pilgrims to Kyoto. Polite rituals played out one after another. A kimono clad woman bowed every time she slid the door open and delivered us another elaborate and elegant, and with all due respect unidentifiable, dish for our evening meal. We sat uncomfortably on the tatami mats and ate at a low table. It was a relief when our attendant cleared the final dishes and said it was time to change into *yukata* robes and head to the communal bath. Like good pilgrims, we soaked. By the time we emerged, warm and relaxed, our room had been transformed: Futons were neatly laid on the tatami floor, covered with fluffy comforters, each made with different, beautiful, colorful fabrics. We climbed under the blankets, and with the help of my handy travel dictionary, Okaasan, Toshie, Masae and I chatted late into the night. We asked random questions to get to know each other better. I mispronounced words in Japanese. They tried to imitate my English pronunciations. "We left Otōsan at home," made us laugh in both languages. I didn't want to go to sleep. This was the best slumber party—ever.

The kind, engaging Maniwa family, the travel, the cherry blossoms, the dreamlike slumber party added up to a great spring of new experiences. For the first time, I felt the magic of the cherry blossoms begging me to lighten up. I so wanted to distance myself from the heavy sadness that clung to my American family in April, much like the way you cannot wait to ditch the heavy woolen winter coat and put on a thin windbreaker in spring.

Inevitably, the cognitive dissonance between my happy spring in Japan and the grief-laden springs I knew in my bones surfaced. It started innocuously, part of the everyday, getting-to-know-you chit chat. Naturally, Japanese people asked me about my American life. I'd say I lived with my father. I had an older brother and an older sister.

"Okaasan ga inai desu ka?" "What, no mother?"

"Okaasan ga inai desu." "No mother."

"Ah sou desu ka." "Is that so?"

"Chisai toki ni nakunatta desu." "She died when I was young."

The earliest Japanese words I learned, after "this is a book," or "this is a pen," were about not existing.

Okaasan ga inai desu. "No mother."

Which in turn taught me how the Japanese can be both empathetic and vague in their responses.

"Sore wa, sore wa taihen deshita ne." "Really, that must have been difficult."

Chapter 12

It was Otōsan's idea to host a foreign exchange student. In 1977, the Maniwa family drugstore business was busy, thriving, even poised for expansion. As a nation, Japan was preparing to emerge as an economic powerhouse, Otōsan wanted to make his mark on this small town. Active in Rotary International, he bought the idea that what postwar Japan needed was to become more international, more open to outsiders. He loved his Rotary Club friends and meetings. His high stature in the club was secured by his fund raising drives, stirring speeches and calls on other small business owners to help poor children in the Philippines or Thailand. What better way to be international, to set an example for the town and his daughters, Otōsan reasoned, than to host an American exchange student?

Initially, Okaasan opposed the idea. Given her circumstances, that was quite understandable. I could tell life wasn't easy for Okaasan. She worked full time in the drugstore, had raised three daughters, and tried hard not to offend her cranky mother-in-law. Her days were long; there was housework and laundry in the morning, followed by a full day of greeting customers and listening to their aches and pains behind the drugstore counter. At the end of the day, she counted the money, ate dinner, bathed and went to bed. Like most people in postwar Japan, she had only rare days off. It would be understandable that once Otōsan's half-siblings, Ayako and Satoru, and then her own daughters, Rie, Toshie and Masae, were out the door to college, Katsuko would crave time and space to herself. But Otōsan was determined; Okaasan relented.

Katsuko Watanabe had married Makoto Maniwa when she was 24 years old in 1953. It was an arranged marriage, motivated by the Maniwa family's drugstore business interests. Makoto's father, Kichitarou Maniwa, had launched the family into the business, dispensing eye medications. Makoto, the oldest son, inherited it around 1947 and wanted to expand. For that, he would need a wife, someone to help him run the drugstore and carry on the family name. Raised by a widowed mother, Katsuko, as a young teenager, spent time doing factory work to make up for labor shortages during World War II. After the war ended, she had the brains and motivation to attend pharmaceutical college in Tokyo. In Katsuko, the Maniwa family found its ideal bride.

Even by Japanese standards, the Maniwa family situation, into which the young bride Katsuko moved, was complicated. Living in the house behind and above the drugstore in downtown Ohtawara were Makoto, his aunt, Hide, (Obaachan) who was also his father's widow, and two half siblings. It wasn't uncommon in Japan for a widower to marry his deceased wife's sister, but that does not make it easier. As the oldest son, Makoto, was responsible for his father's widow and the half siblings. Add to that odd mix, three daughters born to Katsuko and Makoto, and you get a full, complex household.

As welcoming as Otōsan and Okaasan were those first weeks, I felt woefully awkward and out of place. The house was cold, warmed only by kerosene room heaters, whose smell still permeates my memories of Japan, along with the experience of seeing my breath in my room in the morning. I was nervous using the geyser to get hot water in the kitchen sink. What if it blew up? I felt confined wearing the same navy-blue blazer, white blouse and pleated navy-blue skirt to school every day. Dressing in the same uniform as every other high school girl would not make me one of them. Moreover, I dreaded giving speeches in Japanese at school assemblies. My new school had way too many assemblies. The thought of me standing on a stage looking out to a sea of hundreds of black-haired girls, stumbling in a new language, was terrifying.

Feeling alone, I wrote in the blue journal that Phyllis had given me as a going away gift. I took to heart the inscription she wrote in the inside cover:

> "Our love and thoughts are ever with you during your year in Japan. Enjoy and absorb all you can. Use this book to keep a journal of your experiences—it will be a priceless record in the years to come. We love you! Warren and Phyl."

I quickly filled the pages, then moved on to Japanese fabric-covered notebooks. I poured out my thoughts in detailed letters, written on thin sheets of rice paper. I always had something new to report; a revelation about Japanese culture, an outing to a nearby temple or the mountains, or funny language misunderstandings. (Not knowing the Japanese word for swimsuit, for example, I showed up for gym class one day in my regular gym outfit. The other students had their swimsuits on and were ready for the session to begin. *Mizugi* is one Japanese word I will never forget.) Dad copied my letters and mailed them to a long list of relatives and family friends, so they too could read my posts from Japan. Writing was a way to not feel alone in a strange country. I could disappear into my English-speaking brain and feel at ease. I never considered writing for my high school paper or literary magazine, but in Japan, I felt inspired to try poetry. I startled myself with this, my first ever poem to my dead mother:

I miss your loving arms around me
They have been gone for so long
You lived and loved
What else matters?

Thankfully, I could not stay sullen too long. Japan is a country that values rituals and routines, and makes an art out of adhering to them. My new school routine, the demands of learning Japanese and establishing new relationships conspired to pull me out of my discord into new life rhythms. While at times, like other Americans, I balked at the endless rules and the rigidity required to maintain them, I also discovered the comforts of having them. Things are decided. Everyone follows through. There's no need to wonder or worry about how it will all work out. Sigh. Relief.

Without fail, for example, Kakuta-san showed up every morning, on time, to walk me to school. Okaasan led me out through the store, past the shampoos, lotions, lipsticks, boxes of disposable masks, packages of cold medicines and pain relievers. The drugstore shutter whrrrr-ed as Okaasan raised it. Kakuta-san waited anxiously outside.

"*Ohayogozaimasu*," we exchanged greetings and bowed. Kakuta-san was painfully shy, soft spoken, and not too happy with her new job. She hadn't asked for it. But because she lived in my neighborhood and we were both assigned to Homeroom 201 with Mori Sensei, it was decided the job was hers for a year. And so it was.

As Kakuta-san and I walked out to the main street, went one block, turned right and followed the road all the way to the Ohtawara Girls High School, we stuck out, truly an odd pair. We wore the same uniform, but carried different school bags: Hers was the standard issue black leather girls' school bag; I carried a white canvas bag. (I was always so awkward with my purses, I never got the right look.) She wore a navy-blue outer coat; I wore a sky-blue trench coat. Oh, and the socks. While all the Japanese girls wore white ankle socks. I insisted on white knee highs, which is all I brought from Minnesota. We got along, but never became best friends. Blame it on me. Poor Kakuta-san: one day she seamlessly blended in to her junior class, and the next she stood out like a sore thumb. All the other girls flocked to her for the inside scoop on my life; every detail was up for discussion. Arriving at school, we put our outdoor shoes into a cubby, slipped into white sneakers with yellow rubber toes, and headed to class. Having safely delivered me unscathed to our destination, Kakuta-san's job was done for the day.

The Japanese classroom, from the bowing to the teacher etiquette, to the students' sweeping of the classrooms and raking the grounds at the end of the day, shocked my system. All my courses were in Japanese, which at this point sounded like radio static. I found relief in home economics. There, I could sew and cook, so I could participate even without solid Japanese language skills. Between classes, I fended off questions. "Do you like the Bay City Rollers?" "What shampoo do you use to turn your hair blond?" "What do you think about Japanese boys?" Many days, my only true Japanese friend was Kenkyusha, my pocket Japanese-English dictionary.

So, once classes and after-school flower arranging and tea ceremony clubs finished, I couldn't wait to get back to the Maniwa house, my refuge. There, I was left alone to memorize more Chinese characters called *kanji*, that are used in the Japanese writing system, write letters home, and do my laundry. Sometimes I hung out in the kitchen with the drugstore employees on their breaks, sipping green tea, nibbling crunchy *sembei* rice crackers. An accountant who came once or twice a month to reconcile the books was particularly funny and fascinating. He used his trusty abacus to add the columns, his fingers whirring and clicking the beads so fast I couldn't keep up. Then, reluctantly, he checked his work with a new Casio electronic calculator. He swore the abacus was more accurate. Once my homework was done, I often popped into the store. Customers were curious and eager to talk to me. If not, the beautifully made-up girls at the Shiseido counter were willing to discuss makeup.

Surrounded by the busyness of the store, I was never by myself. From this small house, I watched Japanese society unfold. I was in the thick of it, confused at times, but challenged, awakened to new ways of being. As my Japanese improved, I noticed how extra polite Okaasan was to older customers, and how her verb endings changed when she talked to her close friends or younger customers. Eventually, I learned to distinguish different employees' voices by their *irasshaimase* calls when customers entered. And their *arigatō gozaimashitas* when customers left. Bowing thank you. Bowing goodbye. Long, low bows outside on the street until the customer drove away. There were endless bowing nuances to absorb. Would I ever get it right?

More deeply, with the store came something I craved: a steady energy of coming and going. Okaasan sent me off to school with a wave and a bow. "*Gambatte, Kyashi-chan.*" "Good luck. Try hard." "*Itte kimasu,*" "I'm off," I said, ducking under the store front shutter. When I arrived home and declared "*tadaima,*" "I have returned," she and the other store employees chimed in with happy strains of "*okaeri nasai,*" "Welcome back." You leave; your leaving is acknowledged and encouraged. You come back; you are received home.

Just as I was settling into my new family and school routine, a letter from home brought sad news. On long yellow legal pad paper, Dad wrote that Gramps' heart had given out. The funeral in Hayward was "well-attended" and a "wonderful tribute" to him. Gramps was buried next to Grama Nellie and Mom. The time lag imposed by letters made this even harder for me to grasp. International phone calls were expensive back then. And AFS discouraged them, saying it made it harder for students to adjust to their new families. Still, I thought Dad should have bucked the rules when it came to Gramps dying. After all, Gramps had made it financially possible for me to get to Japan. Now, he was dead and buried, and I was learning it two weeks after the fact.

I told Okaasan about Gramps, and asked if I could just skip dinner and have some time alone in my room. Not even 17 years old, I had this gnawing sense that my American family was doomed by people going, leaving and not coming back. I thought about my Dad in our big brick house, how quiet and lonely it must be. And here I was now living above a Japanese drugstore with Otōsan, Okaasan, Obaachan and three new sisters coming and going and a continuous flurry of activity—all thanks to Gramps.

It was a relief I had host sisters older than me. It meant I had some separation between my school friends and my host family, which suited me just right. And they made it possible for me to experience a wider swath of Japanese culture. Rie, the oldest and shortest, had graduated from art college and was living and creating in Tokyo. Her schedule allowed her the most flexibility to return to Ohtawara now and then. Initially, I thought it was because Otōsan and Okaasan wanted someone else around to entertain me. But something bigger was transpiring: Marriage negotiations. Rie had a boyfriend in Tokyo and they wanted to marry. Did I overhear the slightly heated discussion downstairs correctly? Otōsan wanted to hire a private investigator to check out the potential bride groom and his family. Really? Rie will never agree, I thought. But she did. Later, when I summoned the guts to ask her about it, she said she didn't mind, if that's what it took to get permission. Several weeks later, I was sent away, to spend the weekend in Tokyo with the second daughter, Toshie, so that a formal meeting with Rie's fiancé and family could take place at the house.

Visiting Toshie in Tokyo, the neon lights, crowded subways, and gorgeous department stores made Ohtawara seem an even more frumpy small town. Of all three sisters, I found Toshie to be the most light hearted, the most eager for fun and mischief. She took me to the Meidi-ya store in Roppongi, then one of the few western grocery stores in Tokyo, and bought me a jar of peanut butter. Down the street, we indulged in double scoops of ice cream at Baskin Robbins 31 Flavors. After months of only eating Japanese food, I cried tears of joy for Skippy creamy and mint chocolate chip. When I had to make another trip to Tokyo to sit for the SAT exam, I couldn't wait to have another overnight with Toshie. I knew she'd be up for delicious treats.

Toshie was also the one my host parents called on to sort out delicate situations. At the time, she had the best English skills and the most easygoing personality. When I broke a rule or ignored some custom, Toshie did her best to gently explain my errors. After a customer mentioned to Okaasan that she saw me riding my bike on the wrong side of the street, for example, there was a tense family discussion. "Okaasan thinks it is best for you not to ride a bicycle," Toshie explained. Initially, my 16-year-old-self thought Toshie was delivering a warning, not a permanent restriction. But no, I was indefinitely banned from riding a bike in Ohtawara.

Masae was a bigger mystery to me. She didn't come home much, and when she did it was mostly to sleep. The youngest of the three daughters, and four years older than me, Masae carried the weight of the Maniwa drugstore world on her shoulders. While her sisters managed to escape going to pharmaceutical college, Masae couldn't, or didn't. She studied hard in Tokyo, prompting Okaasan to worry whenever Masae had a big test. Okaasan was always sending her food and medicine to keep her spirits up. I often wondered why Masae ever agreed to take over the family business. Did she ever really have a choice?

Obaachan was not really a mystery, just a disconsolate woman: quiet, slow moving, almost a *kabuki* tragedy-like presence in the Maniwa household. Obaachan kept to herself in her room most of the day and hardly spoke at meals. She complained that her back hurt. My bedroom was next to hers, just off the stairs to the second floor. Though tempted to sneak a peek, I didn't. I never summoned the courage to knock and invite myself in to hang out or chat. Instead, I waited and looked for other ways to connect with her. After Gramps died, I suffered a wave of homesickness. Unexpectedly, it was Obaachan who noticed. "Grandma gave me a plant for my room," I wrote in my journal. "She is even trying to be nice and she is normally a crab. I guess if she tries, I can try. My happiest thought of the day."

As the days and weeks passed, Obaachan and I developed our own ways to bridge the linguistic, cultural and age gaps that initially seemed insurmountable. Already skilled in the kitchen, I volunteered to help Obaachan prepare the evening meal. She held up a small green vegetable and said "*piman, piman, piman,*" and I repeated "*piman, piman, piman,*" thereby learning the word for green pepper. We did this with most ingredients, slowing down the cooking process, but rapidly building my Japanese vocabulary. When I pronounced new words badly, I sometimes got a giggle out of her, or a shy smile, one that she tried to hide. She personified her culinary specialty *subuta*, or sweet and sour pork. Sewing also helped me connect to Obaachan. Anticipating the *Obon* summer holiday, when many Japanese believe their dead ancestors return for a visit, Okaasan, who had elegant taste in kimonos, bought me a bolt of cotton with bright orange, yellow and red flowers on a white background. "Obaachan will help you sew a *yukata*," a summer cotton kimono, she told me. "This is going to be so excellent," I wrote in my diary. "When Obaachan and I laid out the material I just wanted to hug her. But nobody ever hugs in Japan."

Obaachan was nothing like my Gram in personality or temperament. But having a grandmother in the house seemed normal. What was new, thrilling and bewildering—all at once—was having a mother in the house—a full-time working mother—who noticed my moods and the tiny details of my appearance. She also set rules. My years of watching Phyllis run a household next door had given me key observational skills. But now there was the added complexity of an immense language barrier. Okaasan never learned to write romanized letters, never studied English, never traveled abroad. She was, however, endlessly patient with my evolving Japanese. Okaasan wore a kimono under her white pharmacist's coat and pulled her black hair back in a tight bun. Occasionally, I had to remind myself not to stare. How did she tie the kimono every day? And how could she stand the white *tabi* socks that separated her big toe from the rest, even if they did make it easier to slip in and out of her *geta*? It would be easy to see her as traditional, or old fashioned. But such labels would be wrong. Okaasan was a remarkable, resilient woman who possessed a very modern sense of the importance of taking time for herself and prioritizing her artistic practices, as well as lovingly caring for her family.

Okaasan started her mornings by getting up before 5.00 a.m. to practice calligraphy. In the quiet of her room, she stroked the black ink stick in water, gently, calmly, until she achieved the right color and consistency. She studied the bright orange corrections her calligraphy *sensei* had made the prior week, and worked hard, thoughtfully, intentionally on her strokes. To me they were bold, elegant and beautiful; but she was aiming for something higher and was never satisfied with her progress. "*Mada mada,*" she said. "I'm not there, yet." When Okaasan came downstairs, she eased into her family duties by offering incense and prayers at the family altar in the living room. By the time I appeared for breakfast, the kitchen smelled of smoldering incense, steaming rice, and strong-smelling miso soup.

Otōsan started his day sitting cross legged on a kitchen chair, steaming green tea and perusing the *Shimotsuke Shimbun,* a daily newspaper that covered Tochigi Prefecture. He clicked his chopsticks on the table, and then dove in for some of the assorted pickles, grilled fish or fried eggs Okaasan had prepared. "*Ano ne,*" he said as he poured me some green tea. "So…" or "Well then." He loved saying "*ano ne…*" It was his way of grabbing my attention, letting me know he had something to explain. "*Ano ne,*" the morning headline today is… The other family members didn't care to discuss current events with Otōsan and were relieved that I engaged with him. Otōsan wanted to know about America, the good things Japan could learn from her. He didn't want to look back, to the bizarre twist of fate: medical reasons made him ineligible to join the army and fight during World War II, where likely he would have died. He was lucky, he said about not fighting in the war. He wanted to keep living that way.

And so I slipped easily and agreeably into the Maniwa household. That was until I came down with a nasty cold. And then our different cultures and remedies clashed. While the Maniwa drugstore dispensed both western and eastern medicines, they clearly favored *kampoyaku*, or ancient Chinese herbal remedies. I couldn't understand why Otōsan wouldn't let me drink orange juice. Instead, he insisted on hot ginger drinks to warm my energies, saying orange juice would only make me colder. Or when I complained of an upset stomach and craved a piece of dry toast, Otōsan insisted I turn to *okayu*, a bland, soupy rice porridge. Instead of a small white pill for a headache, he offered a packet of small beige granules that made me gag. What kind of herbs could make something smell so bad? They may have helped my symptoms, but they also made me nauseous.

Luckily, we found common ground in *umeboshi*. Okaasan and Otōsan argued that *umeboshi* (pickled plums) offered tremendous health benefits. Their powerful acidity has an alkalinizing effect on the body, stimulates digestion and wards off disease, they believed, much as many people today believe probiotics balance the negative effects of antibiotics on intestines. Just like samurai used *umeboshi* to alleviate battle fatigue and cure food poisoning, I should eat an *umeboshi* a day.

From the delicate dish on the breakfast table, the tiny, sassy, shriveled red pickles stared at me. Eat me! Given the surrounding neighbors—gooey fermented soybeans, minuscule dried silver fish with heads (*chirimen jako*), shriveled bluish eggplant, shockingly yellow pickled daikon radishes—the *umeboshi* were probably justified in their poise.

I lifted one, as gracefully as possible with my chopsticks, and plopped it in my mouth. Otōsan, Okaasan, and Obaachan watched my face. Nothing in my dill pickle, sauerkraut childhood had prepared me for the taste of this tiny, tart, salty, pickled plum. I grimaced. I puckered my cheeks.

"*Yappari, suppai desu ne,*" Okaasan said.

"*Yappari, suppai desu ne,*" I agreed.

"Yes, it's a bit sour."

I tried whatever kind of *umeboshi* the Maniwas served—from the tiny, super-dry tart ones, to the semisweet big fleshy ones. To everyone's amazement, I handled them all. And in a bizarre Japanese logic applied to foreigners who actually like Japanese foods, that was practically grounds for making me an honorary Japanese.

After Okaasan noticed I didn't just pick at the *umeboshi* in the morning, but liked them, they started appearing on the top of my rice in my *obento*, or lunch box. She was trying to please me. What she didn't know was that the *umeboshi* actually saved me in home room. Every day as we unwrapped our lunches at school, my classmates couldn't help but glance over and stare at my *obento*. I'm not sure what alien dragons they expected to fly out, but when they saw that my lunch of minced ground pork meat, runny scrambled eggs, sliced cucumbers, and maybe a stewed carrot, all on top of a bed of rice, looked just like their lunches, they were stunned. The *umeboshi* on top sealed the deal. During lunch, for at least thirty minutes, I fit in. I had what everyone else had: a Japanese mother who lovingly and artfully prepared my *obento*.

On the second floor of the Maniwas' house, directly above the drugstore, was what everyone called the "stereo room." Part of the room contained Otōsan's desk, piled with books and magazines, Rotary calendars and miscellaneous posters for the drugstore. The other side had a stereo console and two long tables where I would write, do homework. This was also where I would hang out with my host sisters when they were home, listening over and over to the Eagles' *Hotel California* album and other current hits. One day, I told Rie about how the girls at school noticed every little detail about my *obentos*, including the *umeboshi* on the top. Rie stopped me. "*Urayamashii*," or "I'm jealous," she said. Okaasan was too busy when she and her sisters were growing up to make their *obentos*; "I always had to make my own lunch," she said with not a little touch of attitude. I understood how Rie could feel annoyed that her mother was now making my lunches. But I was not about to let her jealousy get in the way of my new indulgence. I just felt doubly lucky to have such beautiful *obentos*.

Through her smiles and simple gestures, Okaasan, once the nervous bride entering the Maniwa family, empathized with the challenges I faced each day She was kind, patient, and forgiving of my cultural missteps. Though the least outwardly international, she grasped how hard it was to be an outsider. She did her best to make me feel welcome, a part of the family. Even as she rushed to prepare for Rie's wedding, she listened to me practice my speech. She helped dress me in a kimono, tying the *obi* so perfectly, telling me I looked beautiful. She apologized profusely that there was one part of the ceremony restricted to only a very few family members that I would not be able to see. She was sorry to leave me out, but her hands were tied. I was so happy to be at the wedding party, I didn't care. But I knew she hated having to make such insider-outsider distinctions.

Those distinctions between us melted away on New Year's Eve. Masae took me to the Ohtawara Shrine to burn the *daruma* and various decorations from the family altar in the bonfire, along with our 108 sins. We each put five-yen coins in the bin and made a wish. Mine was for happiness for all my family and friends, and acceptance at Stanford. Okaasan was still up when we got home after midnight. She invited me to the family altar and together we lit incense and said the traditional New Year's greeting: "*Kotoshi mo yoroshiku onegaishimasu.*" She prayed for her ancestors. I prayed for mine.

I had lots of questions about Japanese New Year's traditions, and Okaasan was in the mood to talk. So we stayed up. "When I was a little girl," Okaasan began, "I would burn my underwear and old clothes in the same fire as the darumas. I would take a long bath, put on new clean clothes, and then after midnight go to the shrine, clean and fresh and ready to purify myself for the New Year. Sadly, those traditions are dying." One thing lead to another, and before I knew it she admitted that she was a latecomer to Buddhism. In college, she was a Christian. Publicly, she left her Christianity behind when she got married. Privately, she missed it. There were difficult times when she felt unhappy as a young, overworked mother. She dreamed of fleeing the house and drugstore with her daughters to a different life. But she didn't act on those dreams. "Why not?" I asked. "*Goen*," is how she explained it, referring to her abiding sense of fate, destiny and fortune, running between this and former lifetimes.

Sometimes, the Japanese can open up, be more expressive with foreigners than they are with other Japanese. Maybe that's how it started, but that is not where it ended. I listened to Okaasan, late into the night, without judgment. I didn't know enough about life yet to say anything, so I kept listening. What I heard was that she trusted me with her thoughts, her past, her ideas. I felt honored to have her trust. "We ended our talk in tears, saying we loved each other," I wrote in my journal. "And for the first time, we just hugged each other. It felt so good, like we had broken the culture barrier and were close. I won't ever forget that night or all the things she said."

We never lost that trust. Okaasan gave me what I needed most: the emotional space to feel completely safe. That Okaasan stayed in the Maniwa family business, chose to deepen her spirituality through pilgrimages, and loved me was nothing short of "*goen*" for me, too. As with Phyllis, I discovered there are advantages to not being someone's biological daughter. Okaasan worried about me, but I was not her lifelong project, in the same way that her three daughters were. We were close, but we also remained independent. As a family insider, with an outsider's perspective, I was able to talk with her in a luxuriously criticism-free way that biological daughters don't always enjoy with their mothers.

When the plum trees announced spring again, my first year in Japan was coming to an end. In a breakthrough moment, Obaachan invited me into her room to see her flowering bonsai. She was so proud of her plants. She had the perfect temperament for raising bonsai, not aggressive and impatient like me, and the plants rewarded her with incredible blossoms. "*Sugoku kireidesu ne*," I praised their beauty. Obaachan smiled. Then, like characters in an ancient poem, we turned our eyes to the blossoms outside the window.

Chapter 13

My year-long stay in Japan might well have been a one-off, perfectly satisfactory year abroad, if it hadn't been for the Maniwa family. They took me in, taught me Japanese, loved me and sent me home, changed. After, I would never be afraid to hop on a plane and arrive in a distant land. After, I knew the world was full of so many amazing, good, kind people I couldn't wait to explore more. A new Japanese me emerged, one that listened for and embraced politeness and honorifics and vague nuances. I liked the new Japanese-speaking me, especially when I turned on the local Tochigi dialect. That spun Japanese heads every time. Most importantly, I had tasted freedom of expression— writing in my journals, experimenting with poetry and in letters, unedited by anyone. In the surety of Japan, I found a way to let my raw emotions surface and tears flow. After, living in Minneapolis, with a father who dismissed emotional expression would never work

Muto-san, my now trusted advisor, warned me before I left Japan that there would inevitably be return culture shock. I thought I might be immune to the worst of it, given all those aerogramme letters we shared back and forth. But Muto-san said it hit everyone when they went back to a familiar place with new eyes and different reference points. Muto-san didn't lie.

By any measure, I returned to a heartwarming homecoming. Dad, Phyllis, Kristi and the rest of the family met me at the airport holding up bright hand-painted signs: "Welcome home Kathy!" Back at the house, Dad

111

scored the perfect welcome home gift, one he had scoured the entire Twin Cities for. Surprise! He pulled a fresh but dead squid out of the refrigerator and dangled the slippery sea creature in front of me and everyone gathered. "Just like they have in Japan," he said. I laughed. Through the squid, Dad expressed his total affection for me and my adventure. Lucky me. Not everyone returns to the eight arms and two long tentacles of a squid.

Not long after the initial euphoria of my return, turmoil set in. It was culture shock and more. Dad may have been thrilled to have me home, to return to our dinners with me doing the cooking, followed by our after-dinner cribbage games. But I resented going back to my old cooking duties. He had cooked, or otherwise survived my absence, so why return to the old pattern? The very space we occupied—a sprawling house for just two people—seemed a ridiculous waste after living in a compact Japanese house. I questioned everything. Who lives like this? Why are Americans so big and fat and loud and boring? Why is Dad so big and fat and loud and boring?

The first days back at my high school were equally uncomfortable. I was happy to see Kristi and my clump of friends. But I just couldn't get beyond the guy who asked me, "So how was Norway?" As if. Ja Ja. The only place someone from Minnesota would go for a year abroad would be Norway. Or was that Sweden? It was late March and I only had to get through to graduation in June, but with each passing day, I felt smothered by small-mindedness. To add to this angst, I was still waiting to hear from colleges.

Nearly unhinged, I marched into the principal's office to

see if there was any way out. The white-haired man who had been a principal forever and whom everyone tried to avoid, reviewed my Japanese school transcript, which had been translated into English, and said, "Nice work, young lady." Surprisingly, he agreed that keeping me tied to Washburn was futile. He suggested I fulfill my required classes in the morning, take a bus to the University of Minnesota and attend a Japanese language class in the afternoon. No one could believe that's what he said, until I wasn't in school after 11.00 a.m.

At the "U," I loved being in a Japanese language class. I still wasn't sure that's what I wanted to study in college, but I knew I wanted a school that at least offered the option. I was bummed when Middlebury College rejected me. I convinced Dad to let me visit Lewis and Clark College, and after a year in Japan, he let me make the solo trip to Oregon. But when the Japanese professor there told me I'd already test out of what he had to offer, I felt dejected. I still hadn't heard from Stanford. Apparently, my letter had been sent to Ohtawara. Otōsan was forwarding it to me. The Stanford admissions office admitted it was their mistake, but still wouldn't tell me yes or no over the phone. I would have to wait for them to mail me another copy.

For the first time in as long as anyone could remember, two Washburn students received Stanford acceptances that year. Ha. I was not only wildly excited, I felt vindicated. In the end, Stanford was my only real college option; I agreed to go—sight unseen.

With my insufferable "I am so out of here" attitude, I didn't deserve to be asked to senior prom by a nice guy named Sheldon. I turned him down, not so gently. I didn't say that I'd rather be dead than to go to prom. But that's what he might have heard. Dad was appalled, as if I had just blown my first and last date. "Who doesn't want to go to senior prom?" he demanded. (I wasn't worried. In Japan, I had a big crush on another AFS student; we exchanged letters throughout the year, flirted during the summer camp reunion and climbed Mt. Fuji together, none of which I told my dad about. Sheldon wouldn't be my only hope in life.) Kristi hadn't been asked to prom yet, but she still really wanted to go. She was a tad jealous I had been asked and bewildered by my response. I stood by my decision, but realized, too late, I had behaved badly. The Japanese me was embarrassed for my rudeness; the American me couldn't help myself.

The one constant was the open door across the alley. I'd missed Phyllis' hugs, hanging out with Kristi, and the delicious family dinners. It was easy to slip back into those cozy comforts. As usual, Phyllis listened and sympathized with my return culture shock. She said she understood how I was torn between worlds; but it was a good problem to have. In the midst of all these transitions, Phyllis hated to add to my swirling sense of place and emotions. But it was unavoidable. She and Warren had news: the family was moving to Denver. Warren had accepted a call to a new Lutheran congregation, and well, the timing and the job all seemed right. They were leaving one week after graduation.

"Know you will always be welcome, wherever we are," Phyllis tried to reassure me. No matter how much I believed and trusted her, I still felt crushed. My teenage brain reasoned I should be free to come and go, but everyone else was supposed to hold still, remain steady.

That things didn't really work that way was the entire message of the summer. After graduation and goodbye parties, long talks and close hugs, the Sortebergs drove off in their station wagon to Denver, leaving me in a puddle of tears. Living alone with my dad, I felt trapped like one of Gram's green beans in the pressure cooker. I couldn't stand being around my dad and his dates. While I was in Japan, Dad enjoyed his freedom to date without my "you've got to be kidding me" rolling eyes. Now I was home, but he wasn't about to change his successful dashing ways.

In phone calls and letters to Phyllis, I confided that it was so weird being in the middle of a sappy soap opera. I knew that Dad had several girlfriends, but he wasn't as forthcoming with each of them, who, individually, tried to befriend me.

"Would you like to join us for dinner," one woman asked trying to include me.

"No thanks."

"Maybe we could go shopping together sometime," another wondered out loud.

"No thanks. I'm busy... forever."

"I like your purse," one said as she was leaving one day.

"Right," I said dismissing her with a snicker. Everyone said I had terrible taste in purses, so I took her compliment as a suck up. I hoped Dad dumped her soon.

My reactions didn't sway my dad, they just created more tension. "Don't worry," he said. "They are just trying to be nice."

"Leave me out of this," I pleaded.

My only escape was my summer job at the state transportation department in St. Paul. Dad had pulled strings to land me a position in a project to computer code the state's roads, which paid pretty well, considering. But it wasn't really an escape. In a windowless basement room, I poured over country road maps and wrote a lot of zeros and ones on punch cards. I remembered climbing Mt. Fuji with other exchange students the prior summer and now in St. Paul, I had fallen into a dark abyss. Surveying the roads in Minnesota, I concluded the only one I wanted to take was the interstate highway that went south and west to Denver and on to San Francisco.

At home, caught in the dating crossfire made me anxious, and angry. Seething, I tried to warn my siblings, who were not living in the house. I paid a special visit to Aunt Mavis and Uncle Stan, to say my dad seemed to be headed for another relationship disaster, but they dismissed me. Dad was who he was, and basically, I was a disgruntled teenager suffering culture shock. I confided in Phyllis that I thought my dad's dating life was like playing roulette. He seemed to be making random, not introspective, choices.

"What is he thinking? Spin it and see where it lands?" I asked more than once.

Phyllis never directly criticized my dad, instead she wrote me loving, reassuring letters saying, "You don't have to like any of them. You'll make it. Hang in there. You have an amazing future ahead of you."

I was counting the days and minutes until classes and my new life started at Stanford. I was disappointed that instead of wholeheartedly cheering my acceptance, Dad kept telling everyone it was a miracle I got in with my test scores and unconventional school transcript. He was probably still annoyed I handwrote my essay on thin rice paper and mailed it from Japan without giving him or any other advisor a peek at my application. Besides telling me that Stanford existed, he had had no other input. I'm sure he would not have liked my personal essay on cultural stereotypes: How do bonsai plants reflect Japanese culture? What does a baguette say about French people and society? Also, he was miffed I didn't even fake an application to St. Olaf.

I reminded him we had a deal. And a deal is a deal. Generously, Dad had promised me he would pay for four years of college, wherever I got in. After all that we had endured as a family, after all I had done to keep house for him, he was committed to my education, willing to take out the necessary loans under his name. Stanford offered Japanese studies, palm trees and California sunshine, what more could a girl dying to get out of Minnesota ask for?

The car trunk was nearly full. My sister and I were eager to get going. Kari had offered to drive me from Minneapolis to Palo Alto. After our interminable summer together, Dad didn't hesitate to agree. He even approved of the plan to stop for a few days in Denver so I could see Kristi and her family before continuing west. Gram had driven up from Iowa to help me get organized and for the big send-off. At the last minute, she insisted I make room for one more item: my mother's sewing machine. "No one, no one brings a sewing machine to Stanford," I claimed. There was no point arguing with her. Gram insisted that no matter how smart or educated a young woman is or wants to become, sewing is a skill that always comes in handy. So we rearranged the luggage one more time, and the clunky, green Elna found a spot in the trunk. "You won't regret it," she said as she hugged me goodbye.

As I unpacked, my freshman quad mate, Martha, from Vancouver, Canada, was thrilled to see my sewing machine. In addition to wanting to study dance and music, Martha was a sewer. Before the first week of classes even ended, we hurried off to the shopping mall to buy fabric for pillows and curtains for our dorm room. By exam time, we had branched out into sewing burlap boxer shorts as gag gifts for the guys living across the hall. The Elna moved with us all four years from dorm to dorm to off-campus apartment. The Elna made costumes for campus shows, dresses for dances, and kept us in new clothes. Best of all, the green machine helped me make a lifelong friend. In my hurry to move on, away from household duties to loftier, more intellectual dreams, I had wanted to leave my past, and my mother's sewing machine behind. In her infinite wisdom, Gram knew sewing is really about the magical threads that connect us to other women.

Chapter 14

Precariously perched on my bike, I peered into PO Box 8022. This was my window on the world beyond college life at Stanford University. Five days a week, I had mail. PO Box 8022 was stuffed with my personal subscription to *The Wall Street Journal*. Despite our rocky summer together, Dad had thought about how we could stay connected. The subscription was his idea, a college send-off present. New clothes, fresh sheets and towels for the dorm? Any of those would have been appropriate and practical. But as we know from my welcome home squid, my father did not do appropriate, or practical. I grabbed the newspaper, hoping to find a letter from friends in Japan or my various families tucked in the roll. Sometimes I did. But day in and day out during college, the reliable, steady news I received was business and economic.

Seeing the folded newspaper always reminded me of Dad's dirty fingers. First thing every morning, he bounded down the stairs, opened the front door and plucked the *Minneapolis Tribune* from the brick steps. He made coffee and returned to bed with the newspaper. He emerged only after he had finished his morning read. He was oblivious to his messy ten digits, so newspaper ink was a breakfast staple: his thumbprint on a toasted English muffin, or on the white shell of a two-minute soft-boiled egg served in an egg cup. Dad ended his work day with a similar ritual. Returning home from his law office, he poured a glass of Scotch, snatched a handful of crackers, and sat down with the *Minneapolis Star*, the evening paper. Again, he never noticed the news ink transferred to the Triscuits or smeared on the orange Wisconsin cheddar cheese cubes he loved so much. News was all important: keeping current on local and national politics and, on Mondays, reading about his beloved Minnesota Vikings.

Dad did not just scour newspapers to keep himself informed. He wanted to review and discuss the day's news at dinner. The more heated the debate, the better. For a while, I dodged questions about President Lyndon Johnson and the Vietnam War, because I was the youngest, only eight years old. But after my brother and sister both left for college, there was no place to hide at the table. Tricky, unscrupulous President Nixon and the unfolding Watergate scandal flavored my dinners as a 12-year-old.

On most days I tossed the *Journal* into my backpack and rode into the fray of White Plaza knowing I would never read beyond page one. I was happily immersed in the exotic machinations of ancient Japanese literature, world religions, and modern European history, not to mention the excitement of dorm life. The stock market held no appeal. In time, I skimmed the headlines, just in case Dad called. I wanted him to think I was staying current. But I hadn't taken economics yet, and wasn't interested in business, so a full read of the Journal was a stretch. There is no doubt Dad thought that the Journal subscription would help us transcend the turbulence in our relationship that reared in the summer and only increased after that.

After loving my first semester—new friends, classes and the Bay Area, I returned to Minneapolis for Christmas. Dad waited for my return to go into our traditional production of Norwegian Christmas treats:

krumkake, rosettes, fattigman. We made batches and batches and boxed them to give his law partners and close friends every year; he couldn't wait to start. As usual, my siblings ducked out of the annual holiday baking mess. I stayed, in part because I thought it was a worthy family tradition, and we had fun baking. As a family, we delivered our assorted cookies on the afternoon of Christmas Eve, or brought them to family holiday parties. At one gathering, Dad stepped forward and got the attention of the room: "I have an announcement. I'm getting married."

I stood there stunned. To whom?

"Sally and I are engaged," he said triumphantly.

The wheel had stopped at Sally. She's the one who had commented on my purse, the blonde, part-time consultant, who grew up in Arkansas and hadn't completely lost her accent, who was a political activist, on the—gasp— Republican side of things.

I was distraught over Dad's choice for his third wife, and American-me made no effort to hide those feelings. I got it that Dad kept his pledge to wait to remarry until I left the house. But really?

"I'm not even gone three months and you've fallen in love, found the right woman?" I blasted.

I questioned whether his judgment in women had improved since the last wife, who, need I remind him, was such a disaster, emotionally, and financially. But his marching orders were clear: "It's a done deal."

As for Sally, I couldn't fathom why, having raised three kids and only recently divorced, she would want to remarry so soon. Neither of them ever thought to sit down and talk with me about their plans, to even attempt to get things off to a good start. Stubbornly, I didn't take it on myself to act like the grownup in the room.

So, I flew back to California, after a stopover for New Year's in Denver, feeling disconnected from the place I grew up and betrayed by my father. I felt vulnerable: I didn't trust my dad, didn't trust that Sally would want to honor his commitment to pay for my education. My siblings tried to convince me that I was overreacting; they didn't object to Sally. But they had already finished college, were on their own working, and had no financial stake in Dad's newest course. I, on the other hand, needed to plan ahead for all eventualities. Also, I never wanted to be in a position to have to return to Minneapolis. I became a California resident, applied for a California driver's license and filed my own taxes there. That way I could transfer to a University of California school if Dad pulled the plug on my tuition payments. I started a job part time as a "hasher" preparing food and doing dishes in the dorm cafeteria.

Luckily, my Japanese was good enough to land a full-time summer job as a tour guide for Japanese tourists in the Bay Area. I moved into an off-campus house in Palo Alto for the summer and took the first train in the morning up to San Francisco. From there, I put in 13-hour days conducting tours to Yosemite National Park (up and back in the same day) or Carmel-by-the-Sea and Monterey the next. The San Francisco city tours were less taxing, once I memorized that each of the two cables of the Golden Gate Bridge contained 27,572 galvanized wires bundled into 61 strands, and the total length of wire used in both cables runs 80,000 miles. The Japanese appreciated precise facts delivered in Japanese by a blonde American. Many sent me thank you notes on their return home; a few included copies of group photos. It was an ideal summer job: I made good money using my Japanese, sometimes $100 a day plus tips, which were highly dependent on my karaoke efforts on the long bus rides home. I was so busy, waving a flag and leading my Japanese tours, earning as much money as I could, I almost didn't make Dad's third wedding.

Initially, Dad thought that since I was working and so independent, I should buy my own plane ticket to his July wedding. Since I didn't really want to be there, I countered that I was sorry. "I have to work." My friends and Japanese family said I was making a mistake; they encouraged me not to miss the event. Otōsan and Okaasan sent their congratulations to my dad, and Toshie sent me a peppy note on Snoopy stationery saying I should get on with it and just wish my dad happiness. At the last minute, after much haggling, Dad agreed to buy my plane ticket to Minneapolis. Maybe he really wanted me there, but at the time, I was inclined to think he didn't want to answer any questions about why I wasn't there

Dad married Sally on a boat floating down the St. Croix River. This time, St. Olaf and Lutheran traditions were left onshore. This time, there was no pretense we would become the Brady Bunch. Onboard were a few close friends and relatives, Sally's three grown children, my siblings and me. The first time I talked to Sally's son was on the boat. It was awkward. Later, in a nice gesture, Sally sent me a postcard from their honeymoon cruise in the Mediterranean. She addressed it to Katherine Graven. That she hadn't checked the spelling of my name (Kathryn) irritated me to no end. Dad had a new wife; I did not have a new stepmother.

I needed to keep my distance. After running the house alone with Dad for so many years, it was virtually impossible for me to fall placidly under someone else's house rules. On school breaks, I excused myself from returning to Minneapolis by traveling to Vancouver with my roommate Martha, or visiting the Sorterbergs in Denver. Besides, Dad and Sally sold the Tarrymore house soon after they married and bought a townhouse in downtown Minneapolis. So even when I showed up at their new place for a few days over Christmas, it wasn't home.

In the name of furthering my education but also conveniently keeping my distance from Minnesota, the next spring I enrolled in the Stanford program in England for two semesters. Officially, I was there to study history and international relations; unofficially, I took up hitchhiking. On weekends, a friend and I held up signs for our desired destination near the M4 onramp, just outside Maidenhead, and smiled. Typically, we got picked up by kind, elderly couples because, "If you were our daughter, we'd want her to be safe." These kind folks also bought us tea before waving us on our merry way. Hitchhiking and tea: a civilized way to travel. I liked the new freedom to travel so much I decided not to waste my time in summer school.

From the phone booth at Cliveden, the grand Italianate mansion rented by Stanford as an overseas campus, I placed a collect call to my father. "I think I'd learn more traveling around Europe than staying in England." Instead of a summer tuition payment, he agreed to send money for travel expenses.

"Don't worry, I won't be alone. I'll be traveling with my boyfriend."

"What boyfriend? You have a boyfriend?"

"Sorry, gotta go."

I hadn't told anyone in my family about Steve. We met at Stanford's Lathrop House; he lived on the floor below me and was a year ahead. From sunny LA, he wore sandals year-round and played lacrosse. Steve was intelligent, methodical and laid back—the opposite of unsettled, wound up me. My girlfriends gave him mixed reviews, but those who knew me, and my family story, understood how I would go for warm, patient and caring, even if that hinted at boring. We'd only been dating a few months when I decided to go to England. He wrote long letters. I wrote back. Aching to see each other, we hatched a plan to travel to Europe.

When a letter and money order arrived in the mail, Dad didn't mention anything about the boyfriend as traveling companion. Apparently, the boyfriend was not a deal breaker.

May 21, 1980

Dear Bub, (my childhood nickname)

Enclosed is a money order for $1,000.00 I'm delighted to advance you at this time for your summer learning experience. There could be more in the event of a crunch. Since one does not roam round Europe in one's youth every year, opportunities must be maximized.

Upward and Onward,

Dad

With heavy backpacks, rail passes and enough cash in our money belts to survive on bread and cheese, we started in Norway. We visited relatives with names like Jens and Olav. We navigated an unscripted course from Scandinavia to Greece. Steve's trusty musty tent, youth hostels, overnight trains, calling on long-lost relatives and distant family friends made it possible to stretch our adventure out for three months. We returned to Stanford in September, more closely bonded by our pursuit of adventure.

During my junior year, I worked hard at staying away from Minnesota, but my sister's wedding was different. Kari seemed happy and excited, and though I could never imagine settling in South Dakota with anyone—ever—she seemed ready for her June wedding. She looked beautiful in Mom's wedding dress. Everyone said so. Comments like, "She looks just like her mother." Or, "Your mother would be so proud," brought Mom's absence to the fore. That, the presence of some of Mom's relatives, or anxiety about trying to play the role of supportive stepmother all seemed to tip the scales for Sally. She worked herself into an anxious tizzy by the end of the weekend. Up in the guest room, Dad and I lay on the bed and talked about the wedding, the people who came and what a great time it was. I said I thought Sally had behaved badly. He defended her, saying it was a tough situation.

The next morning, Sally confronted me before my father was up. "You are not welcome in my house anymore." What? I thought I was having a private conversation with my dad, but apparently, she had listened to the whole thing. "I've had enough," she said.

At the Minneapolis airport, I told Dad I'd had enough

of Sally, too. He said I was being too dramatic. Of course, I was always welcome to come home. "She was just tired and upset." For once, I knew I wasn't the drama queen. "Talk to her." I said flatly. "I'm going back to California. I love you. But if you want to see me, you'll have to come to California."

I spent the rest of that summer in Berkeley going to summer school. With Steve's help, I figured out that with just one extra summer of classes I could graduate with both a bachelor's degree in history and a master's degree in East Asian studies—in four years. Steve was studying at Berkeley that summer too. We found separate summer apartments within walking distance. To not give Dad any room to object to my Berkeley plan, I paid the summer in-state tuition myself and worked part time. This secured my role as the "black sheep" of the family for both my attitude and distance. My sister and her new husband enjoyed dinners, golfing and playing cards with Dad and Sally; I couldn't imagine how they did it.

After the post-wedding blow up, I didn't return to Minnesota for Christmas. Instead, I drove with Steve to his home in Los Angeles. Dad and I talked on the phone every few weeks, but it wasn't the same. As graduation neared, I thought long and hard about whether I wanted him there or not. My emotionally intelligent roommate Martha said I couldn't invite my father and not invite his wife. It was both or none, she advised. The first and only time Dad and Sally visited me during my four years at Stanford was for my graduation in 1982. My roommates and I hosted an informal after-party outside our apartment. I invited my Aunt Mimi (Grama Nellie's wild and fun sister) and Uncle Cal, Mom's brother, both of whom lived in California. If Sally was uncomfortable with some of Mom's family there, she did a good job hiding it.

And then I felt free. "The day you graduate from college is the day you are on your own financially," my father warned me early and often. I accepted that, and never went to him for money after that. He still tried to offer me career advice: "Go to law school," he exhorted. "You'd make a good lawyer. When in doubt, go to law school." I had many doubts at the time, but I had no desire to go to law school. Instead, I wanted to go back to Japan. Steve and I didn't officially break up. I'd miss him, but I was off to Tokyo on my own.

Chapter 15

Otōsan greeted me at the Nishinasuno Station with a big smile and a boisterous "Welcome back to Japan." He looked the same, though a tad balder. He still walked with a pronounced bounce in his step. Even after four years, the drive along the rice paddies was so familiar, so normal. I exhaled a big ahhh: I'm home. The Maniwas welcomed me back to Ohtawara in September of 1982 with open arms and a delicious sukiyaki dinner.

Otōsan wrote me regularly while I was at Stanford, so I knew the house would feel different without Hide, who I called Obaachan. She died from ovarian cancer the summer I was a tour guide. Hide was only 62, but seemed much older, with her cranky nature and constant lower back pains. As we ate around the *kotatsu*, I sensed the lingering sadness about Rie's husband, who had been killed in a motorcycle accident in India. Rie was living in Tokyo alone, adjusting, but Okaasan worried about her daughter being a widow so young. On the bright side, Toshie had married a local guy, and they were starting their own children's clothing business. Masae had returned to Ohtawara with her pharmacy degree and ran a second drugstore Otōsan had opened in a new shopping mall. They were all delighted I was back in Japan, and eager to help me settle in Tokyo.

Okaasan reviewed the list. Futons, blankets, sheets, towels, pots and pans, rice cooker, rice, miso. "Anything else you want me to send?"

That was already a generous shipment of essentials. "I

am sorry to cause you so much trouble," I said as I thanked her profusely. I had not expected that they would go to such lengths. "Never mind," she said. "We did the same for our girls. Our Tochigi rice is so much better than what you can buy in Tokyo."

After graduation, I knew I was going to be on my own—sink or swim, no family nest to return to. I applied to a nine-month intensive Japanese language program in Tokyo run by Stanford and a consortium of universities. And when they offered a scholarship, I felt like "goen" or good fortune, as Okaasan put it, smiled on me. I wanted to see the Maniwa family again, to take my Japanese language skills to a professional level. This intensive course—9.00 a.m. to 4.00 p.m. five days a week for nine months—helped me to learn to give talks in Japanese and penetrate Japanese newspapers. Japan's pull was stronger than my commitment to a college boyfriend. Dad was stumped that I had not outgrown my "Japan phase," and worried I was going to wind up a professor of esoteric gobbledygook. He didn't get it.

I loved my new life in Tokyo: A new batch of friends with assorted nationalities who also loved studying Japanese; a cozy apartment I shared with a roommate above a professor's house in the residential but still trendy neighborhood of *Toritsudaigaku*. I loved shopping for fresh vegetables and tofu or just-fried *tonkatsu*. My regular shopkeepers loved me back with their greetings, smiles and bonus samples, earned simply because I was a blonde-haired Japanese speaker. I had a steady Saturday morning English teaching job to keep me afloat financially. Steve visited at Christmas, but we wanted different things. After he left, I wrote that it was time for us both to move on. It was hard to cut a tie to such a stable, kind guy, and I was probably not eloquent in my conveyance, but I was ready.

When my language classes ended in May, despite what President Reagan said about it being "Morning in America," my job prospects seemed brighter in Tokyo than back in the US. Responding to an ad in the *Japan Times*, I landed an unlikely entry level job on the bond sales and trading desk in the Tokyo office of the US investment bank First Boston Corp. My boss said being fluent in Japanese outweighed my obvious deficit of having no experience or expertise in financial markets. I also believe it didn't hurt that in the interview, I said with a straight face and without a trace of a white lie, that throughout college, "I subscribed to *The Wall Street Journal*."

"You what?" was Dad's reaction. "What do you know about financial markets?"

"Not much," I agreed. "But I speak Japanese!"

The jumpy, high energy sales and trading desk was the perfect window to see how Japan was beginning to recycle its vast trade surplus. Flush with cash from auto and electronics exports, Japanese investors gobbled US treasury bonds, and dabbled in currency swaps. Think the sound of yen sloshing around. On the first day, my boss handed me a thick book containing stock and bond market terms and an outline of how the financial markets worked and said "go read." Beyond that, I learned on the job, listening in on conference calls with traders in London and New York. Part of my job was to recap market activity by sending a sum of the day's trades on a teletype machine back to New York. I was a quick study but a lousy salesperson.

"Tanaka-san. I understand your hesitation to buy today. Sure, I'll call again tomorrow." Five million dollars a pop for some US treasury bonds seemed a big investment to me. I didn't want to be responsible for someone I had never met making or losing big money. I lacked the killer sales instinct: I was not meant to sell bonds.

But I didn't let on my doubts during my Dad's first visit to Japan. Now that I was settled with my first "real job," he wrote he wanted to visit. It was a huge step, more than a symbolic gesture on Dad's part to see me in my Japanese world. But how could I deal with him and his wife for 10 days? That's when I realized the power of the home turf advantage. I joked with my friends that if Sally gave me trouble, I could abandon her in Shinjuku station at rush hour—only a few million Japanese pass through that metro stop. I never needed to. But at a sushi bar, I let her know I was in charge. I ordered *"odori ebi"* dancing shrimp just to see the look on her face. The sushi chef beheads the live shrimp in front of you, and they are still wriggling on top of the vinegary rice when served. Dad (squid man) thought it was great fun, but his wife looked pale, and refused to eat the dancers. When the deep-fried shrimp heads came later, a nice gesture from the chef, I felt confident in my position.

The Maniwa family warmly welcomed Dad and Sally to Ohtawara. Toshie and Masae prepared a beautiful feast. Otōsan brought out his best whiskey to drink with my dad. They drank and I translated late into the night. Of anyone, Otōsan seemed the happiest. Two families from two different cultures coming together at his house was something special to share at his next Rotary meeting.

After that, the overnight stay at a temple on Mt. Koya tested Dad's limits—he would get up for a 5.00 a.m. Zen chant once, to be a good sport, but not twice. "If you've seen one temple, you've seen them all." he quipped. I disagreed: Kyoto was full of amazing temples they had to see. On their return home, Dad wrote me a gracious thank you, saying he appreciated my openness to Sally, declaring it a fantastic trip. "Better than any of my three honeymoons."

Riding Tokyo's overcrowded subways, foreigners can't help but stand out in the sea of black-haired commuters. On the Toyoko Line, which I took to work every day, I befriended another blonde American who got off one stop before me. He worked for ABC News. Comparing jobs, I calculated that he won, hands down, for more exciting job and career. When my friend informed me that he was leaving Japan, I applied to be his replacement.

The night editor's shift from 4:00 p.m. to midnight was a serious step down in pay and lousy hours, my father duly noted. It was hardly glamorous to spend evenings alone, ripping sheets off the AP and UPI wire services, and watching Japanese news broadcasts. But it was a genuine job in a news bureau, and when the bureau chief offered it to me, I was thrilled.

During the day, before I reported to my night shift job at ABC News, I poked around for ways to break into print journalism. That's the advice I was picking up from people who worked in the bureau and in the foreign press corps. Most reporters started off in print: wire service jobs led to newspapers, or maybe a national news weekly. Becoming an on-air television reporter was a remote possibility.

People told me to write what I knew. From my stint at First Boston, I knew about Japanese banks and brokerage firms, and international financial markets. I pitched a story to *The American Banker* newspaper in New York.

I experienced my first byline joy when the *Banker* ran my story on nascent credit card use in Japan. Equally exciting, the editor asked how soon I could deliver another story. Japanese banking could be my beat, I thought optimistically. This coincided with big news events in Asia that unfolded on my watch on the night desk: Corazon Aquino rose to the Presidency of the Philippines after the assassination of her husband, Benigno Aquino. In India, a trusted Sikh bodyguard assassinated Prime Minister Indira Ghandi. Several months later, pro-democracy leader Kim Dae Jung returned to South Korea from exile in the US. The political turnovers, filled with both pain and promise, sucked me in. I didn't want to just read about current events, I wanted to cover them. I had no experience covering breaking news, but decided not to let that deter me.

I had, in fact, been a keen follower of Japanese news since my first year at the Ohtwara Girls High School. I dashed to the third-floor library during study hall, nabbed the *Japan Times* from the news rack, and settled into a corner. My brief but regular dates with the largest English language newspaper in Japan were a legitimate escape from the constant Japanese static ringing in my ears. I was lost in Mori Sensei's classical Japanese language class; Ban Sensei's biology class also bewildered. Reading the news in English about President Jimmy Carter and US-Japan trade disputes over beef and oranges, or about Japanese productivity and manufacturing successes, I processed the words in my "normal" brain. I learned about Japan's rising role in the world economy from the devastation of World War II. It was intriguing, exciting, and as the headlines screamed, a "miracle." For the first time—ever—I felt I was living in an exhilarating time and place.

Access to news in English helped me make sense of Japanese household life. I devoured food columns which detailed how to prepare local seasonal vegetables, such as daikon radishes, wild mushrooms, eggplant and sweet potatoes. These served as talking points with Obaachan in the kitchen after school. I struggled to comprehend the opaque maneuverings of the Liberal Democratic Party, which gave me plenty of fodder to discuss with Otōsan. Pushing the limits of my sports interests, I followed sumo wrestling tournaments and humored all of them with questions about the huge wrestlers' eating habits. I never failed to glance at the television listings for upcoming movies in English.

At Stanford, I never considered writing for the *Daily*. My Journal subscription taught me that Dad's love of news was a double-edged sword, one I couldn't quite handle. Reading and analyzing current events gave us something to talk about, but the endless unfolding also made it possible for us never to talk about other things: family cracks, personal hurts, underlying grief.

Back in Japan for the second time, I saw things differently. Once again, I picked up journals like the one Phyllis had given me, and took notes. I loved observing Japanese culture, sorting it out through writing. I didn't equate writing in my journals, making notes on everything people did and said in Japan, with news until I started working at ABC. I had a sense I was in the right place at the right time with the right skills. What might have been an esoteric language skill now positioned me to do exciting work. To be 25 years old, fluent in Japanese, living and working in Tokyo in 1985 was not so wild a dream after all.

Witnessing unfolding events has the bizarre effect of hooking reporters into making awkward cold calls to complete strangers to ask deeply personal questions. Figuring out how to turn a vague outline of events into a compelling new story then becomes an urgent necessity. Tight deadlines add to the pressure. Why does anyone do this? There are as many answers as journalists, but for me, it was the challenge of overcoming my worst deficits: discombobulation, self-absorption and procrastination. Looking for the key details, listening to others, writing on deadline—those would be good skills to have—in English or Japanese.

Generously, veteran American journalists in Tokyo helped me map a path. They warned of long hours, low pay and an absurd amount of fun. A correspondent for *Business Week* opened my eyes to a full scholarship possibility to attend Columbia University's Graduate School of Journalism. A special, little known program there, funded by the Japan-US Friendship Commission, was looking for Japanese speakers who wanted to become journalists.

That was me.

Chapter 16

"いって来ます" "*Itte kimasu*," I said to Okaasan in the entryway of the Maniwa home in Ohtawara. "I will go and come back." To see you, to eat delicious meals under the *kotatsu*, to sleep soundly on a fluffy futon.

"いっていらしゃい" "*Itte rasshai*," Okaasan replied, with a huge smile, followed by a deep bow, and finally a loving wave. "Please go and come back."

"I'll be back," I promised. Funny. It was 1985. I was 25 years old, and this is the first time I made—and kept—such a promise.

I never promised I'd go back to Minneapolis. To my father's credit, he never, ever, tried to lure, pressure or beg me to come back to live in Minnesota. His love, caring and guidance, for all its difficulties, and disappointments, was deep and strong—strong enough to let me go. I was always welcome and felt at home at Phyllis and Warren's, even after they moved from Minneapolis, to Denver and later to Chicago. But I only visited those cities because of them. I moved on when they did. I never returned to Los Angeles to fetch the thin-wheeled blue bike I left in Steve's parents' garage. Put another way: I excelled at leaving. I made sure to keep moving in a straight line to somewhere new before anyone could leave me.

As I prepared to leave Japan, after three years of studying and working in Tokyo, I began to see another possibility. "*Itte rasshai*" "Please go and come back," Okaasan said. The Maniwa home had been a place of comfort, belonging and excitement. Otōsan and Okaasan always seemed to like it when I came "home" for a night or two, alone, or with a few friends. So, I wasn't being too bold when, after I left my job at ABC News in Tokyo and my tiny, trendy apartment, I asked if I could store my stuff with them. Graciously, they agreed to keep my futons, pots and pans and other household and electronic items.

But actually learning where you want to go and come back to, how to make comings and goings work and to embed them in a way of life, involves more than just packing, storing and retrieving cardboard boxes. It requires shifting from a straight-line mindset of leave, or be left, to discovering the people and places that matter, nurturing those connections, and using them to draw circles. Coming and going, coming and going. Making the world turn.

After I whittled my baggage down to one brown backpack and a sleeping bag, Okaasan insisted I make room for one small gift. "びょうきにならないように" "These will keep you healthy," she said, handing me a clear plastic container filled with a three-month supply of my favorite type of *umeboshi*, salted plums. Yes, I would gladly take an *umeboshi* a day, to ward off stomach troubles, and more importantly to think of her. Since high school, Okaasan had kept me going with *umeboshi*. Of course, they would fit in my backpack.

"*Itte kimasu.*" I was embarking on a three-month journey through Asia on my way to graduate school in New York. "This trip is filled with uncertainty—only a vague course and plan," I wrote in my journal. In a way, it was going to be a personal test. I had come to hate uncertainty, my Dad's impetuous decisions, preferring instead Gram's steady planning and organizing. But I was also sick of always being the responsible one; I wanted to lighten up, see where the winds sent me, extend my edges. I had no idea if Richard, an American friend from Tokyo, and I would be compatible as travelers, but I didn't let that deter me. I traveled for a week in Thailand and met Richard in Bangkok. From there, it was on to Burma and India.

I had Eric Sevareid's tales of Burma as a historical guide. Severaid, author of *Not So Wild a Dream*, was my journalistic hero for parachuting into the "Hump" of the Indo-Burmese mountains just as his plane plunged into a mountainside during World War II. But it was Richard who fully grasped what would be necessary for a successful Burma trip. He came prepared to deal in the Burmese black market: a backpack laden with Japanese calculators, lipstick, nail polish, perfumes and cigarette lighters. Before boarding our Burmese Air flight in Bangkok, I scurried to buy my allotment of duty free: Johnny Walker Red whiskey and a carton of 555 cigarettes. I had to get with Richard's program. I had a lot to learn about surviving outside of Japan.

Time stopped in Rangoon. In 1985, The Socialist Republic of Burma was trying to rebuild the nation without outside help. Progress was slower than slow. World War II era jeeps cruised the streets. The taxi drivers wanted to be paid in cigarettes not the local currency called "chat." At the official Tourist Burma Office, our efforts to book a flight to Mandalay for the next day were met with blank stares, until the official spied the red Johnny Walker box peeking out of Richard's backpack. "I would like to give a present to my manager," the official said, unofficially.

Richard nodded. "I believe I've just had two cancellations," the official offered with a big smile.

From Mandalay, we traveled by boat up the Irawaddy River to Mingun, home of the world's largest uncracked bell and the Mingun Pagoda. I liked the bell but was more impressed by the river scenes of water buffalos and villagers coexisting in close quarters. Next, a hot, bumpy bus ride took us to Pagan, an ancient city of temples and pagodas. Bus is a misnomer for the rickety Datsun pickup truck with 15 of us crammed into seats and stools in the back. The seating arrangement provided a close-up of men chewing betel, their gums and teeth stained bright red. I arrived in Pagan with a splitting headache and upset stomach. I was too sick that night to take in the sights. *Umeboshi* couldn't quite stand up to Burmese food poisoning. It was the sickest I've been in all my travels.

Two days later, I had recovered enough to continue back to Rangoon. We checked into the Strand Hotel, once one of the most famous colonial era hotels in the British Empire. In 1985, the Strand had a name, but it was a dump. Not much had been done to it since the post-colonial Burmese government took it over from the British in 1948. But it still served some Western style food, which, along with a good nap, was what I needed to regroup. Recharged, we headed for the Shwedagon, a city of stupas with one grand and golden pagoda. "Michael," a local, heavyset Burmese taxi driver with a light-up cross on his dashboard offered to be our guide. The next day he drove us to Pegu, the ancient capital city of the Mon Kingdom, easing us through military check points with 555 cigarettes. What could be better than driving to see a colossal reclining Buddha with Michael snapping his fingers to Richard's cassette tapes of Billy Joel hits?

Thailand. "Bangkok never seemed so modern and civilized," I wrote. While Burma was an education in military dictatorships, socialism, black markets and roughing-it travel, I was more than happy to leave Burma and return to Thailand. We spent a day doing laundry and replenishing essentials before flying on to India. Plopped on the floor of an ABC News colleague's house in New Delhi, we got our bearings. By now, it was apparent Richard and I had different travel objectives. I wanted to head up to Kashmir, to trek in the Himalayas. Richard decided to peel off and join another group. We agreed to meet up again in a couple of weeks. I surprised myself with my flexibility and independence.

Excited and nervous, I traveled solo to Srinagar. In 1985, Kashmir was as magical as the original story of the Goddess Parvati who created the city by using a mountain to crush a demon that lurked in Dal Lake. That June, I slept peacefully on a houseboat, waking to the smells of hot masala chai and the gentle sounds of men in the *shikaras*, Kashmir's version of a Venetian gondola, paddling by to sell fruits, nuts, and flowers. I asked around to see about joining a three-night four-day trek. I snared a pair of green canvas boots with black rubber soles for only 60 rupees. Decidedly ugly, the boots were perfect for hiking from Pahalgam to Aru and through the Lidderwat Valley. Taking notes in my journal, I was practicing for my future career:

"The Himalayas surround me, rushing streams crash over the rocks. Pines give the air an alpine smell. Mohamed, our guide and cook, squats near the kerosene stove. Mutton and curries waft through the mess tent. Rajiv looks on. Here in the mountains, boundaries are only a product of the imagination. Here we are, close to Pakistan, not far from China. The geography makes more sense as I walk the hills and see the faces of the shepherds."

Returning briefly to Srinigar, I faced the hardest decision of the trip. My next big idea was to take a two-day bus ride to Leh in Ladak. But my on-the-ground research about the trip returned bad reviews. The mountain roads were notoriously dangerous and there was no guarantee I could easily return. Two days of nail-biting, hairpin turns was so not me. I was ready to abandon the whole idea until a Kashimiri on the houseboat challenged me. "Kathy, you wanted adventure and you came to India. Why are you scared now?" The 434-kilometer bus trip along the Indus River from Srinigar to Leh was beyond scary—but also superb.

"The mountains touch the sky and the waterfalls rush down to greet you." I wrote. It felt liberating to be taking in the natural world after the banking beat. I covered so many pages with my observations of rocks and geological formations: "Fascinating and formidable," "glacial and rugged," "cliff hanging" were the words I used. It's possible the very energy that created this part of the earth, the energy pushing up the growing Himalayas, was having the same effect on me. Day by day, I felt taller, stronger.

Surviving the hair-raising adventure to Ladak gave me new confidence.

Several miles outside Leh, I visited the Thikse Monastery, a "Mini-Potala" perched on a hill with vast views of the surrounding Indus Valley and snow-capped mountains. The colorful prayer flags and imposing Buddha statues paled in comparison to the funeral of an important lama that just happened to be taking place on the hillside that day. Monks in unusual, tall yellow hats chanted and waved incense as they honored their brother. I hadn't considered Tibet for this trip, but now I had to.

But first, reunited, Richard and I covered a lot of ground: from the love story of the Taj Mahal, to the turbans and forts of Rajasthan, to Varanasi and the holy waters of the Ganges. I convinced Richard that Tibet was a must see. In Varanasi, we put the Tibet plan into action and bought bus tickets to Kathmandu. At our last dinner in Varanasi, we pledged to return to India. We were in her grip. Then the sag paneer arrived. The odd brownish color of the spinach made me suspicious. I lost my appetite and stuck with plain rice. Richard was hungry and ate. One bad meal is all it took. By the time we reached Kathmandu, 24 tortuous hours later, Richard was sick, frighteningly sick. There was no choice but to put him on a flight home via Hong Kong and figure out how to get to Lhasa.

In 1985, China's control made access to Tibet tricky, but not impossible. In a Kathmandu cafe, other foreigners explained how it could be done: Join an overpriced three-day tour into Tibet, which affords you a temporary alien registration pass. Ditch the tour on the last night, find a driver on his way to Lhasa, and hitch a ride. The currency to pay for this? Photos, buttons, souvenirs—anything with a picture of the Dalai Lama. They were all easy to find in tiny shops in Kathmandu, easy also to hide in sleeping bags, and to roll up in underwear. Caroline, an Australian woman about my age, just happened to be staying in the same cheap, but clean, guest house in Kathmandu. The only thing we shared was a not-completely-sane desire to cross Tibet into China. That was enough.

The 875-kilometer drive from Kathmandu to Lhasa is not for the faint of heart. As long as I am confessing here, I should also say I wasn't completely honest with my father about my Tibetan plans. I called him—collect—from Kathmandu.

"Can you spell Kathmandu for me?" his secretary asked.

"It doesn't really matter," I replied. "Can I talk to Dad?" I filled my father in on Richard's departure and my new travel mate. I gave him a vague sketch of my new itinerary: overland from Kathmandu to Lhasa then a flight to Chengdu, China.

"How are the roads there?" Dad asked.

"I'm sure they're just fine." I reassured.

But in truth, I knew they were so not fine. Also, not paved for long stretches. Narrow. Winding. Dusty. But on the other hand, this was Shangri La in the Himalayas: remote, beautiful perfection. This was the Potala, the highest building in the world, that holy Buddhist palace surrounded by snow-capped peaks reaching even higher. I was determined to get there. What my father didn't know wouldn't hurt him. Caroline and I joined a tour. After the third day, in the dark of the Tibetan night, we left our tour guide a thank you note. "Please don't worry. We love Tibet so much. We want to see more and stay longer." In the parking lot of the guest house area, we approached several drivers waiting in their trucks for daybreak to begin their haul to Lhasa. Eventually, "*Wo men yao chu Lhasa*," (we want to go to Lhasa) was enough shared basic Mandarin to get us the lift we wanted. Calm, with a dark, leathery wrinkled face that made him look older than he was, Tempe smiled and motioned us to climb in. Quickly, he became our new best Tibetan friend. Tempe agreed to take us to Lhasa in his robin's-egg blue Isuzu truck. He found us safe, decent lodgings, mud-floored accommodations with yak hair mattresses.

Just outside Shigatse, Tempe explained we would be staying a couple of nights. His family lived nearby, and he needed to pay an overdue visit. We worried that maybe this was just an excuse for him not to come the next day. But when he arrived at the scheduled time and invited us to join him for the day, I felt badly that my trust had flagged, even momentarily. Caroline wasn't well, the high altitude made her head hurt, her legs ache, and her stomach nauseous. But I insisted she come anyway. "You can nap in Temp's truck."

In a small hillside village, a stout, slightly grey-haired woman emerged to greet us. Just how her son explained he was in town with two white women from America and Australia was hard to fathom. But she welcomed us warmly, without hesitation. She led Caroline to a dark corner, and pointed to the mattress, where she laid for the remainder of the visit. Tempe's mother led me to the open-air kitchen courtyard and a ball of dough. We bypassed the language barrier by making *momo*, Tibetan dumplings.

Tempe's mother watched as I stuffed the ground yak meat into the circle of dough and twisted the top to seal in the goodness. (It helped I had *gyoza*-making experience from Japan.) A goat wandered through the courtyard, indifferent to the foreign visitors. Soon more relatives arrived: aunties, uncles, cousins, a curious neighbor or two.

Surrounded by Tempe's family, in the high Tibetan plateau far from everyone and everything I have known, relying on my cooking wits and nonverbal communication skills, I felt a oneness with the world. We ate the steamed dumplings. We drank more yak butter tea. Then everyone smiled, huge, unbroken smiles, when I pulled out my Dalai Lama photos. While I had plenty to go around, it hardly seemed enough. Maybe it was the altitude talking, but I noticed my whole body shifting, and wondered if the universe was changing too. As I hugged Tempe's mother goodbye, I understood that in the farthest reaches, remotest corners, unlikeliest of addresses, good, loving people could and did transcend cultural barriers.

Om Mani Padme Hum. That's the six-syllable mantra of Chenrezig, the Tibetan Bodhisattva of Compassion. The mantra, not reducible to a simple translation, embodies all the compassion of all the Buddhas. Om Mani Padme Hum. I absorbed the vibration of compassion.

I was incredibly lucky to make it unscratched from Kathmandu, Nepal, to Lhasa, Tibet, first by tour, then hitchhiking. But smart girls know when the gig is up. So after arriving in Lhasa, and reserving a bed in the dorm for foreign travelers, Caroline and I headed straight to the police station. Of course, I'd like to remember turning myself in as something I did on my own initiative. But it was Tempe's idea. After making such lasting memories, the last thing I wanted to do was to give Tempe trouble with the Chinese authorities.

Caroline and I approached the windowless counter. Deep breathing was required, not only because of the task at hand, but because Tibet's capital city sits nearly 12,000 feet above sea level.

"We have a small problem," I said slowly to the Chinese officer. "We just arrived in Lhasa. I'm afraid we might not have all the correct documents." The officer said we needed an alien visitor's pass to enter Tibet.

"We left Kathmandu in such a hurry," I explained. "We had no time to apply. Can we apply now?"

Caroline and I waited anxiously. One hour, then two. What was taking so long? The officer had already briefed his colleagues. No paperwork was being blatantly shuffled. Maybe they just wanted to watch us squirm. We tried to look cool, relaxed, not as wickedly nervous as our swirling stomachs suggested. Maybe they had to wait until after the tea break? It occurred to me that all my previous travel experiences had led me to this critical juncture. They had informed my instincts to assess new situations, observe people. They formed the bedrock of my trust in myself to overcome language barriers and loss of comfort. Yes, all these travel experiences had seasoned me, hardened me, delivered me to this police station in Lhasa. But the real questions were: Would they matter? Would they be enough?

The Chinese official walked to the windowless counter and called our names. Without revealing any emotion, he granted us the alien visitor's pass for Tibet. We smiled, gratefully. But we were not home free yet. We were in Lhasa, a week from Kathmandu, or an airplane flight away from Chengdu, China. Which way would he send us? Caroline and I bantered about how long the journey from Nepal was and how we very much would like to see China.

"You see, we have already come this far," we said. He pointed for us to go sit, again. The wait was interminable. Finally, another official called us to the counter. He handed us back our passports. We peeked inside: The 30-day China tourist visa stamp consumed a full page.

Our good fortune was doubly fortunate. Later that night, after flashlights were out in the foreigners' dormitory, a handful of armed Chinese army officers threw open the doors and demanded everyone's travel documents. No one was hauled off that night, but the armed men had made their point. "Saved by Tempe," I whispered to Caroline.

Om Mani Padme Hum.

The relief and gratitude that flowed after I narrowly missed seeing the inside of a Chinese jail—or worse— stayed with me. After that, climbing the endless stairs to the Potala, the standby flight to Chengdu, several weeks solo in China seemed doable. After that, being rejected for a Mongolian visa, thereby dashing hopes of an Ulan Bator to Moscow train route back to Europe and then New York, was disappointing but not devastating. After that, I was willing to board a ship in Shanghai for a two-and-half-day voyage to Hong Kong, even though I'm not one for ocean cruising. After that, New York City's crime and grime bothered me but didn't overwhelm.

I called it "my Tibetan perspective." I could look around

and see terrifying, horrific injustices playing out everywhere. But at the top of the world, where the air was thin, and centuries of meditation and chanting had cleared away negative vibrations, I learned that the world can and does look out for us. The world looked out for me. And that Tibetan perspective, of knowing my own strengths *and* that the bigger world cared, was what allowed me to stop leaving, and to begin drawing circles. Circles of coming and going. *Itte kimasu.* I will go and come back.

Chapter 17

Fresh from my first solo trip in Asia, I arrived in New York City in the fall of 1985 weighing a scant 104 pounds. Eager to dive into reporting and writing, I felt so clueless about America. I must have looked as vulnerable as I felt. As I stood on a corner at 110th and Lexington Avenue at dusk, a New York City police officer approached me.

"You shouldn't really be out here by yourself for too much longer, young lady," he admonished.

It was only the first full week of graduate school, but my political reporting professor had dispatched us to various neighborhoods for our first lengthy assignment. I was wandering around Spanish Harlem trying to assess how the neighborhood might vote in the upcoming primary election, I explained.

"Try the post office. Someone who mails letters and pays bills is more likely to vote," he suggested.

I took his advice, which only confirmed the worst stereotypes about crime and illiteracy in America. Compared to Tokyo, New York seemed dirtier, dicier, and wholly unpredictable. But there was no denying its deliciousness. I developed an insatiable craving for liverwurst and mustard on rye bread, which I needed to try in all parts of the city. As I ran around Manhattan covering everything from bankruptcy court, to schools, to press conferences with big names such as Henry Kissinger, I availed myself of every opportunity to pop into a new deli and check out the sandwiches.

Unlike my classmates, plagued by doubts about

whether a journalism degree would ever be worth the cost, I was lucky my Japanese language skills had helped me hit the jackpot. I had a full scholarship from the Japan-US Friendship Commission with a living stipend for New York, as well as a generous financial writing scholarship from *The American Banker*, supporting my studies in New York. My father softened his stance that maybe law school was not the only admirable career path. One fall weekend, Dad flew east on legal business. At the last minute, Sally canceled because of a family illness. After years and many tense moments, finally, it was just the two of us.

It was the perfect father-daughter weekend in New York City—a magical weekend to savor, again and again. On Saturday, we walked and shopped in Soho. In one small boutique, he insisted I try on a sweater coat. Since my birthday is in November, he often bought me a new winter coat or jacket as a birthday gift. The Soho coat cost more money than my student budget allowed, but Dad said it was worth the splurge. I remember dinner that night, because it marked a point of no return. Dad considered eating raw oysters a true coming-of-age test. He ordered a half dozen on the half shell, and encouraged me to slip the slimy things down my throat in one gulp, brine and all. I had savored my share of raw fish in Japan by now, so I slurped the raw oysters without the slightest gag reflex. He ordered more, and some Chablis. We capped the flawless New York City day watching the musical *42nd Street* on Broadway.

After that, Dad stopped talking to me about law school.

My scholarship to Columbia came with a paid internship back in Tokyo after graduation. Lucky for me, but to the chagrin of my classmates, I had a choice of several news organizations willing to take me for nine months. Sometimes, I wonder if I made the right decision but in the end my choice was probably inevitable. Confident in my Japanese skills, but plagued by doubts about my journalistic abilities, I picked the most familiar: *The Wall Street Journal.*

"Now we're talking," were not Dad's exact words but they fit his sentiment. He read the Journal, his colleagues and friends read the Journal. He had something concrete to show off now: my byline with our same last name. Pretty soon, if he talked it up enough, the extended family and complete strangers would be reading the Journal.

"*Itte kimasu,*" I said to New York.

Chapter 18

It was so much easier returning to Tokyo, now a familiar city, for my third stint in Japan. I was slipping back into a culture that I knew, a network of Japanese friends through AFS, with the backing of a supportive Japanese family. Looking ahead to long weekends, holidays, or when I just needed a break from urban life, I knew I could hop the newly completed *shinkansen* line from Ueno to Nasushiobara and Otōsan would pick me up. In Japan, I felt the intangible connectivity of being "home" that eluded me in Minneapolis.

"*Tadaima*," I'm home, is how I felt seeing Okaasan's smile.

"*Okaerinasai*," Okaasan replied, so pleased to have me back.

On a hot August day in 1986, I received my first assignment from my Tokyo bureau chief. Japanese companies were turning the global auto industry on its head, moving their manufacturing overseas, touting their streamlined supply chains and innovative designs. But in auto-obsessed Japan, it was still difficult and expensive to get a driver's license. Why?

To find out, I traveled to Yonezawa, a mountain city 200 miles from Tokyo, to a residential driver's education boot camp. The course lasted 17 days and 16 nights, but I spent just a few days observing student drivers, listening to the instructors who practiced and effused calm, with an occasional bout of barking. My story began:

"After an hour of driving in circles practicing right-hand

turns, Tsuneyoshi Yagi is ready to change directions. Forty minutes later he almost has the hang of left-hand turns."

Not exactly earth-shattering. To my shock, the piece ran on Page One in the middle column slot, called the A-head because of the shape of the headline. "In Japan, the Road to a Driver's License is Uphill and Bumpy," read the headline.

The bureau celebrated my first success over beer and yakitori in the pub located in the *Nihon Keizai* Building. It was a great start, but too soon to feel confident. Editors are always wondering what your next story will be. And the next one after.

In the late 1980s, Japan's rising role in the world and its postwar economic strides were a compelling backdrop to any story. I wrote about American companies trying to get a toehold in the booming Japanese market. I went behind the facade of the obedient Japanese work force to uncover how illegal foreign workers were penetrating the cracks, taking jobs Japanese no longer wanted to do. I followed regulators trying to shape the Tokyo stock market into something other than an insider's trading den. Hot on the money trail, I tracked the Nikkei stock index, to see where nouveau riche Japanese were investing their cash.

On several occasions, I had to interview my former boss at First Boston. He was not happy with my decision to leave the investment bank for ABC News and had sent me off with a memorable put-down: "So, I suppose you think you are going to be the next Barbara Walters." Two years later when I called and identified myself as a reporter for *The Wall Street Journal*, his first response was dead silence. Then, he invited me to a fancy lunch at the Imperial Hotel.

More satisfying for me than financial topics were the personal stories. I sat with Japanese housewives, giving them the opportunity to speak about their hopes and dreams for women and family. Their stories revealed the long shadows cast by a work culture that valued company loyalty and long hours above all else. And I took my turn in the foreign press pool waiting for hours in the Imperial Household briefing room, listening to earnest officials give non-informative details of the declining health of the Showa Emperor, Hirohito, until his death in 1989.

I worked 80-hour weeks, lived and breathed the stories, the deadlines, the rewrites, the 4:00 a.m. phone calls from editors across the world. It was exciting, demanding, all-out fun work. I was deep into global financial markets, international trade disputes, the machinations of the Japanese economy, the competitiveness of the Japanese auto industry. But what I enjoyed most were the quirky stories that spoke to how the Japanese thought about their culture.

"For Tetsuro Ozawa, daily life in Japan can be a real pain. Mr. Ozawa is forever bumping his head. He also has trouble scrunching his legs under dinner tables while sitting on the floor. He is more than six feet tall, 6-feet-1 in fact."

That beginning to an April 1990 front page piece about how the Japanese were getting taller and what that meant in terms of their psyche, not to mention the changes in industrial design standards it necessitated, was a favorite. When I first pitched the story to my bureau chief, he balked. It couldn't be true and there was no way to prove it, he argued. I knew it was true from my own experience. At five feet four inches tall, I sat in the back of my Japanese high school class because I was considered tall. My height stayed constant, but in 1990 riding the Tokyo subways to work, I noticed the adults towered over me. The Japanese government, it turned out, keeps meticulous measurements of all grade school students' heights; the data backed me up.

I was often asked what was it like to be a woman reporter in Japan. People expected to hear how disadvantaged a woman must be in the Japanese workplace. Japanese women were, but I never felt disadvantaged. In most interviews, even with high-ranking Japanese executives, I was taken seriously as a journalist, not in small part because I arrived without an interpreter, ready to conduct the interview in Japanese. Inevitably, a conversation ensued about where I had learned the language. I explained that I had spent a year at a Japanese girls' high school in Ohtawara, had lived with a Japanese family, studied Japanese intensively. Once I had demonstrated both my provincial Tochigi and urban Tokyo accents—we had broken the ice.

The biggest hurdles I faced came from Americans, not Japanese. Never having worked a full-time job in America, I didn't know how to navigate the politics and personalities of the foreign desk, let alone the other sections of the paper. I was at the mercy of my Tokyo bureau chiefs, who, not surprisingly, had their own priorities and office politics. In theory, I had a mentor in the highest-ranking woman at the Journal and my foreign editor based in New York. She took me on as an intern and then hired me as a Tokyo correspondent. But there were workplace issues I could never discuss with her. Like when the chairman of Dow Jones came to Tokyo and the bureau chief insisted the entire office go out after work to show the boss "Golden Gai," an area near Shinjuku famous after World War II for its houses of prostitution. By the 1980s, the tiny bars and narrow alleys of Golden Gai were still seedy, a home to strip clubs and karaoke clubs serving pricey drinks. However inappropriate the sex-club bar hopping, I never complained to the foreign editor in New York. How could I? She was married to the chairman. I chalked up such after-work demands as the price of working in an overseas bureau of a prestigious American newspaper.

I was never going to be one of those women who let love dictate her career or life path. I was too independent, too resourceful, too ambitious. Anyway, finding someone globally compatible, lovable and trustworthy was a tall order. Then a friend from my former Japanese language center asked me to meet his Ph.D. thesis advisor newly arrived in Japan for a sabbatical year. My friend was returning to the US and wanted to leave his professor with some local contacts. The three of us met for a *shabu-shabu* meal in Roppongi. For hours, we dipped meat in boiling broth, slurped udon noodles and drank sake. The professor, Dennis, was smart, curious, talkative and grounded, with very basic Japanese language skills. Dennis didn't fit my image of a Harvard Business School Professor. Sure, I'd be happy to help him adjust to life in Tokyo, I told my friend afterwards.

Not too many friends, old or new, took me up on my

invitation to experience my favorite Japanese *shiatsu* massage place in Akasaka-mitsuke. I swore by the *senseis* who dug their thumbs deep into my neck and shoulders—so tight after hours at the computer. But Dennis was game. He didn't flinch at the sight of six or eight futons lying in one open tatami room. He bowed politely to the receptionist who handed him a locker key and a pair of pajamas to change into. "*Domo domo*," he mustered in Japanese. Thursday nights after work, we met at the Namikoshi Shiastu Clinic and joined other tired Japanese on the floor for *shiatsu* heaven.

"We're just friends," I insisted to the receptionist, who kept giving me a certain look as I checked in week after week with Dennis. "My work is very busy. The professor won't be staying in Japan long."

Yet, as I started my fourth year of my Tokyo assignment, I wasn't sure what to do next. The idea I would turn thirty in Tokyo, stay single and live only for my career seemed a real possibility. A terrifying thought: Is that what I really wanted? Could the safety I loved about Japan turn into a trap, just as complacency and security do anywhere? Perhaps the long work hours were taking their toll. My mind wandered to other possible foreign assignments. My mind wandered to Dennis. This kind, energetic guy from South Carolina was breaking up with his long-time girlfriend who had left Japan mid-sabbatical. He wasn't my type. He spoke with a slight southern accent; he had a beard he never wanted to shave. But then, he was keen on global adventure. A few months later, he returned to Boston and I refocused on my day job. I kept my Thursday shiatsu appointments. I missed him. The *senseis* asked about the professor. He wrote me letters, long letters. We ran up huge international phone bills. Maybe he was worth a gamble. Maybe I should pay attention to my personal life. My heart and mind agreed it was time to figure out if I could live, work and love in America.

The Japanese host gracious sayonara parties for foreigners about to return to their home countries. In my years in Japan, I'd attended many for fellow students or journalists and came to appreciate how important they are to mark life's passages, when one moment ends and another is about to begin. But none was sweeter than the one hosted by my *shiatsu senseis*. "Make sure to invite the professor," they pleaded. So as I wound up my days in Japan, Dennis flew from Boston for a final visit in Tokyo and to join in some of the sayonara fun. Together we arrived at our favorite *kushikatsu* bar down the street from the *shiatsu* clinic. Four of my favorite *senseis* dressed in regular street clothes, not their work uniforms, were seated at a table decorated with small Japanese and American flags. We drank beer, nibbled delicious fried skewers, poured sake for each other and toasted: "*Yoi nichibei kankei wo*," or, "To happy Japan-US relations."

Chapter 19

I had a vague sense of *"tadaima"* or "I'm back" when I arrived in Manhattan to take up my new assignment at the Journal's headquarters. Realistically, however, after four years in Tokyo, I returned to America fully expecting culture shock. I anticipated feeling like an odd duck in a big office. I was prescient: the newsroom buzzed with reporters and editors working in real time to get stories ready by 4:00 p.m. Filing stories from Tokyo, with its 12-hour time difference from the editors, lacked the same urgency. Working with new editors and reporters spread out over several floors was exciting, but most were depressingly chained to their desks and phones. I missed the coziness of the Tokyo bureau and the freedom of reporting stories in person.

One early assignment to a corporate annual meeting proved that I had a lot to learn about covering news in the US. I had reported on plenty of such meetings in Tokyo, so I knew to position myself close to the right executives for questions after the briefing. I talked one-on-one with the chief executive officer, and returned to the office with spicy quotes and a decent story. As I was typing away at my desk, the editor shouted across the newsroom: "Graven! Where the hell are you? You are two hours behind the other wires." My glaring mistake: I had not phoned in the story to the Dow Jones wire service immediately after the meeting. That had not been part of my job in Tokyo; the wire service had its own reporters. Ah, so that's why I had the CEO all to myself. The other reporters had dashed to pay phones to

file their stories. Never again.

What I had no way of anticipating as part of my return culture shock was a phone call from my father in January 1991, just four months into my New York life. I was in my Battery Park City apartment eating dinner alone and watching the evening news; President Bush was declaring war in Iraq. My father called to say his bout with pneumonia during Christmas was not going away. In fact, he had lung cancer. "I'm a fighter. I'll beat this thing," he declared defiantly. But his cancer was the bad kind. The kind that took off and raced to the brain and spread to the liver.

I hung up the phone and called Dennis. "My dad has lung cancer. It doesn't sound good." I started sobbing. My mind raced from guilt about having spent so many years overseas, to panic about what to do next. Should I hop on a plane to Minneapolis? What about my job? Dennis tried to reassure me that things might not be as bad as I imagined. Then he helped strategize.

Shaken by the news, but trying to be a better American me, the next night I called Dad and asked if Sally could get on the line too. "I'd like to help, spend time with you, and not worry about old fights. Can we draw a line in the sand and start fresh from here?" I asked.

"What do you say, Sal?" Dad asked.

There was a slight pause, and then she said, "Okay."

And that was that. Years of feuding ended because we decided to stop. We didn't have any time to fight. Dad was dying.

Every other week during my Dad's cancer treatments, before there was internet and telecommuting, I crammed my reporting into four long days in New York, and then wrote and filed my stories over the weekend from Minneapolis.

After a combined eight years of living overseas, I reconnected with my father and made peace with Sally. Dad and I played cribbage, talked about what everyone in the family was doing. That gave Sally time to run errands or take a nap. I stepped gingerly around the kitchen—willing to cook if Sally didn't feel up to it, happy to stay out and let her rule. I suggested we keep a notebook to track Dad's medicines and leave it by the phone where it would be handy when the doctor called. She liked that idea. I appreciated that she gave Dad's family, friends and colleagues ample time to visit with him. When Dad wanted to move his regular bridge game to the hospital, she helped set it up. That was remarkably generous.

"I will go and come back," I promised. I went back to work in New York, and returned to Minneapolis to spend time with Dad. We talked about my news stories. He bragged about a Page One story I wrote to his many visitors. "I will go and come back," became a way of life for a few short months.

"Play some hymns," Dad said from his comfy living room chair by the window, the same chair where he had always read the newspaper and smoked his pipe. Only now that he had lung cancer, he had given up the pipe. In a very un-Lutheran-like way, we made the first line of hymns into a game. I played through the green Lutheran Hymnal and he sang along. We rated the hymns for their hum-ability. Could you hum back the first line after only singing it once? If so, it was a keeper. If not, best to skip that dirge.

Dad argued that hum-ability applied to Broadway show tunes as well. If you couldn't hum at least one or two songs after a musical, it wasn't going to make it.

My playing and singing hymns eased him into a calmer, contemplative place. His physical body weakened. He lost his hair and the chemotherapy and radiation zapped his cells. But emotionally, he started opening up. Certain hymns reminded him of "Tweeps." It was strange and deeply touching for me to hear him refer to my mother by her childhood nickname. "Tweeps." That sounded nice. Some of my anger, built up like an ice dam after years of his blanket stubborn refusal to talk about her, thawed.

The music also created the opening for him to discuss what he termed "an ingenious solution to a difficult problem."

"What's that?" I asked.

"What to do with me when I am gone."

Dad had devised a tri-state plan. He wanted to be cremated, with his remains divided between three cemeteries. For his kids' sake, the cemetery in Hayward next to our mother. For his 90-year-old mother's sake, the cemetery in Greene, Iowa, near his father. And for Sally's sake, a plot up in Nisswa, Minnesota, near the lake home that they shared. Ingenious.

As for the hymns? He trusted me to make sure they would be peppy, uplifting and above all hum-able.

Then he told me to leave. "Go back east. Make a nice life with Dennis," he said. He didn't want a morbid death watch. Besides, he and Sally needed time alone. I didn't want to leave. But I also understood that what he really wanted was to know that I had a promising life to go back to. I flew to Boston; I needed to be with Dennis.

Though I wished circumstances were different, I didn't turn to my older siblings for support. The difficult truth for me was that my siblings and I were in such different places it made it hard for us to come together and share our sorrow. My brother was working in Hawaii and unable to make frequent trips to Minneapolis. My sister had just moved to St. Louis and given birth to her third child when Dad got diagnosed. She was beyond sleep deprived trying to nurse an infant and care for two other kids. Adding to the terra incognita of it all, I, the black sheep of the family, was making peace with Sally, living in the US and the one child positioned to help care for my dad.

But in fact, my siblings and I had never shared our grief over our mom or our pain from Dad's failed marriage. We shared biological parents but experienced their living and dying in different ways. I was always jealous that they had more time with our mother. Now we all knew Dad's days were numbered.

Days later, Sally called and said Dad was slipping fast and I should return. Dad wanted to die at home, lulled by the sounds of his favorite Gilbert and Sullivan album, the *Pirates of Penzance*. Sally made that possible. My tears flowed uncontrollably to the plucky lyrics: "In matters vegetable, animal, and mineral, I am the very model of a modern Major-General."

Dad's death at age 61 couldn't have been more different than my mother's at age 36. His cancer was swift, but I had time just to sit with him. He thanked me for massaging his head and feet. Together, we practiced breathing techniques to ease his pain. He never wanted to go deep or dwell on emotional questions. While that was disappointing and unsatisfying to me and many others, I started to understand why: People die how they live. I never had the chance to ask my mother, but I knew where Dad stood on the concept of heaven. I heard him tell a slightly cloying hospital chaplain: "I'm not sure there's a heaven. But I am a betting man. As for heaven, I have nothing to lose on betting there is one."

Twenty-five years after my mother died, we celebrated Dad's life in the same church where we three kids were confirmed, where my sister was married. We opened with the classic, rousing hymn "Praise to the Lord the Almighty." Warren was honored to give the homily, and I was comforted knowing he and Phyllis and Kristi were there for me. The pews were packed, overflowing with nearly 800 guests. We went out with "Ode to Joy." Beethoven always wins when it comes to hum-ability.

Then we carried out Dad's wishes. My sister and her family, my brother and his sort-of girlfriend, Dennis and I and my uncles drove to Hayward and placed Dad's ashes next to Mom. The next day, we drove with Gram to Iowa and had a quiet graveside ceremony in Greene. Sally opted to wait and do her own thing at a later time in Nisswa.

Exhausted after completing the tri-state plan, I returned to Battery Park City, to the different hum of the newsroom. I went to work each day, eager for distraction. I lay awake at night wondering: What did it mean to be an orphan at age 30? Removed from Japan, on my own in Manhattan, who was my family now? I struggled to find a way to get my inner and outer lives in sync. They didn't line up. If there is no past, no parent begging or expecting you home for holidays, there is only the future.

I needed time with Phyllis and Warren, who were living in Chicago. I visited them for long weekends whenever I could. Phyllis and I dashed to the fabric store and sewed together. We took long walks, and drank tea. I trusted both Warren and Phyllis with my grief and sadness, with the tough assertion that I loved my dad but hated how he dismissed emotions. With them, I could let my tears flow. In time, I saw that my tears were not just for Dad, but for Mom, for the family I wanted us to be, the one we never were again after the accident left us cracked and broken. I had stuffed a lot of tears over the years, but with Dad gone I didn't have to do that anymore. With Phyllis holding me tight, I learned that crying didn't lead to falling apart. Crying made healing possible. Slowly, I saw my tears as a victory: finally, the courage to be me. I'd never let anyone stop me from tasting my own salt—even if I made a mess of my face.

Dennis had heard me talk about Phyllis and Warren, but now he understood that they were not just old family friends; they were my "other parents," integral to my life and sanity. After Dennis, the person I talked to on the phone longest and most frequently was Phyllis. "*Kathy!*" I needed to hear Phyllis' voice. "*Phyllis!*" She needed to hear mine. Dennis recognized I needed time alone with Phyllis. Steady and solid, he held me and loved me when I needed it; he gave me space when I needed to be alone. Bereft, unfocused and unsteady me wasn't sure what to make of this man, but Dennis said not to worry; he wasn't going anywhere.

After months of going through the motions in the

newsroom, I wondered aloud if I should take a break, step away from the day-to-day news cycle. Dennis invited me to move in with him in Boston. I applied for a spot for a year as a visiting fellow at Harvard University's Program on US—Japan relations. I asked the Journal for a leave of absence. Unsure of anything, I decided to take our relationship to the next level. Like Dennis, the plan was compelling: I could keep my Japan connection alive, spend time with him, and have a way out at the end of a year if I needed it.

Gram was more worried than Phyllis about me moving in with Dennis. She wasn't prudish. Rather, at 91 she found my open-ended plans unsettling. She hoped we'd get married soon so she could be at the wedding.

At Harvard, I dutifully attended the Japan seminars. But afterwards, allowed to audit classes elsewhere in the university, I walked straight to the music department and took an anonymous seat in a course on the History of Western Music. I spent hours listening to the CDs that came with the textbook and looked for more in the music library. Listening to music, just letting it roll through my body, was a break from the spontaneous waves of grief that washed over me while I waited at an innocent stop light, or when my nose tricked me into smelling Borkum Riff pipe tobacco instead of simmering soup. Escaping to other centuries via a Gregorian chant was calming, soothing. It kept me going. The journey from classical music to the unsettling sound of John Cage—whose indeterminacy ideas offered that a "piece can be performed in substantially different ways"—mirrored my inner wanderings. Did I want to enjoy the comforts of a prescribed career path? Or did I want to make my own sounds? Could I have both?

Enveloped in a cloud of "expect the worst," I was surprised how easy and comfortable living with Dennis was. I had worried I'd feel smothered, but I didn't. I thought it a bit strange he brushed his teeth in the shower. But in the scheme of things, that was minor. He worked hard, long hours researching and writing, preparing to teach, which left me to my own rhythms. He didn't cook, didn't even try to fake that he could. But he loved that I cooked and was so appreciative of our meals together. In the late afternoon, we made a ritual of taking a walk along the Charles River.

Though our paths crossed in Japan, Dennis and I also shared a passion for India. Dennis came to our relationship with his own experiences of living and working in India, as a Fulbright Scholar at the Delhi School of Economics. That, in addition to his other previously mentioned charms, earned him significant points with Gram. She was even more pleased, however, when six months after my father died, I told her Dennis and I were going to southern India.

Gram delighted in writing the address of the girls' school where she taught, so Dennis and I could try to find it. Her memory was intact: the Methodist Episcopal Girls High School was right across from the YMCA, on Ritherdon Road in Madras, now called Chennai. It was just where Gram described, though the building numberings had changed. Dennis and I met current teachers, watched the uniformed girls chatting happily on the school grounds. We could report back to Gram that the school was indeed still thriving.

The trip to India brought me to a new point with Dennis. My father's death not only reminded me that life is short, but that it is never fully sorted out. We have to grieve, but we also have to resurface and grab our own happiness. Ever since we had met, Dennis demonstrated he could be both steady and spontaneous. After losing both my parents, reliability mattered. But so did a zest for adventure and living. After Madras, we traveled to Trivandrum at the southern tip of India. Swimming in waters mixed by the Arabian Sea and Indian Ocean, I asked Dennis to marry me. He said "yes," and has joked many times since that he didn't have much choice: "Kathy is a much better swimmer."

Back in Minneapolis, we shared pictures with Gram, rekindling old memories. It was, she said, both just like yesterday and a lifetime ago. She was excited about my engagement. She offered me her bridal veil to wear at my wedding, the delicate lace a piece of India we shared.

It was immensely important to me to have found a partner who understood the emotional complexities of moving between two cultures. As a Southern man moving to the Northeast, Dennis knew about difficult cultural transitions. He had weathered bouts of cultural shock after living in India, and again after his sabbatical to Japan. He was with me in Japan, but also when I moved back to the US and adjusted to life in New York. Dennis, more than anyone else I had dated, knew about coming and going.

And now with Dad gone, Dennis knew we had to make a trip to Ohtawara to ask Otōsan for my hand in marriage. Otōsan made the most of his evening with Dennis. They ate. They drank Otōsan's best whiskey. With each toast,

Dennis' Japanese improved, as did Otōsan's English. Until neither could remember how fluent they really were. Otōsan gave Dennis his blessing. "I will fly to America for the wedding," Otōsan announced.

Dennis and I planned our own simple wedding at Harvard's Memorial Church. We asked Warren to perform the service. I dissolved into tears at the thought of the vacant position: who would walk me down the aisle? Warren offered the winning solution. "Why not Phyllis?" he said. "Why should a man have to give you away to another man?" Warren counseled in his true progressive voice. Without hesitation, I knew I could walk down any aisle with her by my side. Phyllis offered to sew a beautiful banner for the occasion to decorate the church, and she agreed to make her famous chocolate mousse cheesecakes with fresh whipped cream and raspberries for the reception.

Many friends have whined about how planning a wedding strains the mother-daughter bond. There were times I wished I had someone watching over my shoulder, questioning my decisions, offering unsolicited advice. I flew solo, accepting the first tip that came my way for location, photographer, caterer. To keep things simple, I decided to wear my mother's wedding dress, which fit perfectly thanks to Jane Lee. Mrs. Lee and her husband owned a dry-cleaning business on Newbury Street in Boston. When I first moved to the neighborhood she and I often talked well beyond the typical "it will be ready tomorrow after five" greetings. Mrs. Lee was from Taiwan; I had been to Taiwan on a reporting trip to cover an election. Oh, yes, the food was so so good in Taipei. She recommended preserved turnip when roasting chicken or turkey—to take away the fowl taste. "Here, you can buy it in Chinatown," she said handing me a piece of paper with the item written in Chinese characters.

So, I wasn't too forward when I walked in one morning with my mother's wedding dress, which had been in a box since my sister had worn it a decade earlier. "Do you think you can dry-clean and tailor this," I asked. "Of course," she replied. Mrs. Lee being Mrs. Lee, quickly understood that this was more than a simple dry-cleaning drop-off. She took me under her wing. "I'll make the dress perfect for you." It took multiple fittings, and each time she told me, "You will be a beautiful bride."

Boston hosts a spectacular Fourth of July party. We planned our 1992 July 5th wedding to take advantage of the festivities. Gram loved the weekend. She didn't let the several flights of stairs to our new condo deter her from seeing where Dennis and I would make our new home. A once-in-a-blue moon thick fog on July 4 forced the mayor to postpone the fireworks until the next day. At the last minute, Warren got sick and couldn't perform the ceremony, so another friend, Reverend David Killian, stepped in.

My parents' absence was a deep, noticeable hole.

But wearing Gram's veil and my mother's dress, I felt the love of so many women surrounding me as I held Phyllis' arm down the aisle. My siblings, the extended Graven family, Sally, Dennis' family, and dear friends, far flung from Japan and America, traveled to Boston to celebrate with us. Stacey, a fellow exchange student to Japan, stood as my maid of honor and helped bridge the different cultures mixing at the event. Kari's daughter, Hallie, was my adorable, perfectly poised flower girl. Kristi and my cousin Nadine sang "Simple Gifts." Otōsan offered a heartfelt Japanese toast: "*Kampai.*"

Dennis often jokes I am his Japanese wife, which bewilders most who don't understand his humor, or the story of how we met in Tokyo. We got married knowing we were soul mates when it comes to maximizing travel. I left the Journal to stay in Boston as a freelance writer. As newlyweds, we didn't stay put in Boston long. Book projects in mind, we applied for travel research grants and roamed Asia trying to understand how globalization works. We alternated three months abroad, three months in Boston for two years. We explored the Mekong Delta in Vietnam, reached beyond the Chinese cities of Beijing and Shanghai to the northeast province of Liaoning, became semi-experts on hawker street food in Thailand, Singapore, and Malaysia, returned to India for a breather before flying south to Australia and Indonesia.

While the vagaries of travel in developing countries might push some couples to the brink, our traveling deepened our love. We could be our true selves anywhere, in bargain third-world guest houses with squat toilets and mosquito nets, or eating barbecued emu under the skies of the Southern Cross.

Sometimes our research took us to the same place, sometimes we needed to part ways. Either way, we each knew the other could handle new situations. I will always love Dennis for coming with me to a rural village outside Dalian, in northeast China, to interview a Communist Party official about rice policy. With us was a 20-

something Chinese student fluent in Japanese. He was the closest person I could find to be an interpreter. I asked my questions in Japanese, and he translated them into Mandarin. For hours, Dennis sat quietly, diligently scribbling in his notebook, unable to understand a word.

On other occasions, I was the one who had to fill in the blanks. In Bangalore, India, Dennis spoke at a conference of industry leaders about the global economy. I took advantage of our stay at the Windsor Manor hotel in ways Dennis had not dreamed of. After eating one of the best meals of my life in the hotel's Bukhara restaurant, I couldn't contain myself. I phoned the hotel general manager with an unusual request: "Can I work in the kitchen?" There was a long pause, followed by a promise to consult the head chef. An hour later, he answered: "The chefs would be delighted to have Madame in the kitchen."

I spent the week following sous-chef, Gopal, to the markets for spices for his signature garam masala, and to the butcher for lamb. Back at the Windsor Manor, I rotated around the various kitchen stations rolling out chapati and naan, stuffing shrimp with exotic spice pastes, and manning the hot tandoori oven. My last night there, the chefs asked me to cook for them. What could I pull together that wouldn't involve hard-to-get western ingredients, but still show my deep appreciation? My menu: a huge pan of paella, a side salad of creamy cucumbers (Gram's tried and true recipe) finished off with an apple crisp and vanilla ice cream. "You cook very well. Yes, very well," they praised. The next morning, Gopal and I exchanged goodbyes—both of us in tears. I'm sure Dennis' lectures were most illuminating. But I think I came closer to making globalization tangible.

After two years of coming and going, Dennis and I ended our final three-month stint in Jakarta, Indonesia, visiting friends stationed there. The thick smog and sweltering heat overpowered the rewards of a delicious chicken satay or a spicy beef rendang. It was time to pause the travel. Time to think about having kids. That was a big idea for me. For most of my life, I hadn't pictured myself as a mother. How would I know what to do with kids? In Minneapolis, I was a terrible babysitter for the neighbor's kids. I was at my wits end caring for my sister's three little kids for just a few days. My motherless self was scared. But Dennis wasn't. He grew up distant from his mother, who never liked the role, or cooking or homemaking, and made that clear. By comparison, he said, I was more than qualified. He loved my cooking, how I made our home happy and colorful and hosted holiday parties and invited strays from assorted countries to join us. He told me I'd make a great mother. I'd have to trust him.

Satisfied with our travels, and as ready as we'd ever be to settle down, we returned to the US. Occasionally, we'd look at each other and discuss again whether having a family would kill our individual and combined wanderlust. "No way." "Not us." We worried that feeling trapped would be our biggest challenge.

In late March, as Boston's winter dragged on, Dennis and I escaped to Florida for a quick visit with Sally. While we were there, my uncle called with news that Gram had died from an apparent stroke. She never knew what hit her. Dennis and I flew with Sally to Minneapolis to gather with the extended family for a memorial service in Greene.

Gram had requested her body be donated to science. Even in her death, she didn't want to miss an opportunity for someone to learn something.

As sad as I was to lose the woman who had taught me survival skills and so much more, I wanted to celebrate her well-lived 94 years. Sharing Gram stories late into the night with my siblings and first cousins, it became obvious Gram had found a way to connect with each of us through our own interests and passions. "I was her favorite," declared Cousin Paul, who studied aeronautical engineering. "No, I was definitely her favorite," countered Cousin Mike, who became a neonatologist. I didn't say anything. I knew I was her favorite. Eleven grandkids—each one convinced they mattered.

Chapter 20

Stories abound about how some women just think about wanting a baby and the next minute they are pregnant. Not me. I didn't think 35 was too late to start a family. But when I wasn't pregnant after months of trying, I heard a different story from the doctor.

"Well, you are not exactly a spring chicken."

Besides my age, he said, there was no medical reason I couldn't have a child. He counseled patience. Patience wasn't in my vocabulary.

My mind said something else must be going on. Deep inside, I couldn't help but wonder if my body resisted a baby because I was holding on to something. Walking along the Charles River, I rolled back my up-tight shoulders, took a deep breath and tried to hear myself, not my disappointed hormones talking. Nothing. Then a flicker of anger. I was so sick of defining myself by my parents' deaths. "You had your chance," I said to Mom and Dad, as if they were right beside me listening. "It's my turn."

And that's how I went from not imagining motherhood, to being obsessed with becoming a mother, to fervently wanting my own chance to have kids and raise a family.

Thank goodness I had Phyllis. She's the one person besides Dennis who I could really talk to about my new quest.

"How can I become a mom when I don't remember my mom, or what a mom does?" I asked. "Do you think those thoughts are why I am not getting pregnant?"

Phyllis laughed sympathetically. "Would you have relied on those thoughts *not* to get pregnant?"

"Right. Crazy me."

Probing, tests and more tests, and the doctor still couldn't explain why I wasn't getting pregnant. A specialist suggested hormones to boost my ovaries to release more than one egg at a time. They made my moods wobbly and skewed my thinking.

"Do you think I am not meant to be a mother," I moaned to Phyllis. "Is this a sign?" When my periods came, they were painful and depressing. Returning to my Japanese drugstore roots, I added acupuncture and herbs to counter the every-other-month hormone boosts. Alternative therapies were not for everyone, Phyllis said, but they might help. "You are part Japanese, after all," she joked.

In the midst of all this no-baby-yet business, I was so excited when Phyllis called and floated the idea of her and Warren spending the Christmas holiday with me and Dennis. It was a first. "Yes! Come! But won't the others be upset?" I asked directly. Now that their four children were married and on their own, they took turns visiting different ones on holidays. "We need to spend a Christmas with you. You're our daughter too," she said. "If anyone is mad, they will have to get over it."

Phyllis arrived in Boston with a shoebox tucked under her arm. Her precious cargo: perfectly round cardamom rolls blanketed in tin foil. "I always have these rolls on Christmas Eve. I hope you don't mind." Along with the delicate and delicious cardamom rolls, I served roast duck with forty cloves of garlic and braised red cabbage—a

Danish must. Warren complimented my Norwegian flatbread, saying I rolled it "thinner than the master ladies at his church." Phyllis made *Rommegrot,* a rum pudding for dessert. Dennis poured aquavit shots to wash it down. I was as content as I can ever remember being. This was a big deal: having two parents come to Christmas dinner at my home with my husband was a miracle.

The Christmas visit with Warren and Phyllis went so well, we planned more visits: stopovers in Chicago, ski trips to Colorado. After each rendezvous, Phyllis wrote me lovely notes, exclaiming "we made new memories." The four of us became adult friends. But this came with some new family tensions. Without kids, Dennis and I were free and eager to travel. Warren and Phyllis' other kids had toddlers, or spouses who didn't crave time with the in-laws. Dennis and Warren, however, bonded over heated discussions about politics and economics. Dennis challenged Warren's preachy side with humor, and Warren loved that no topic was off-limits for Dennis. Phyllis understood that the dynamics made it hard for Kristi, who was juggling three kids, a career and a husband who often clashed with Warren. But for Phyllis, there was always enough love to go around, and tensions in one part of the family need not sour other relationships. I felt guilty at times that somehow, without intending, I had stolen my best friend's family right out from under her. Mostly, I hoped and trusted that with a mother like Phyllis, that wasn't possible. The power of her unconditional love and hugs had to be big enough.

What I loved most about Phyllis is that, with her, I could drop my guard and say anything. Over the phone,

together taking long walks or sipping afternoon tea, we talked about our friends, books, family machinations, politics and *Oprah*. Phyllis loved *Oprah*. I never watched, but I loved hearing Phyllis' take on the show. The way Oprah got people to bare their deepest feelings was the emotional world Phyllis thrived in. So even when I wondered out loud some illogical, irrational thoughts, Phyllis wasn't fazed.

Three years later, Dennis and I had not given up our dreams of having kids. We alternated between Eastern and Western medical remedies, and discovered we could be more patient than we thought, when the alternative was to give up. And then the phone rang.

Toshie called wondering if I could possibly come to Ohtawara. The surgery Okaasan had had several months ago? Well, that was really stomach cancer that no one was talking about. And now the doctors said Otōsan had cancer of the peritoneum, which I had to look up to learn was the membrane lining the abdominal cavity. They weren't telling him that either. Both my Japanese parents had cancer that nobody was talking about except that we were now talking about it. At the time, many Japanese believed it best to avoid the "C" word, or *gan*, with Japanese patients because they might take it as a death sentence and pack their bags too soon. Many doctors agreed and obfuscated their diagnosis in front of patients. "We are all taking turns going to the hospital and making food. We think you should take your turn," Toshie said on behalf of the other sisters.

Of course.

Mostly, it annoyed me when people act out of

obligation. But in this case, I felt so proud to be considered enough of a daughter that it didn't feel like any obligation to drop everything and spend two weeks in Ohtawara, the town surrounded by summer's lushest green rice fields. At the local, unimpressive hospital, Okaasan was in good spirits, though she could only eat tiny amounts of food. Combine that with her medical background, and I guessed she knew she had cancer. But if Okaasan could be kind enough to play along, so could I.

"Otōsan really liked the cold tomato soup you brought him," she reported.

"It's called gazpacho."

She repeated "gazpacho," and laughed at her Japanese pronunciation of the Spanish word.

In a different room, Otōsan was happy when I showed up with mail from home, fresh laundry, and a Kathy-cooked meal. He bragged to the nurses about his daughter's cooking skills. I watched the confused looks on their faces.

"Yes, this is Kyashi. She's our fourth daughter." "*Yonbanme no musume desu.*" I loved being called fourth daughter.

"*Osewa ni narimashita,*" I said with a bow and a slight smile. "I'm indebted to you for your care."

Back at the house, I helped with shopping, laundry, chores, cleaning, anything the sisters needed. Again, I didn't feel like an outsider. The Maniwas treated me as a daughter, and a sister. I thanked them for allowing me in, inside the family at its hardest, most vulnerable time: two parents straddling life and death on the rim of a tea cup. I felt at home, strangely safe, even as the tea cup was about to tip. I never said it out loud, but I wanted to know what kind of karma called for both Okaasan and Otōsan to wind up with cancer at the same time? Instead, I asked gentle questions to understand the situation so I could figure out where I should spend my time at the hospital.

"Saah," my Japanese sisters sighed. "Muzukashii desu." "It was hard to know for sure."

If I spent more time with Otōsan, it's because I thought his case seemed more dire. Somehow, I had this feeling that Okaasan would pull through and out of this cancer mess. Of course, we would have more time. Maybe that's because, as Rie said, she insisted on sharing a hospital room with others: not wanting to be alone, wanting to hear others talk of their lives and illnesses. I've never thought about hospital rooms that way. Most people want privacy. Okaasan was always thinking of ways to heal others. For sure, she would lick this thing.

Several weeks later, looking out from my Boston bedroom window, the night lights of the John Hancock Tower reached for the October sky. Across the world, Otōsan's voice was weak, softer than ever. Still foggy from my own medical procedure earlier that day, I mustered words of gratitude. "Thank you for wanting an exchange student. You changed my life." His reply was enduringly polite: "Kochirakoso." "こちらこそ," which means "the feeling is mutual." "I love you. I love your family," I told him. I couldn't say goodbye. "じゃね、またね" "So, until next time," was how we left it. I think I might have bowed as I said it, the way Otōsan and Okaasan did in the store, or hanging up with a customer on the phone. Funny, the way mannerisms sink in over the years.

181

Two days later, Okaasan called to tell me that Otōsan had died. I wanted to reach out across the Pacific and hold her tight. Instead, I grabbed the conviction in her voice: "だいじょうぶです。" "I'm okay." I could not grasp how she could be so strong, so assured. And then several weeks later, on top of Otōsan's funeral, and her own health, she managed to send me bright, bold flowers on my birthday.

Around this time, my doctor confirmed my craziest suspicions. Could it be? Yes, I was finally pregnant. I called Okaasan. She lifted me again, with her cheerful voice claiming delight at our good news. "キャシーチャン、おめでとう。" "Kyashi-chan, Congratulations!" After the first ultrasound, I called her back: "We are having a baby boy!" But I could hear in her weaker voice that her own health was deteriorating. As my uterus swelled with new life, Okaasan's stomach was succumbing to rogue, life devouring cells. She cheered me through my first trimester with cards and short phone calls. I tried to do the same for her. Our exchanges, as they had been for so many years, were rooted in trust and love that transcended cultural differences.

Ever so gracefully, Okaasan bowed out before the New Year, two months after Otōsan. The doctors insisted a long flight to Tokyo was too risky for me, and for the baby growing in me. I was so sad I couldn't be there to pray, light incense, and cry with my three Japanese sisters.

Phyllis tried to keep my sagging spirits up with more frequent phone chats. Each time, she listened to my doctor's reports and updates as if she'd never been through it before, though she'd already had four kids of her own and a bunch of grandkids. Yes, she was so excited to welcome our baby boy in July. Oh, she picked out a beautiful baby book just like the one she gave to Mary, her youngest daughter, who had just had a little girl in early March. Between the new babies, she and Warren were off to Malta and Greece to celebrate their 40th wedding anniversary with friends. We talked the night before they left as she was packing.

"I'm craving mangoes. I can't eat enough mangoes or drink enough mango-flavored tea. What do you think that means?" I asked, not expecting a serious answer.

"Nothing," she reassured. "Kathy, you'll be fine."

Chapter 21

The morning sun was just starting to hit the brick wall in our bedroom on April 16, 1998, when I picked up the phone and heard Warren's shaking voice. It was almost unrecognizable, so I thought I might be having a bad dream. "Phyllis went to bed, suffered a heart attack in the night, and didn't wake up," he said. "She didn't wake up." I leaned over, shook Dennis, and said it out loud. "Phyllis is dead. No, this is not a dream. It's Warren calling from Athens."

I hated April. "Why does everyone die in April," I screamed. "I don't want to answer the phone again. Ever."

It hadn't occurred to me when Phyllis and I last talked about my growing belly and pregnant state of mind that she wouldn't be here to see Dennis' and my baby come into this world. She was the one who had reassured me that losing both my Japanese parents would not hurt my baby. I played our last phone conversation over and over in my mind: She was in Chicago, packing, I was in Boston craving mangoes. And I can't remember a moment, a hesitation, the slightest difference in her 64-year-old voice that might have hinted she was on her way out of this world.

Phyllis celebrated life's happy moments so well. I had kept imagining how it was going to be. She would say "Welcome, baby!" and draw him up in her arms. And, what about me? I wanted another Phyllis hug too. And now? I found myself in an unusual, unsustainable vortex: Caught between the dead and the unborn.

My mind swayed between the two unknowable realms, trying to grasp how I was going to say goodbye to Phyllis and welcome a baby in one breath. The Sortebergs had family living in South Dakota, Warren's home state, so that's where they decided to bury Phyllis. Two of the four kids, Kristi and Karin, were both married and living in Sioux Falls, so it was a natural place for the family to gather.

For Phyllis' funeral, we decorated the Gloria Dei church with her large, colorful banners, the ones she had sewn for all of us to celebrate our special life moments and rites of passage. I brought my two: "And God said YES," the bright orangish one with yellow felt letters that she had made for my confirmation. And the one with purple and gold words of wisdom, "Love and Be Loved," which she had made for our wedding. Her kids and friends brought even more, shouting: "Live Love, Love Life," or simply "Amazing Grace." Hung together, the banners were an impressive body of artwork and an equally amazing proclamation of faith.

The family asked me to speak during the service. I thanked Phyllis for teaching me to take time for tea. Over tea, we shifted from a mother-daughter relationship to being close friends. What didn't we discuss over tea? We laughed. We cried. We poured more tea. After a long late afternoon walk, and before dinner, there was tea with a special Phyllis scone or a dunkable Swedish toast. Where would we all be if Phyllis hadn't learned the art and beauty of tea from Marjorie, the childless Englishwoman who lived a few doors down from us in Minneapolis? She loved Phyllis as a daughter and friend; Phyllis in turn did that for me. We would all think of Phyllis at teatime because she's the one who taught us that angels come to tea.

After the funeral, Mary and her husband decided to go ahead and baptize their new baby. Nothing made much sense then, but somehow since we were all there, and no one could say when we would gather again, it seemed a good idea. Baby Brynne looked so beautiful in the baptismal gown Phyllis had designed for her grandkids. Shaken to the core, Warren, bless him, blessed the water and the baby. Just six weeks old, she was still fresh from God. Hopefully she could live in that freshness for a while, protected from the grief of this world.

My oldest friend and her siblings had lost their mother, Warren had lost his soul mate, and I had lost another mother. It was all so terribly sad. I wasn't the only one shocked and hurting. It wasn't right, I knew, but I nevertheless felt sorry for myself—a stupid place for a 38-year-old woman to be sitting, because Phyllis was the one who had died, and I was the one about to have a baby. She had promised to be here for the birth. And now she was buried in a Greek-made coffin in Sioux Falls, which was so far away, so dark, so cold. And it wasn't like I could just stop this baby from growing and being born while I figured it all out, got a grip. No, this new soul was kicking soccer balls and coming soon.

Back in Boston, I dropped the piece I was working on for the *New York Times* Sunday magazine. I had been so thrilled when the editor accepted my query, but that was already lifetimes ago, when I was still fine answering the phone. Sitting at the computer, I couldn't fathom why I should write the damn piece. I'll take the "kill" fee, the depressing journalistic term that seemed entirely appropriate now. Put everyone—reporter, editor, reader—out of their misery by killing the story before it sees print.

I'm sure my raging hormones made my grieving a million times worse. Possibly, I'd regret not having the stamina, the drive to see the story through. I might be letting my journalistic breakthrough slip through the cracks. But at the moment, my story about a sketchy rice mogul from New Jersey trying to corner the market on the global rice trade seemed about as compelling as cold, weak tea.

Instead, I kept my doctor's appointments and took long walks. I wanted to scream my rage at April, the month of Easter, the one that took Mom and Dad, and now Phyllis, from me. But the yellow daffodils and purple crocuses popping up on Marlborough Street and along the Charles River begged me to be more hopeful. They reminded me that I so wanted to become a mother, so wanted a baby. No matter how sad I was, I couldn't let my latest loss affect my unborn son.

Chapter 22

Adrift in an abstract sea of unknowing, wondering where Phyllis' soul wandered now and what our son would look like, I started thinking about tangible ways to bridge the gap between the dead and the unborn. I decided to sew. I'd make a baptismal gown for my baby-to-be. I'd use the same pattern Phyllis had used but I'd add my own touches. Gram, I thought, would have approved of my logic and purposefulness.

The first few weeks after Phyllis died were rocky. In addition to my perpetually puffy eyes, I looked like a beached whale and I was as hungry as a horse. But I made progress on the baptismal gown for baby-boy-to-be. I found just the perfect 100-percent white cotton sateen for the gown itself in Chinatown. It felt like a mini trip to China—without the jet lag. Rummaging through Gram's old linens, I found a beautiful piece of Norwegian Hardanger lace on a stained table runner. I tossed the linen runner and used the lace for the main front piece. Stanford sewing buddy Martha sent beautiful lace she found in France that would work nicely for around the collar and sleeves. I found some "pineapple" lace, the Southern symbol of welcome, for around the bottom of the gown. That's me, lucky in pineapple.

I finished the gown and decided that even by Gram's exacting standards it was exquisite. But my tears still wouldn't stop. Maybe they were trying to tell me something? If tears are memories seeping out, I needed a way to catch them. I must catch them and turn them into something else. For that I needed handkerchiefs. I had a bunch of old hankies in my special dresser drawer, some from Gram, some from Great-Aunt Mimi. A few more and I could make a quilt.

I wrote to Phyllis' daughters, to Katsuko's daughters, to Dennis' mother, to Gram's last living sister, my Great-Aunt Margaret: Can you please send me a handkerchief? They all agreed; I waited for the hankies to arrive in the mail.

I thought of the hanky quilt as a conversation with my unborn son, admittedly a one-way one.

Hi. I am your mother. Hi. Again. I'd like you to know about some women who have been so special to me. They loved and cared and held me tight, like I am doing to you right now. I'm so sorry you will never meet them. But still, it's important that you know them. Your dad has met many of them so he knows what I am talking about here, if you ever think I am just a little crazy for doing this. Let me explain: The assorted handkerchiefs are from different women, the women who mattered to me. And in the way that the universe weaves some amazing, loving, silvery threads, these women helped me bring you into this world. They are your grandmothers in the most elegant, exquisite, expansive sense of grand.

The quilt I made measured three handkerchiefs by three handkerchiefs, roughly 36 inches by 36 inches. That's the size tablecloth I had to work with. "Go with what you've got," is a classic pointer for fledgling journalists unsure if they have reported enough to tell a story. "Go with what you've got," lights a fire under any writer on a deadline. "Go with what you've got," turns out to be solid advice for all kinds of life situations. You can't tell I used a tablecloth as a base because just the lace edges stick out now. There are a total of fourteen hankies. Why? Because not all hankies are the same size, and three spots needed layering.

Life is so many layers. Try not to let yourself get too hung up on the surface. Look deeper sometimes. Then again, don't forget to resurface.

Phyllis' hanky, white linen with light pink and darker fuchsia flowers, green leaves and stems, has a scalloped finished edge. The fuchsia edging pops against the pure white larger, and the textured handkerchief beneath that holds it. At first blush, the petite flowers don't scream Phyllis; they are a bit fussy, and she wasn't. But the hanky is sweet, feminine and colorful, which is the Phyllis I knew.

Okaasan's off-white linen hanky is simple elegance. Only one corner is embroidered, and it's a single plum blossom with barely noticeable leaves. I layered that atop a light blue handkerchief with blue and white flowers on the corner. To expose that corner of the underlayer, I folded and stitched down the corner of Okaasan's hanky. Handkerchiefs are ubiquitous in Japan. Both men and women carry one every day. In summer, it is so humid they use hankies to wipe the sweat off their faces waiting for the bus or a train. In winter, the handkerchiefs are necessary to wipe up after a steaming bowl of spicy miso ramen has cleared the sinuses. Is it because everyone carries a ハンカ (*hankachi*) that public restrooms don't offer paper towels? Or is it the other way around? I like to imagine Okaasan stepping into a Japanese department store on a trip to Tokyo, treating herself to a new *hankachi* from the beautiful ones on display.

I hope you will go out into the world and discover the deep, rich wonders of other cultures. When you do, don't believe the stereotypes people try to impress on you. Japanese women are said to be meek, follow three steps behind their men, without a voice of their own. Katsuko was a professional working mother, devoted to her calling of healing, to her children and her brush strokes. Her eclectic spiritual commitments fed her soul. Even when she was exhausted, she kept her daily calligraphy practice for herself. That's a lesson I want to hold dear. Okaasan taught me about inner landscapes. They need to be loved, challenged and accepted. We all have inner and outer worlds, different ways of being in each. What will yours be?

Gram's hanky might also be my great-grandmother's hanky. On fine white linen, there is a pink, blue and white butterfly crocheted on the corner. My great-grandmother used to crochet like this on the end of hand towels, which is why it might be hers, via Gram. Some gifts and connections are not always obvious. Elizabeth Davis' weakness forced her daughter, Helen, to become stronger, more competent, determined to see the world.

Turning weakness on its head, making it a source of strength is how I see the butterfly on this hanky. When in doubt, look to the butterfly.

Indeed, the Davis women liked butterflies, so I placed the handkerchief from my Great-Aunt Margaret, the last surviving Davis sister next to the one from Gram. Great-Aunt Margaret's hanky is white with green embroidery; two green butterflies hover over a flower.

Great-Aunt Mimi took her hankies out to dance at the Arthur Murray Dance Studio in San Francisco. At Stanford, I used to visit Grama Nellie's sister, in Corte

Madera, for lunch and laughs. Mimi could make the room stop and notice her with that laugh. After Mimi died, I helped my mother's cousins clean out her house. I left with a box of dresses, a stack of gloves, and a pile of well-used handkerchiefs. Several of Mimi's hankies are the under-layers in the quilt.

No matter how bad things might seem, Mimi reminds us: It's good to dance. It's good to laugh.

The smallest hanky forms the centerpiece of the quilt: Elizabeth Edmundson Encarnation's wedding handkerchief.

Your Grandma Betty helped raise so many of her mother's 13 kids, that by the time she got to your aunt and your dad she'd had enough diapers. It wasn't her fault that her mama had three sets of twins. Yes, that's two times three. You can't blame Betty for wanting to put Adam's Run behind her. In Charleston, she met a handsome Portuguese sailor and that's as far away as she needed to go. There's a vast gully between Northern girls like me and Southern women like your grandmother, but handkerchiefs, or tear catchers, help bridge the differences. Grandma Betty sent me, us, her wedding hanky. I guess that means we're in—even if we have a funny accent. Sometimes a handkerchief offered is more precious than words.

On top of Betty's Wedding Hanky is Gram's crocheted pink cross.

Get over the pinkness. Why Gram had a pink cross sitting in her sewing box is beyond me. But she did. And it is perfect. This quilt is for your baptism, after all. You may or may not choose Christianity or any religion in your life but I feel compelled to start you out with something to reject. I like the part in the Lutheran baptismal service that calls you a child of God. As an orphan, I take comfort that I am still someone's child. Later rather than sooner, I hope you will understand. You are beyond me; you are beyond your father. You are a child of something infinitely bigger, whatever shape or form bigger means to you.

The other four top-layer handkerchiefs on the quilt are a mix of Gram's and Mimi's. By virtue of the power in me, because I hand-stitched this quilt, I dedicated two hankies to all the other women who helped me along the way. Finally, the most contemporary one, the textured lace hanky, I saved to honor women who will, no doubt, emerge in the future and matter to me, to us, in dramatic, yet unknown ways.

But what about a handkerchief from your maternal grandmother, Arlene, you ask, wisely?

There isn't one in the quilt that was hers. Technically, if one can get technical about hankies, my Great-Aunt Mimi's would be the closest to it, since they are related.

If I had Grama Arlene's hanky, I might not have had all the others. Don't ask me if I had a choice which I'd choose? There is no mathematical calculation that can solve that equation. I think my life would have been good either way, just different. Anyway, you'll see. Some things in life choose you, not the other way around. Believe it or not, I was not always in charge.

As I finished stitching, a wave of exhaustion and relief rolled over me. Tears turned to new pressing questions: What kind of mother do I want to be? What does a mother do? What if my baby hates me? Stop. Babies don't know how to hate. They want food, love, sleep. That's what

I want, too. It's going to be okay. I have Dennis. I have the best of so many mothers with me. We can do this.

Dear Family and Friends:

Please join us to celebrate the baptism of Luke Graven Encarnation. Reverend Warren Sorteberg will officiate. Martha, Logan, Ken and Christopher are the godparents. The informal baptismal service will be at our home, with food and drink to follow. Luke doesn't know it yet, but he will look precious in the baptismal gown I've made for him. Please join us, together in love, as we wrap him in the hanky quilt. I'll be at the piano opening with one of Phyllis' favorite hymns, one we sang at her funeral. Together we will sing: "I Was There to Hear Your Borning Cry."

PART II

Chapter 23

Now what?

That's the question best avoided when overwhelmed by postpartum hormones and lack of sleep. After Luke was born, my Aunt Lori came from Minneapolis to help for a few days. Other friends came over to cheer me, push the stroller, let me sleep a wee bit more. A wider circle of my favorite people came for Luke's baptism. But then, Dennis' work schedule pulled him back on the road. I was home alone with Luke and the question wouldn't go away. Just how did this whole new mother thing work?

One rainy October afternoon, having tea with a friend, I noticed the track holding the dining room lights seemed slightly off. Was I delirious or was the ceiling about to come down? My friend confirmed my worst fears: The ceiling was caving. Water was leaking from the roof into the dining room and who knows where else. Apparently, a worker thought hammering a few extra nails into the new rubber roof would keep it from blowing away.

Now what? Luke's gorgeous dark brown eyes looked to me for a solution.

Newborns and new ceilings don't mix. Dennis agreed that Luke and I should accept our friend's offer of his home in Provincetown while the plaster guys made repairs. As I drove out to the tip of Cape Cod, banners proclaiming "Women's Week" in P-town welcomed us. But walking down Commercial Street with Luke cuddled next to my chest, it was clear that a sleep deprived new mother and baby were not on the same wavelength as the lesbian crowd gathered for a week of revelry. I ducked into a coffee shop. Joe, the owner, gushed over Luke: "He's adorable." He then emerged from behind the counter to take Luke off my hands so I could enjoy my coffee. Joe was my new best friend. Luke and I went to Joe's every day after that. With each visit, that amazing feeling of "the world is really there for me" kicked in. Om Mani Padme Hum.

That's it. Luke and I will travel. I will take advantage of my time off and we will go out into the world. We will take Manhattan. I pushed Luke's stroller from Midtown to the Village to visit a former journalism colleague. On my return, I opted for the subway. Inside the West 14th Street station, I faced a steep set of stairs; I stopped to consider options. In the pause, a young kid, wearing a green and white New York Jets jacket offered to help me carry Luke and the stroller down the stairs. "That was unbelievably nice of you," I said as we reached the train platform."

"No problem, lady. You have a cool-looking kid."

"Yes!" I said to baby Luke. "We did it."

Back in Boston, "Now what?" led me to a part-time position at Boston University teaching business reporting and feature writing in the graduate school of journalism, starting in January. I needed someone to take care of Luke. Mrs. Lee came to my rescue. "I'll ask around," she offered one morning as I dropped off a bag of dry-cleaning. Which is how I found Ginny, Luke's first babysitter—a college student from Alabama. She came highly recommended by one of Mrs. Lee's other customers, and I quickly realized Ginny was a gift to me from the goddesses. Ginny made it possible to work part time. And the university teaching schedule allowed me to build on my Manhattan triumph during school and summer breaks. Luke and I ventured to South Dakota to visit my sister Kari, to Florida to visit Sally. Then we got Luke a passport and headed west to British Columbia to visit Martha. And then we flew east and joined Dennis in London. The three of us sang "London Bridge is Falling Down" while picnicking in the park near the real London Bridge.

I was amazed at how present and playful Dennis was with Luke. I knew Dennis was smart, but hadn't given much thought to his building prowess. But in true gung-ho Dennis fashion, he dove into building things with Tinkertoys and Duplos. Which was great because that's what Luke woke up at 6.00 a.m. eager to do. I lacked the building knack and the early morning "let's play" vibe. All of which made me realize how critical it was having two parents to balance each other and trade off duties for day-to-day sanity. I had that until I was five—but after, my life with Dad was so lopsided. I hoped not to ever inflict that on Luke.

Emotionally, having a child pulled me in new directions. Seeing Dennis, I wished to be more playful too. My natural inclination was to create order, not let it rip for the hell of it. One winter day, when it was too cold to go out, I was going stir crazy chasing Luke, crawling around on our ancient wooden floors searching between the cracks for lost Cheerios. I pulled out a big soup pot, filled it with water and set it in the middle of the kitchen floor. I ran and got some bath toys and invited Luke to put the ducks in the pond. Together we sat on the kitchen floor and played ducks in the pond, splashing water all over. Silly fun was a major maternal triumph for me.

After London, even Japan seemed doable with a kid. Being pregnant with Luke, I missed both Otōsan's and Okaasan's funerals. I tried to console myself with the idea that not being there was maybe a good thing. How many childhood homes can one woman unwind? Mourning, sorting through belongings, deciding what to toss and keep, rearranging the furniture, is hard work. But when Dennis announced a business trip to Tokyo, I thought Luke and I should tag along. My timing was terrible. At 13 months, Luke was walking and exploring life. Sitting or eating at low tables on tatami floors, Luke was like a chicken given free-range to peck at anything. Keeping him from grabbing the miso soup or tipping the rice bowls was a constant battle.

None of this bothered Masae or Toshie, who welcomed us home with delicious food, cozy futons and a deep soaking bathtub. But for me the visit was acutely surreal. With my two Japanese parents' voices gone, the rhythm of the daily routine felt off, so disconnected from what I had known. Making an offering at the family alter in the morning, I stared deeply, sadly at the photos of Obaachan, Otōsan and Okaasan on display. Masae was now the sole and heavily burdened owner of the family drugstore business. She was working hard, long hours, but the slumping Japanese economy hit small business owners hardest. Suffering marital heartbreak, Toshie and her daughter, Yoko, had moved back into the family house with Masae. The three of them stoically coped with a miserable dose of misfortune.

For now, Okaasan's faith in good fortune was remote. Rie, the oldest daughter, was living in the San Francisco

Bay area. Rie, like me, was one step removed from the death-altered Maniwa household. (Rie lost her first husband in an accident. She later married Steve, an American friend whom I had introduced her to. The Maniwa family welcomed Steve, another *gaijin*, into their fold. Eventually, Steve and Rie, together with their two sons, moved to the US.) The Maniwa sisters lost both their parents within three months of each other. They were orphans, too. Rie and I frequently conferred on the phone about the turn of events in Ohtawara, worrying together, and individually, about the fate of the Maniwa household.

Still, I accomplished my main goal on that trip: *Ohaka mairi*, or visiting the graves. With Luke in tow, I paid my respects to Otōsan and Okaasan in the local cemetery. But between chasing Luke around and worrying about the endless possibilities of him bonking his head or grabbing something, I honestly couldn't take much in. Instead, I remember the smell of the incense made me sick. The upheaval in the family, in the home, in Japan, the corner of the world that I counted on for security, was bigger than momentary nausea. It made me want to flee. Soon after returning to Boston, I found I was pregnant again. "No wonder the incense was too much," I quipped to Dennis.

I was happy Luke would not be an only child. But with two kids, I conceded, travel might need to be put on hold—at least initially. The idea of one woman—me— traveling long distances with two babies to meet Dennis struck even me as exhausting. Meanwhile, Dennis' consulting business thrived. He was traveling regularly to Asia and Europe. Though he once boldly proclaimed having kids would never change him, I saw him wrestle with shifting priorities. More than once, he flew to Beijing, gave a talk, and flew home—spending more time in the air than on the ground in China, just so he would not miss out on what Luke was up to.

But our excitement for baby number two was soon dampened by the stunning news that Warren, Phyllis' widower, my last remaining "other" parent, was sick; seriously sick with a rare lymphoma. I was going to have a new baby and someone else was dying. How could this be? Warren had seemed fine at Luke's first birthday party in Maine in July. Trying to do what he knew Phyllis would have done, he joined us for the celebration and brought a soft pointy-headed, red-white-and-blue sailor toy as a gift. "Grampa" for the occasion, he held out his hand and tried to coax Luke to walk to him. We ate blueberry pie and lobster together. We talked about the first time he and Phyllis came to Maine with us. We both cried over missing Phyllis. Warren said he was thinking of moving back to Minneapolis from Chicago when he retired. He and Dennis discussed whether he should still retire. What would he do retired without Phyllis?

Now what? The three flights of stairs to our apartment seemed even longer when I was pregnant with baby number two and whiny Luke begged to be carried up. As my belly swelled, I couldn't do it. "We will just have to rest right here on this step until you keep walking," I'd tell Luke. Once, the trek took us thirty minutes. "Stairs or traffic?" I asked myself. "I'd rather be stuck on my urban stairs than in traffic," I mumbled. No more complaining about the stairs.

I read plenty of books on how to prepare your child for

a new sibling. But I must have missed the good ones. Or failed to grasp the key points. Luke was not remotely interested in becoming a big brother. Dennis brought Luke to visit me and baby David in the hospital. It didn't turn out like all the other cozy family photos I'd seen. Luke hugged and kissed me, balked at posing for a photo and ran off down the hall. When we brought David home, Luke's welcome greeting was "Go away baby Day." At 22 months old, Luke also knew how to get my attention. I'd just get David to sleep and Luke would run to his brother's crib and say: "Wake up baby Day."

As a mother of two boys, I felt in way over my head.

David was born in May. As soon as we were both able to travel, in July, I flew with him to visit Warren, who was now in hospice. The tears wouldn't stop as I made my way to Sioux Falls to introduce our new baby David to Warren, Kristi and the family. Gaunt and weak, Warren held and blessed my son. I didn't know how much longer Warren had to live, but we both knew then he wouldn't be there to baptize David or watch him grow up. Warren told me he loved me like a daughter. It "wasn't much," he said, but he was leaving me some money to help with all my travel expenses. I was touched. "How about I put it in a ski fund for the boys?" I asked. Warren, Dennis and I were downhill skiing buddies and had shared great times skiing in Colorado. I promised him my boys would learn to ski. Holding my hand, he blinked back a tear and smiled: "That would be great."

Warren, only 67, died on September 11, 2000, not quite two and a half years after we lost Phyllis. Once again, Dennis and I, with our two sons, gathered with the

Sorteberg family and friends in Sioux Falls for a funeral. Sadly, Kristi, David, Karin, and Mary joined me in the club that no one wants to be a member of: we were all orphans.

Six parents gone never coming back. What were the chances? There is a reason I hated math: Numbers never captured the magnitude of the situation for me. We baptized David at home in Boston in the same gown I had made for Luke. David's godparents wrapped him in the handkerchief quilt. Together with friends, my tears leaked out as we sang once again "I Was There to Hear Your Borning Cry."

And then Dennis and I turned our focus to living. And to loving our two little boys.

In time, I saw more clearly the reasons we create sacred spaces for the dead. We, the living, need those fixed spots so we can go on breathing. Sometimes it is enough to remember a person, the way she laughed or talked, or that he loved barbecue chicken and corn on the cob. But sometimes we need to see the unchanged stillness of a grave to accept the separation. In time, I told myself that if I could do *Ohaka mairi* in Japan and South Dakota, it was time I revisited Wisconsin.

When Luke and David were not quite four and two, old Wildwood friends invited my sister and me up to the lake for a weekend in late June. Swatting at big, nasty black flies, my sister, the boys and I stomped through puddles on the road to Cabin 8, the same road that she had driven the golf cart on so many lifetimes ago. We played and splashed with the boys on the same sandy beach where I'd left toys idle. We laughed at simple water fun. It had all the necessary ingredients for a perfect mother's moment. Yet, I felt unsettled. One minute I was playing with my sons, the next I found myself staring through them, staving off notions that I must not die suddenly and leave them motherless.

What could I do to put those fears to rest?

Just because my mother died suddenly, unexpectedly, freakishly, did not mean I was destined for the same fate. That's what our logical brain says to such deeply seated fears. But I decided logic wasn't enough to thwart my embedded fears of inflicting my motherlessness on my own children. I needed to shatter, literally break, outdated, unhelpful patterns of avoiding the grave in the Graven family. So, after leaving Wildwood, instead of driving straight back to Minneapolis, I drove to Greenwood Cemetery. I located the Lindholm family plot, and unbuckled the two car seats. Holding hands, with one trusting little boy on either side, we approached my parents' graves.

"We can't see Grama Arlene and Grandpa Dave, but this is one place we can come to remember them," I tried to explain. That sounded right. The boys stared at me blankly. Quickly, I changed tactics: "What can we play?" I wondered out loud. We formed a circle around the granite gravestones to dance and sing. "Ring-around-the-rosy, pocket full of posies." We giggled as we shouted, "We all fall down." We got up, sang and danced it again and again.

I like to think my parents were happy I brought my two boys from Boston to Wisconsin for a visit. I hope they agreed that, with two little boys growing into their own future, it was time for me to put away April sorrow. I like to believe that wherever my parents' souls float, through time and eternity, they know to show up for "ring-around-the-rosy." Of course their souls showed up. Dancing around their graves was one of my greatest moments of healing. With childlike simplicity, with what I perceived as my parents' benevolent approval and my future holding onto my hands, I claimed what I had lost. I replaced my parents' hopes and dreams with my own, saying boldly: "It is my turn to play."

Chapter 24

As a mother myself, seeing my mother's grave made me aware of how little I really knew about her. There was a time when I knew from the tone of Mom's voice that I was in trouble and about to be sent to my little white rocking chair to "think about it." I used to know how she combed her hair, and exactly how she stood at the kitchen sink, not from photographs but because we spent time together. But then, as we as a family moved on from surviving our own injuries to accepting the unacceptable, those memories got pushed aside. For me, they were pushed to the point of unknowing. Today, I can't muster my own clear memory of the sounds, smells and touch of my mother's physical being. Left unattended, just how long do those primitive maternal-child bonds last? If she walked into a room today, would I know her?

Over time, I became so successful at filling her void with other loving women who cared for me, I didn't brood over what I was missing. That Dad, out of both guilt and fortitude, moved on to new wives, made it acceptable to leave Mom in the past. But now with all of them dead, gone, I had the desire and resolve to look into the void, to wonder on a deeper level who my mother was.

Luckily, Arlene was a scrapper. In Wisconsin, that meant she lovingly saved favorite school assignments, programs, ticket stubs, photos and letters in leather-bound scrapbooks. In the 1930s and 40s, lots of young women were scrappers in the Midwest. Girls got together, sat around the kitchen table, drank coffee, smoked cigarettes, gabbed, and worked on their scrapbooks.

Mom's scrapbooks survived my Dad's subsequent wives and his move from the Tarrymore house. For years, they were in the attic in the townhouse he bought with Sally. I didn't specifically ask for them, but somehow, after Dad died, and Sally sold the townhouse and moved to Florida, the box marked "Mom's Scrapbooks" in blue Sharpie was shipped to me in Boston. Besides the scrapbooks, the box contained one neatly ordered folder of "Kennedy for President" campaign materials from 1960, a "Mondale for Attorney General" bumper sticker, Mom's wedding photo album and stray black and white photos that never made it into an album. This suggests someone other than Mom packed the box.

I've moved the box from one closet to another in my house, many times over the years, as we've remodeled, or rearranged sleeping and storage spaces. Each time, I've opened it, explored inside and gotten distracted from the cleaning at hand. Each perusal seems fresh because I am in a different place in my life.

When Dennis and I were newlyweds, I looked at her wedding album more closely, comparing how she looked in the dress to how I looked in the same gown decades later. I was 32 years old when I got married; she was a young-looking 23 years old. She looked happy at her wedding. I was happy to be married too.

When Dennis and I hopped around Japan and Asia on our research grants, I arranged a meeting in Tokyo with the then Ambassador to Japan, Walter Mondale, at the US Embassy. Back home, seeing the aged, not-so-sticky bumper sticker in the box, made me think how far back my parents went politically and how far I'd come internationally.

Years later, as an emerging artist, I looked for traces of her artistic bent and organizational talents. Judging from the looks of the books, she was dedicated to scrapping as a craft but wasn't overzealous, overtly artsy, or an extreme doodler. I saw that she organized things straightforwardly. She didn't embellish with exclamation points or sappy hearts or smiley faces or extraneous decorating papers or backgrounds. Sometimes she included dates, but not always, suggesting, perhaps, a slight weakness for detail that might explain mine.

From her scraps, it was easy to picture this attractive, brown-haired, bright-eyed young woman as organized, fun-loving, caring, ambitious, adventurous, and outdoorsy. She valued school assignments, holding papers together with colorful threads, and sticking on hole protectors to prevent the hole punches from damaging the paper. In her widely spaced, hand-written autobiography, "Only Yesterday," written in May 1946 for a high school assignment, she described an early adventure with a neighborhood kid named Bobbie Parker.

"We walked down to Shue's pond and picked all the dandelions there and came back and put them in a kettle. Deciding we didn't have enough, we started out again only this time we went in the direction of the creek. We took our time and picked all the flowers we saw before we started home. It was almost dinner time and when we were almost home, we discovered our mothers were looking for us.

Anyway we were both home in a hurry. My mother made me stay in the house the rest of the day. Bobbie only got a spanking so he rode up and down the sidewalk in front of my house on his tricycle, shouting, 'Hey, Arlene, why don't 'cha come out.' I think I got the worst end of the deal."

I paused and thought a moment about Grama Nellie. Here, young Arlene leads us to believe her mother was stricter than the other mothers, dishing out a day of staying inside as punishment for an innocent girl wandering off to pick dandelions. Maybe Grama was really never happy.

In the same essay, Arlene recounts her formative years in the kitchen.

"When I was ten years old, I did my first baking. I made pineapple cupcakes. I made my mother stay out of the room while I did everything by myself. They turned out to be very delicious so I took some down to Mrs. 'Macs' to have her taste. She thought they were wonderful and I was proud of having made them all by myself. After that I would come home after school and make a surprise for my mother. Shortcakes were my specialty."

I laughed at the idea of pineapple cupcakes—yuck. I have no clue who Mrs. Mac was but I loved that Arlene had a woman nearby who she liked, trusted and wanted to share her baked goods with. I savored this image of her telling Grama Nellie to stay out of the kitchen while she measured and mixed on her own. Maybe my kitchen bossiness was genetic. Funny, who knew we both specialized in shortcakes?

Civic pride was another big theme of Arlene's scrapbooks. She saved the program of the dedication of Hayward's new post office from 1941, when she would have been 12 years old. She saved a short clip and photo of her father when he was selected for the board of directors of the Wisconsin Indian Head Association, a local business promotion group. She gave a full page spread to an article about the Chippewa Indian ceremonial dances held in Hayward. And then there is palpable local excitement in this headline: "Hayward Unveils World's Largest Muskie." The Governor of Wisconsin flew in from Madison to celebrate a stuffed specimen of "Old Evil Eye," the world's largest muskellunge taken by rod and reel. From her early small-town beginnings, I could begin to imagine how and why she might have thrived in Albert Lea and loved politics.

She saved school essays, which gave me insight into her self-image. By the time she was in high school, by her own account, she was known as an ambitious young woman about town.

"One day I entered the small one room repair shop of Shoemaker Melby who is known to all Hayward-ites as the best old shoemaker in town. I was greeted with the usual smell of leather and oils, but even more familiar were the faces and figures of some of Hayward's old timers who were seated around the old-fashioned wood stove in the middle of the room engaged in one of their typical discussions.

"They were people I had often seen, but rarely had occasion to talk to. One of them remarks that he knew whose daughter I was and wondered how it was possible for one person to look like both of his parents. Then he went on to say that he knew my grandfathers. Others in the crowd joined in the conversation and I was surprised to find out how much more they knew about my ancestors than I did. They knew, too, that I was going to college and practically everything else about me."

The details about the shoe leather and oils helped me imagine her as a living, smelling young woman. She appeared confident in who she was, proud of herself that she was heading off to college. Looking back to myself at that age, I could see those same traits in me as I headed off to Japan and then on to Stanford. Her words reassured that she would have understood my need to leave home to seek a bigger world.

Mom's scrapping picked up steam when she arrived at St. Olaf College. She kept letters from her secret dorm sisters, playbills from college stage productions, bus ticket stubs to Minneapolis, and napkins and coasters from restaurants. The drink menu from the Nankin, a landmark downtown Minneapolis restaurant, offered a Dubonnet cocktail for 55 cents, a glass of Burgundy for 25 cents, or $2.25 for a bottle. Knowing she occasionally fled Northfield for some good food and partying made her seem entirely more fun and human.

Each time I've flipped through her scrapbook pages, different aspects of my mother's life leap out. A bit like magnets, they jump out and stick only when there's a pull from the receiving side. A couple of years ago, I noticed a tiny scrap, about half the size of a small index card. It's an inexplicable gem: A handwritten note addressed to my mother from one of her professors.

> "Office of the Dean of Women
> St. Olaf College, Northfield, Minn.
> Dec. 9
> I have sent a note to Dr. Paulson, telling him that I have suggested that you make an appointment with him soon to discuss your choice of journalism as a profession.
> E. Jerdee"

This small detail sent my head and heart spinning.

I knew my parents met working on the *Manitou Messenger*, the St. Olaf College newspaper. Dad rose to become co-managing editor. He coauthored the neatly typed "Style Book" imploring aspiring journalists to follow strict rules and the highest ethical standards. Old photos show them smiling, goofing off in funny hats, posing around a cluster of typewriters; the hum, the click-clacking, the energy of the newsroom enveloping both of them. Dad infused his dating life with newsroom jargon. On a half-sheet of three-ring notepaper he dashed off this practically illegible date invitation, while on his way to check on the printing presses.

Dear Arlene,

Voice la grandes nouvelles (sic)!! According to the latest scoop, tonight's "Whing Ding" will be a picnic. We're supposed to congregate at Mohn Hall, Friday Oct. 29, 5:30 p.m. Following any sort of code of ethics, etiquette or morals, I would therefore pick you up at 720 at around 5:15—however—I've got football practice until ???? p.m. I shouldn't be as late as usual because it is Friday, but probably around 5:30. Perhaps I could meet you at Mohn Hall? (The main thing, of course, is to meet you, regardless of place and time.) See you then? If you can think of any more "suitable" arrangement, I'll be at Mohn Printing Co (Ph 34) until 2:00 p.m.

Anticipatingly Yours,
Dave

But after college, instead of pursuing journalism, Dad followed in his father's footsteps to law school. But I didn't know, or it never fully registered with me, that my mother wanted to be a journalist. Somehow, the lasting family story was that she wanted to be a social worker and an English teacher because those are the jobs she held while my dad was in law school. But what if she took those jobs because she had to forgo her real desire? How could I not have known?

I think back to that wonderful father-daughter weekend in Manhattan. That would have been the perfect setting for Dad to say something like, "Gee, your mother would be so proud. You know, she wanted to be a journalist too." But no, that conversation never happened. After I returned to New York City four years later to work at the Journal's headquarters in lower Manhattan and he was battling cancer, he might have mentioned it then. "Gee, you've really made a go of this journalism career…You know, your mother once…" But no, it never came up.

Maybe he didn't know. Maybe my mother changed her mind before she met him, or it was a fleeting ambition that she never shared. English teacher, social worker, were acceptable roles for women in the early 1960s; maybe journalism was just too big of a stretch?

I can't know what my father knew, what they shared or did not share. But this snippet made me wonder if it's true that somehow we grow up—unwittingly or not—wanting to complete our parents' unfinished business, to be what they could not. All along, I lived with the illusion I was bucking the family business, the legal business. I would not add another Graven esquire to any law firm shingle. But what if, instead of being the rebel, I was following the family calling, a quiet one that never fully found its voice?

I can't say whether knowing my mother wanted a journalism career would have helped or deterred me. But when I was stressed out on a deadline, or irritated a story got killed, or annoyed with an editor, let's just say it would have been soothing to know another woman—my mother—might have understood.

Discovering the power one little detail had to reshape my understanding of her and myself, I went through the scrapbooks and family newspaper clips again, with a fresh reporter's eye. I asked myself what other details I might have overlooked that could resonate with me as an adult, as a mother?

Sitting on the floor, I joked with myself that this old box and I had something in common: we were unlikely survivors. As I flipped through Arlene's typewritten essays, I wondered about the woman whose years I had already outlived. Did she imagine me as a grown daughter? No, she wrote about her hometown and traveling the world beyond. She was full of civic pride and busting with curiosity. Was there anything, even the slightest hint, in her telling of herself that might give me comfort, even fortitude for my own family tasks at hand?

I turned to the worn, brown leather-covered scrapbook. Oddly, I felt free to search her pages, to sit with her creative work for as long as I liked. I no longer felt like I was the little girl hiding in the closet, secretly searching for a whiff of her perfume, hoping not to be caught. I was no longer compelled to tiptoe around my dad's guilt to learn something about her. Instead, I felt newly summoned to wield my own imaginary highlighter, to discover the snippets most important to me.

Before long, my mind wandered to the essence of scrapbook making. My mother relished sitting at a table and (perhaps sipping coffee and smoking a cigarette) pasting her piano recital programs, theatre playbills and restaurant menus into her books.

"Damn." I didn't recognize a whisper of that part of her in me. I have saved all kinds of memorabilia, but I don't get around to sorting let alone gluing stuff into memory books. It strikes me as fussy, annoying work, but I'm probably wrong about that.

Unsatisfied, I performed some different rapid mental calculations: She wrote; I write. She scrapped; I create mixed media paintings. Maybe, yes most certainly, when looked at from various other angles, I could be her daughter. I continued to explore my mother's world. Seeing what mattered to her as a young woman, what tickled her funny side and stoked her curiosity, brought me to a new place. I felt her with me.

I didn't want to move.

Our communion was abruptly interrupted by loose sheets of paper spilling from the back of the scrapbook. They were shoved in for safekeeping, but never glued. My mother wouldn't have done that, I thought. Of course not. On quick inspection, I saw they were multiple copies of the same thing: my mother's obituary in the *Minneapolis Tribune* from April 1966. Her scrapping days were over. My life without her was just beginning.

Along with the obituary, I found a diamond in an Albert Lea Tribune newspaper column: "Love Notes," by Love Cruikshank. I must have read this article before but once again it seemed new. Maybe I wasn't ready to absorb it until now. Instead of writing about National Library Week in April 1966, the Albert Lea columnist apologized to readers that she had another story to tell, a story about the untimely death of a friend. She wrote a stirring tribute to my mother.

"She was a beautiful blend of yesterday's and today's woman, never neglecting her home for her civic responsibilities, but never using her home as an excuse to avoid them."

This made me think about my own community efforts. I have aspired to be both globally minded and domestically involved in my son's schools, and our neighborhood.

Maybe I got this notion of juggling two worlds from her?

Cruikshank ended with an impressive and soothing list of Mom's work on the war on poverty, her love of people, and politics, her volunteer work for the church and the community with this:

"Indeed one of the keenest recollections I have is of watching her in her kitchen planning a political campaign, while at the same time keeping her young daughter out of the electric mixer in which Arlene was mixing a cake for a neighbor's birthday."

I paused. Then read it again. This tiny detail—my mother holding me and a mixer while talking to a reporter—was a wonderful journalistic moment. The reader knows the reporter is on the scene; the reporter notices the mixer. Miraculously, instead of dismissing it as just a mundane, kitchen moment, the reporter included it, and thereby elevated the scene to a lasting, truthful image of who a person was and what she stood for.

Reading that column, I fell in love with the power of good journalism to comfort, excite, explain—all over again.

Alas, I must confess my mother's wonderful scrapping is not genetic. I didn't inherit her orderly gene. To be sure, I've saved programs from school events, my best essays, articles and tons of photos—all the things that could lend themselves to a wonderful scrapbook. And I've done the same for my two boys' school plays, music recitals and sporting events. But at this point, they are still a disorganized mess of a collection.

Chapter 25

I realize that if I died tomorrow, I'd be leaving this untidy mess of memorabilia to my kids—unsorted—as is. I really don't wish that on them, and I really do plan to put it all in order before I go. But I've also come to accept that there are worse things I could do to them. I think all mothers worry about leaving their kids with unfinished business.

There are no hard rules when it comes to unfinished business. There are practical things that may, legally, require handling. But there are emotional pieces, bequests that require more time and sorting.

I remember Gram was unusually anxious holding the small white box in both hands. The package wasn't wrapped in beautiful paper or tied with a colorful ribbon. But then, why would it be? It wasn't my birthday or any other special occasion. Steady and sturdy, Gram wasn't one for spontaneous surprises. I couldn't imagine what she was up to.

The Gift Nook
Interesting Gifts
612 W 54th St
Mpls, MN

The red label on the box, while curious, did not offer hints to the occasion or the contents.

"What's this?"

"Well, I've had this for a long time. I've been waiting for the right moment to give it to you. But I don't know if I'll ever be sure there is a right time for this, "Gram's voice quivered. "I guess now is as good a time as any."

The exact date of this exchange has faded from my memory. My best recollection is that she brought it with her when she visited me in Palo Alto, CA during my senior year in college. But what remains firmly etched in my mind was Gram's uneasiness, her lack of surety.

"Your mother was working on this at the time of the accident," Gram explained.

Inside the box Gram had protected for many years, was a 36-inch-square ivory-colored linen table cloth, embroidery yarns and a wooden embroidery hoop. The pattern of a large arching palm tree, shading a temple, from which three tiny figures are walking over a hill to their small home in the corner, repeats on each side of the square. The stitching in dark brown, lighter brown, gold, off-white and sky-blue is maybe seven-eighths complete. What's left to stitch on each side is the little hatted figures walking home. A needle threaded with the light-blue embroidery yarn is poised to continue the next left-to-right cross stitch. Only it hasn't.

"Once I thought I would finish it. But I never could."

Her confession that she was not up to the task only magnified the moment. Gram, ever so smart, educated, hardworking and disciplined had been my guiding spirit throughout my childhood. I'd never seen her not do what she set her mind to. Back in 1923, she left her parents, five siblings and an ardent suitor in Minneapolis, and traveled by train to New York, by ship across the Atlantic and on to India via the Suez Canal. She spent two years teaching young girls to read in Madras, India, before returning to

220

Minnesota and her husband-to-be. She lost one stillborn son, but raised three more, including my father, her oldest. What did she mean, she couldn't finish it?

I looked at the threaded needle, a moment frozen in time. I didn't even know Mom embroidered. Stunned, I didn't know what to say.

Gram didn't expect an immediate answer. "I hope you'll finish it someday. Finish it and use the tablecloth. Your mother would have wanted that." She closed the box, handed me the gift, and regained her usual composure.

"Thank you," I said, as we hugged.

It was an open-ended gift: Gram left it to me to figure out what to do with my mother's unfinished work. At first glance, it looked simple. But in fact, the box contained a lifetime of work.

I tucked the box away. I didn't need to see the needle to feel its shape prick. Deep within, I knew how life changes in an instant. Needle threaded, aren't we all somewhere between waiting breathless for the next stitch and just one short stitch away from breathing our last?

Even without re-opening the *Interesting Gifts* box I received from Gram, as a grown daughter, a mother myself, I see in my mind's eye my mother's unfinished needlework. It can awaken old aches.

Yet, as I've come to know my mother, my guess is she would have dismissed the unfinished tablecloth as no big deal. In the scheme of things, she would have been far more devastated by her unfinished business as a mother of three.

This fear of leaving unfinished business, I believe, prompts many women to keep "to do" lists. Every time I get on an airplane, the image of boxes of my sons' baby photos waiting to be put into those empty, archive-quality, acid-free albums flashes across my mind. If the plane crashes, no one but me will know the right caption for each image, I despair. Unfinished business. I need to get right on that when I get home.

In any family's life, artist's studio, or writer's notebook, lurks plenty of unfinished business, even more tangled threads. The trick is to figure out which ones matter most, and tend to those with heart and mind.

For me, India, not my mother's tablecloth, was the unfinished business I felt compelled to complete. Gram never made it back to India. My father was born in 1929, just as the Great Depression started, followed by two more sons. The demands of raising and educating a family during World War II, followed by my grandfather's appointment as a federal judge, left little extra time or money for a journey back. The decades passed. As a widow, she traveled overseas to Norway, to visit me in Japan on a tour of the Far East and Alaska. But not India. Perhaps she thought some places are best left as youthful memories.

That no one else in the Graven family, my parents, uncles, siblings or cousins has ever gone to India seemed so sad, so unsatisfying to me. For Dennis, no one in his South Carolinian family had ever been interested in his years of Indian experiences. Someday, we wanted our kids to see the delights and problems of a developing country. The bigger world Gram opened my eyes to had become important to my life and choices. That was the thread I wanted to keep pulling.

After my Boston wedding, it was harder for Gram to travel. But, even as her traveling days waned, Gram's intellectual world stayed open. She was sharp until she died at age 94. She was in the midst of writing histories of small churches in the Midwest. She left scads of notes and notebooks of her research on congregations, all of which she was deeply immersed in. She left boxes of slides of her photographs of flowers—fairly organized but not perfectly culled. More importantly, she died with film in her camera.

So, consider this: If we are deeply engaged in the messy art of living, we can't possibly finish it all. We can't tidy everything up.

Chapter 26

As Dennis and I began our own family, we were painfully aware that neither of us had a physical or emotional "home" to return to. Our home, the one we made, however we defined it, would have to be the place from which we would come and go. Obviously, we needed to create our own holiday traditions for Thanksgiving, Christmas and Easter. Dennis offered to sing "Jingle Bells" as a Thanksgiving grace. I look charge of Christmas baking, teaching the boys to make delicious Scandinavian treats. Together, we would decorate a chocolate bunny cake at Easter with jelly beans and red licorice. We nurtured friendships and counted that circle as family.

But we also wanted to ground it all in something bigger. We wanted to plant some new roots.

The summer after we got married, Dennis and I rented a house owned by Harvard University on Sutton Island off the coast of Acadia National Park in Maine. We invited friends, Warren and Phyllis and even Sally, to join us for a week of hiking and biking, lobsters and mussels. We walked to the house along a long narrow path through the woods, since Sutton has no roads, no stores or businesses. The island post office is a galvanized metal trash can chained to the town dock. Sally was a good sport to come along, but she did offer that Harvard could have provided a better wheelbarrow than the sorry, rickety one left at the dock for us to use.

We loved the quirky island location and funky passenger ferry access, so Dennis and I returned for several summers after. Eventually, we wanted to stay longer than the Harvard rental rules allowed, so we migrated to neighboring Little Cranberry Island and tacked on more time at a rented boathouse on Sand Beach. I sewed the baptismal gown and hanky quilt there; Luke celebrated his first birthday there with a homemade blueberry pie served in his high chair out on the deck. Two years later, in the same spot, same high chair, David made the same blue-faced mess. Back then, our big family adventure was to walk down to the dock to catch island legend and lobsterman Warren Fernald, as he moored his boat, the "Mother Ann," and rowed his dingy to the dock. He let the boys pick out the lobsters for dinner. Sometimes, he'd offer us crab claws. The boys squirmed as he ripped off the claws with his bare hands and tossed the crabs back in the ocean to regrow their digits. This summer bliss lasted until the year our toddlers broke a lamp throwing a ball indoors. Clearly, we had overstayed our rental welcome.

Time to find our own summer place. Unlike many other summer residents, Dennis and I were not returning to our childhood haunts. Instead, we were intent on building new memories and traditions for ourselves and our kids. To us, the distinctions between the islands that make up the township are subtle at best; mostly they are incomprehensible. The issues, rivalries, perhaps a few fishing vendettas, go back for generations. Not bound by island or family traditions, we were free to invent.

Having spent almost six weeks each summer on Sand Beach, we were considered by locals to be Little Cranberry people. It was most alarming, practically unthinkable, to some that we ended up moving on to the next island over,

Great Cranberry Island. In 2002, we bought a modest home built by an artist—quirks and all. The artist had given the neighbors perpetual permission to have half their summer vegetable garden on the property. And he had designated a small area as a cemetery, where he, his wife and their daughter's cremains would all be interred. But the house's location, only a short quarter-mile wheelbarrow schlep up from the dock, and the stunning views overlooking the Western Way, more than compensated.

The grey shingled house came with a separate but small studio tilting over itself. The studio had been moved here from near the town dock, after serving, some say, as the island telephone booth for years. Water seeped in through the skylights. The weathered grey cedar shingles resembled the fog's habit of creeping in and hanging around in the mornings, or clinging to the rocky shore for days, too lazy to move on. With a little love and care, the art studio became "The Barn," our offbeat guest cottage.

Like any new settlers, we spent the first few summers learning the island's ways. Attendance at the firemen's potluck suppers, for example, was not optional. When a woman arrived at the door to collect our "covered dish" for the supper, I had no idea what she was referring to. We had failed to notice the sign at the post office. "Everyone donates a dish," the woman said. "It supports the volunteer fire department." I promised to deliver something myself within the hour. The event was well worth it beyond the assorted casseroles and decadent desserts. That's where I learned that the island's pumper trucks and a driver were available for birthday parties.

Further up the main road, the Great Cranberry Island Library, with its small, but gem-like collection of books on Maine and island life, was our favorite resource for getting to know the island. The children's story hour gave me a luxurious mini-break and the boys a chance to meet other kids. Ruth, the librarian, knew everyone on the island and offered advice and counsel as we checked out books. Until a few years ago, people checked out books by signing their names on the cards inside the last page. You could easily see who on the island had read the book before you and use that speck of information to decide to check it out or not. Then to preserve anonymity, big city libraries and privacy rights folks decided everyone should have a library number. It made sense. Except as I volunteered to weed through the library's collection at the end of one recent summer, I was heartened to see the names of islanders now gone and to remember them as readers.

For other island news and gossip, the Cranberry General Store, a few steps across the parking lot from the dock, was the place to go. "Get a pound of butter, and everything else you need to know," longtime islander Charlene used to say about the store. She said it enough that after she died, the store put up a sign quoting her. The general store has had many owners over the years; each tried to figure out how to make a viable business in a place that swells to several hundred residents in the summer but slims to only 50 in winter. One constant: the odd, old codgers who gather on the front porch to drink coffee in the morning. They like to intimidate with purported combined wisdom. Often, they succeed. But if a storm is coming, they are the ones to ask if it is time to haul in the boats.

What has knitted the island community together is the Ladies Aid Fair. This fair is not like the Minnesota State Fair my father abhorred and refused to take us to, having had enough of 4-H clubs growing up in Greene. No, on the first Wednesday in August, islanders and tourists alike show up for the 10:30 a.m. starting bell. Colorful streamers run from the church across the main road to the telephone pole. In the white elephant tent, one person's clutter is magically transformed into the next person's bargain treasure: silver pitchers, deviled egg holders, glass teacups that nest in their own luncheon plates. The island fashion section can come back to bite. That pink hat you bought as silly afterthought for a dollar? That was your neighbor's favorite for years. Make a mad dash to the baked goods table for homemade bread, blueberry muffins or one of Beverly's famous lemon meringue pies. Always buy raffle tickets for the quilt. You want one of the quilts made by the island women; these are masterpieces of art, history and love stitched together with grace. Choose your water balloon toss partner carefully; one of you will wind up wet. Stop by the fish pond, it always delights. Throw a line with a clothes-pin over the mysterious curtain and see what you catch. At our first Ladies Aid Fair, a wide-eyed and incredulous David came running from the fish pond with his prize, and this report: "The fish talked."

I loved this island—feuds and all. Whatever else happened, whether we stayed living in downtown Boston or not, I wanted my sons to know a caring community. Dennis and I wanted this for ourselves too. At the same time, we did not want to let go of our dream of raising global kids. So much had happened since we paused our global wanderings after Jakarta to have kids: the loss of my other parents, not to mention the September 11 attacks on the World Trade Center. New airport security measures and a fear of rippling terrorist strikes made many people reluctant to travel. We saw it as a call to make sure our sons were prepared for the new global world. Even if we didn't move from country to country, unworkable given our career choices, we would maximize our kids' exposure to foreign cultures during sabbaticals and school breaks. In effect, the 9-11 attacks made us think harder about the places we could safely take a family.

"Itte kimasu." Have baby, push a buggy, will travel. Have two babies, push two buggies, will travel. "Itte kimasu," we said as we headed to Spain, France, England, Australia, New Zealand, the Caribbean, Canada, Mexico. We discovered a playground with a pirate ship in London; we became global pirates. In Nice, we played freeze tag: *Glace*—you're frozen! Baseball was a blast in Sydney. Not everyone can brag that they played baseball with a red and white striped Cat in the Hat bat with the Sydney Opera House as a backstop.

"But the kids are too young. They will never remember this," one friend implored as I announced plans for a sabbatical year. Luke was five; David three. "But I will," I answered. I wanted to maximize travel opportunities before we were hemmed in with a strict school schedule.

"You can't just pull a kid out of kindergarten. It will destroy his social skills," a preschool teacher admonished one morning. I didn't believe her. I thought both boys would pick up valuable social skills, maybe even foreign language skills. Dennis had consulting work that took us to Europe and Asia. I needed to find new perspectives on parenting, on myself. I needed the world's reassurance that despite my losses and new terrorism threats it was still there for me. I needed to draw more circles.

Pick olives. Pick a good cheese. That's what the boys remember from their first time in Spain and France. Olives, all sorts of olives, are delicious. David saw olive trees alongside the road. He begged us to pull over so he could pick. Uh oh, unripe olives were bitter and hard, he learned. "No way," Luke stammered before he tasted a warm creamy goat cheese at a farmer's market in the south of France. Just as Sam I Am discovered he could eat green eggs and ham, Luke discovered he liked goat cheese, here, there, anywhere, in a house, maybe even with a mouse, for the rest of the trip, and even today.

And we all remember the big train blunder in France. Dressed for a warm fall day in Aix en Provence, we experienced an unusual delay waiting for the TGV to take us one stop to Avignon. We boarded singing the French nursery song, "Sur le Pont D'Avignon" in anticipation of our destination. Politely, I told the woman who was sitting in our row, "*Nous avons un petit problème.*" Gruffly, she informed me that we were on the wrong train. We were on a super-express, nonstop train to Paris. A group of Japanese tourists and folks from Kentucky all made the same mistake, so my French wasn't the problem. For the next four hours the boys squirmed in their strollers. Dennis and I sat on the floor between two rail cars. The French countryside scrolled by. Musical David kept humming "Sur le Pont D'Avignon," until we couldn't stand it.

"We aren't going to see the bridge," I admitted.

Seriously underdressed, we stepped out in cold, rainy Paris to grab a meal, but only after we scored the last seats, on the last train, heading south that night. Ever since, the boys have been a bit skittish about train travel. Back home, months later, as we boarded an Amtrak train to New York, they hesitated.

"Hurry up," I pushed.

"Mom, are you sure we aren't going to Paris?" David asked.

Miserable missteps come with adventures. It's part of building character, resilience, stamina and curiosity. It's what the boys would need to tackle family trips to India and Japan, places Dennis and I planned to return to again and again. It's what we think they will need to make their way in a global world. Without our big adventures when they were small, Luke and David would not have been as well prepared to take their places in a classroom in India.

In 2009, as the US economy tanked and Dennis' consulting business slowed, I argued for a family sabbatical to India. "If not now, when?" I asked.

We contacted our friend Shukla Bose to see if we could join the Parikrma Humanity Foundation's efforts to help the poorest, most disadvantaged kids who live in the shadows of Bangalore's high-tech boom. Shukla agreed to enroll Luke and David, then 11 and 9, in the Parikrma School in Jayanagar. Shukla educates, feeds, clothes and nurtures kids who live without enough food, electricity and running water at home. Little by little, day by day, she works to break the cycle of poverty. For the first time, single moms, who carry bricks on their heads at dusty construction sites, see their kids going off to school. Shukla's determination gives me hope for India and the world. I wanted to dive into that effort for however long. I wanted our sons to witness devotion and hard work, passion and a mission.

For sure, not everyone would have chosen India for a family sabbatical. And a trip of this length and distance would not have been possible without Dennis' talents, academic interests and career success and my choice to be a stay-at-home mom. But from the beginning, Dennis and I bonded over international travel; we vowed that seeing the world and experiencing foreign cultures was the gift we could and would give our kids. Put another way: given the choice between an auto rickshaw ride in India or a roller coaster ride at Disney World, we both would choose the auto rickshaw any day—even with the jet lag.

In Boston, the boys walked across Marlborough Street to their elementary school, The Learning Project. The headmaster was reluctant to excuse them for two months, but we argued, persuasively, the merits of this opportunity to learn and serve. He agreed, after we promised they would keep up with their American school work, even as they did homework for their Indian school.

The neighborhood school idea worked for us. We looked for a similar arrangement in Bangalore. We booked a doable but spartan two-bedroom service apartment in the Homestead Brigade building half a block down and across the street from Parikrma. Part short-term apartment, part hostel, part business hotel, Homestead offered a simple Indian breakfast of *idly* and *sambar*, or porridge, on the top floor every morning. Or, we could also cook on a two-burner stove in the unit's kitchenette. As we got ready for the first day of school, Dennis told the boys that today might feel like being thrown into the deep end of a swimming pool. "Well, we will just have to swim," Luke offered bravely.

On January 8, 2010, at 8:45 a.m., Dennis and I walked Luke and David, dressed in their new green and blue Parikrma school shirts, across Mariyappa Road. We dodged cars, buses, motorcycles, auto rickshaws, bicycles, and pedestrians. We walked past the guy selling plastic buckets, the guy selling fresh coconuts, past the popular *masala dosa* takeaway stand, through the gate to their new school. Shukla, dressed in a colorful, flowing sari, emerged into the playground to give us a warm welcome.

We timed our arrival to the start of the school assembly. The principal, dressed in a vibrant green sari, stood in front of some 300 squirming students seated on the floor. On the blackboard, she had drawn a bouquet of flowers and a message of welcome back to school for the new year. She then announced two new boys, Luke and David, would be joining the school for seven weeks. She asked two students to be their guides for the first day, to show them to their new classes. David was in the Mars class; Luke was in Saturn.

Watching Luke and David set down their backpacks and walk with an unknown classmate to sit in the sea of Indian school kids made my heart sing. Gram's thread of desire to see the world had come around, almost *nine* decades later, to her great-grandchildren stepping up to learn from that world. As Luke and David took their spots on the floor, they didn't look back at us, even when everyone stood to sing the Indian National Anthem. The principal adjourned the assembly with a reminder to each student to follow the school rules: speak in English, never waste water, paper or *time*, keep their school clean and neat, and learn something new every day.

When we picked them up, Luke and David appeared stunned. But they were still standing, and managed weak smiles. They had new text books, which on first glance had intriguing stories about elephants and Indus Valley civilization. "I learned some Hindi," David boasted, showing me a notebook in which he had dutifully copied the vocabulary. "I didn't have Hindi, but I had physics. It was more advanced than my science class in Boston," Luke reported. Their reward for the first day: a fresh pomegranate, which they ate out on our little balcony overlooking the cows in the alley. We took a short rest and then headed down the street for some groceries. Coming home, in front of our apartment, a group of girls from Parikrma spotted David and called his name. He waved to them and turned to me: "Oh, Mom, those are just some girls in my class." After a long day, the boys said the best dinner would be a grilled cheese sandwich and a glass of milk. Grilled cheese it was.

Days later, David had had it. He hated being the center of attention at school. He was tired of the kids wanting to touch him. In America, the teachers tell kids to mind their own "personal space." Sitting on his classroom floor, crowded to begin with, he concluded that there was no such thing as personal space in India. "I'm going home," he announced. "How?" I asked. "I'll book a flight on the internet. I'll go through London Heathrow." "How about we take a day off from school and think about it," I countered. I let him sleep in the next day. We took it easy. We ate cereal for breakfast—no *idly* and *sambar*. We hung out on the balcony and ate pomegranates. Luke came home from school and told David he had a solution. "When the kids come near you, put up your hands to make a high five. That way they can't come too close. It works for me." David agreed to try, and for now, to cancel his return flight.

Without the confidence earned by surviving adventures, the boys would not have jumped as enthusiastically into the car as we set out on our first trip from Bangalore to Mysore, the former capital of the state of Karnataka. There they were quickly captivated by the cool blend of Hindu, Muslim, and Rajput styles at the Palace of Mysore. Grand rooms filled with exotic images: The octagonal wedding hall, with a peacock-motif glass ceiling; the glittering golden *howda*, for elegant royal elephant riding; and to Luke's delight, a vast, silvery armory. The motto of the royal family, the Wadiyars of Mysore, who ruled this part of India for five hundred years, is written in Sanskrit above the palace entrance gate. "Never Terrified." Perfect advice for the boys as they climbed for their first elephant ride around the palace grounds.

At dinner, I learned what their eyes had taken in that day. When the food took forever to arrive, I suggested we play a version of the telephone tag game. There was a collective groan: "Oh, Mom." I insisted. After repeating the previous line, each person added a new element. I started:

"On the road from Bangalore to Mysore we saw:
Sugar cane being harvested,
Trucks loaded with coconuts,
A flat tire,
A water buffalo,
Funky rock formations,
Thali lunch on banana leaf,
Giant golden Ganesha statues,
Cows pooping next to a car,
Rice paddies,
Another auto-rickshaw with a flat tire,
Old men driving ox carts loaded with more coconuts,
Families packed into small compact cars,
More water buffalos…"

I call this our family's "Mysore Perspective." See how the world goes by. See us out in the world. See us coming together, sharing a meal, talking about the day. That's home. Listen: hear us smile.

I don't know what our family time in India or subsequent return visits will ultimately mean to Luke or David. I'd like to think the experience of sticking out because you are white and foreign will teach them to be compassionate towards other races, as well as defenders of diversity. I'd like to imagine they will not be afraid to go out and see the world. I'd like to dream that one day, a day of their choosing, they will arrive in Bangalore and experience a tiny "I'm home" sigh.

In their own time, I hope they will see how old, thin, knotty, messy family threads can lead to new adventures. A great-grandmother, a grandmother, a mother and a daughter can dream these threads of peace and offer them up to the world. But we can't predict what snags a family will encounter, which threads will break, and which hold.

Now what? At the moment, the only thing I know for sure is that my sons don't want Indian food for breakfast.

Chapter 27

I got dahlias. I got cosmos. I got sweet peas. Who could ask for anything more?

From the moment I open the bamboo gate and enter our garden on Great Cranberry Island, I feel like singing and dancing to Gershwin. It's been almost two decades since we bought our summer place here. It's where Dennis, Luke, David and I have grown up as a family. Each year, our garden has expanded.

In the Northeast, especially Maine, where the winter sun is asleep by 4:00 p.m. and the summer sun stays up until 8:00 p.m., gardens are about dreams. From the beginning, at night, Dennis and I lay in bed and aspired to have a garden view from every window.

From the kitchen, we wanted to see flowers and vegetables. Dennis sketched a design for raised beds protected by a deer fence. We dug a trench and laid a pipe for water. We hauled in soil and mixed in bags of compost.

I got climbing peas and pole beans and Sungold tomatoes.

For the back of the house, we fantasized about picking cherries, peaches and *nashi* (Asian pears, a cross between an apple and a pear) from our own trees. The fruity thoughts connected us, to our island home, to our shared love of Japan. We planted an "orchard" behind our bedroom window: Reliance peaches, Montmorency cherries, Japanese *Shiro* plums, and *Housui* and *Chojuro* Asian Pears.

I got fruit—enough for jams and pies and my mighty

juice machine.

Over meals, we critiqued vegetable varieties, analyzed hardiness zones, and weighed the benefits of earthworm castings versus compost tea. Pretending to be garden gumshoes, we were certain that the Concord grapes, left too long to their own devices, ran amok and murdered the back fence. We had a strong hunch that the white raspberries and thornless blackberries, constricted by thriving chives, might do better in their own space. And we were confident the rhubarb and asparagus could survive fine outside the deer fence. We realized it was time to think about a vineyard.

It was back to the graph paper. Hunched over the plans on the dining room table, we bickered over the "vineyard's" possible dimensions, not wanting to go too big or too small. We made peace by pounding in stakes to mark off the new area, so everyone could imagine what it would look like. Finally, we settled on a plan that took advantage of the shed to support the horizontal cables we hoped to train the fruit to love. We moved the "vines" into their new digs, gave them extra handfuls of cow manure to ease the transition. This freed space in the raised beds for more potatoes and kohlrabi, besides new prime real estate for more dahlias, cosmos and sweat peas.

To see Dennis and me working together out in the raised bed gardens, you'd conclude we are not compatible gardening companions. He brings out long metal rulers and measures the distances between the thumb holes the seeds go in. I like to eyeball things. On my own, I wouldn't bother with labeling. I figure when the plants come up, I'll know what they are. Dennis, however, is ever ready with the popsicle sticks and Sharpies to mark each variety planted; he then takes the extra step to make notes on the garden master plan. I am more worried about whether we have planted enough sweet peas along the fence. Their germination rate is iffy in Maine. Dennis does not lose sleep over my sweet pea concerns.

Actually, we have come a long way. Or, at least I have. In the true spirit of gratitude, I must admit without Dennis, my inner gardener might never have seen the New England summer sun. He learned to love plants from his mother, Betty, who had little education and few life skills except for gardening. In Charleston, gardens are a big deal. Betty lived for her garden club meetings. Azaleas connected mother and son.

When we bought our Marlborough Street brownstone apartment as newlyweds, one of the things Dennis loved about it was the roof deck. It offered so many container gardening possibilities, he said. We had to haul soil up three flights of stairs plus an internal winding staircase to get to the roof. I hated the hauling but liked the idea of a roof garden, so I went along. One gardening success led to another and soon Dennis wanted to put up a "temporary" greenhouse, one that never permanently altered the historic neighborhood look, but allowed us to grow tomatoes. The tomatoes grew steadily in the greenhouse in spring, and judging from their prolific production, thrived on the hot roof in the summer. Pansies, roses, and Gerbera daisies flourished in our urban container garden.

But even just starting seedlings in the greenhouse together revealed so much about our gardening personalities. One year, I planted a few too many seeds in those perky peat pellets that swell up in water and hold moisture around the seeds. Not really thinking about yield rates, more focused on the mystery of germination, I hit the germination jackpot. Nearly all the sunflower seeds sprouted. Much too close together for Dennis' comfort. It called for thinning and transplanting, Dennis' expertise. To avoid that extra effort, I was willing to let quite a few little sunflower souls die ignobly. Dennis refused. Patiently with the plants, less so with me, he separated the seedlings, giving each their own black pot on the roof. By August, several dozen giant sunflowers waved to the Catholic priest who lived in the penthouse across the street. He waved back.

My random approach to gardening tested Dennis' well defined sense of order and methodical problem-solving. "You can't just sprinkle seeds and hope," he muttered. "And why not?" I countered. Whether positive or negative, we all have our gardening influences. At this point, I was being too much of my father's daughter, and not enough of my grandma Helen's granddaughter.

Growing up, our yard was always one step above disaster. Around the house, the weeds and the perennials were indistinguishable, like identical twins. Plant annuals? My dad would mend the basketball hoop before he'd think of planting impatiens. And being a single dad, he took years before he got around to fixing the hoop.

Gram, however, was a gardener's gardener. She took pride in her gorgeous peonies in early June. Her roses made you forget you were in Greene, momentarily transporting anyone who sniffed them to a charming English cottage. Never one to slough duties, Gram poured even more

241

energy into her garden after Granddad died. She hired a handyman named Elmer, who came dressed in overalls and a straw hat. Elmer weathered Gram's bossiness, "water this, stake that."

Gardening was one way Gram tended her grief. It strengthened her soul, gave her pleasure and purpose. She put any visiting grandchild—including me—to work, not just for the help, but true to her den mother role in scouts, to teach us a thing or two. Before it was chic, Gram was an avid composter. We stuffed cantaloupe and watermelon rinds near the base of plants. The rinds attracted the earthworms, which aerated the soil as they tunneled through to the fruit, leaving nutritious waste in their wake. We picked beans and tomatoes. We triple-washed lettuce in the sink, careful not to bruise the delicate leaves. As our reward, she let us make lettuce rollups: sugar sprinkled on the lettuce leaves made the leafy greens go down. Once we were hooked on the just-picked freshness, she hid the sugar.

But the most exciting part of gardening with Gram came via the US mail. Every summer she ordered live ladybugs from a ladybug farm in California. They arrived in a small, ventilated cardboard container, which we picked up at the post office. Standing in line, I felt self-conscious. Probably the whole town knew our Gram was a bit out there, on the edge, with her organic gardening methods. We'd rush home to open the box at the kitchen sink, anxious to know whether the aphid-eating ladybugs had survived the journey. They moved slowly at first, but a tiny splash of water woke them. Out in the garden, we let a third of the troops crawl out of the burlap sack, onto the back of our hands and arms, on their merry way to the roses. According to Gram, the nasty bugs, the ones that are out to eat anything and everything, did not stand a chance against our ladybugs. Inside, the remainder of the ladybugs chilled for weeks in the refrigerator, waiting their turn to join the front line.

After the roof deck sunflower fiasco, or triumph, I'm not sure which, I faced a critical choice. Step aside and let Dennis rule the garden or get into gardening. Was it the mystery of living plants, the endless possibilities of nurturing something beautiful that caused me to make a shift? Or was I tired of hearing in my own head the excuses for why we never got around to making the yard beautiful after Mom died. Or both?

To Dennis' amazement, I gradually shifted my focus to the details. I read the instructions on the back of seed packets: How deep to sow the seeds, how many per inch. With a bit more attention on my part, and a slight bending of the rules here and there on his, we managed not to kill each other—or the garden on the roof. I ordered ladybugs from California. Dennis and I found we shared a love of gardening.

In ways big and small, having a garden in Maine has changed how we, as a family, roam in the world. From our own gardening life, it was not much of a stretch to walk through new gardens and wonder how other gardeners did it. We scoped out our neighbor's gardens, as well as famous Maine gardens designed by Beatrix Ferrand. And then we set out on more exotic gardening expeditions.

On our first family trip to India, our curiosity for gardens helped ease us into daily life. From our apartment near Ashoka Pillar in Bangalore, we were just a short auto-rickshaw ride away from the Lalbagh Botanical Gardens. We visited this vast Mughal garden regularly and still didn't make a dent in one of the largest collections of plant and tree species in Southern India. At the end of January, when Lalbagh was in full glory for the Republic Day Flower show, we had to restrain ourselves from plotting how we could transplant the entire exotic flower show back to Maine.

Bangalore is known as the garden city of India, but the screeching auto-rickshaws and urban grime can still be overwhelming. Goa is a common getaway from Banglore, so one long weekend we decided to check out the former Portuguese state. We made Cuidad de Goa, a small Indian family hotel with Portuguese flare, our base. We were about as far from Maine, physically and psychologically, as one could imagine. Yet, we felt at home riding a water taxi to lunch at a pier (a warmer version of our summer life in Maine.) We feasted on Goan seafood and coconut curries. Afterwards, the boys joined a pickup cricket game on the beach. But we were really here to see what had brought Vasco da Gama to India: spices.

The long, circuitous road to our first spice plantation outside Ponda gave Dennis ample time to regale the boys with stories of Portuguese explorers. Local Indian rulers, he said, were underwhelmed by the gifts the Portuguese explorers brought. At the time, European silks and spices could not come close to the quality and variety the Indians already had. On arrival, we were happy and grateful for the local guide, who took over from Dennis as the authority on spices. We looked up to towering palm trees, wrapped in pepper vines. We gazed horizontally at vanilla pods strung between tree trunks. Our eyes followed the hanging banana plants down, past the dangling flowers to discover tiny insects that thrive in the underbrush. We watched elephants bathing in the water. Intoxicated by the smells of cinnamon, cloves, allspice and cardamom, Dennis accepted the guide's dare, and the boys' double dare, to try the elephant chili pepper. The tiniest of red peppers is known as the elephant chili because of the elephant-like scream it inspires. "My Dad likes hot food," David advised the guide as he offered Dennis a taste. Instant perspiration, red face, a bit of panic, gave way to an uncontrollable ahhhhh. "My whole face is numb," Dennis cried. "Things have a way of coming back to bite you," I joked. Dennis didn't laugh. It took an hour for the capsicum-inspired pain to wear off, by which point we were on to a lunch of vegetables in fresh spices served on bamboo plates and banana leaves, with lime pickles on the side. "Have some feni," I said, pouring him a shot of a strong cashew moonshine.

"Elephant watching and hiking spice plantations are now some of our favorite family interests," I wrote to friends and family back in the US. Of course, we wanted more elephant watching and spices.

It is hard to imagine anything topping Goa. But a different weekend trip to Nagarhole National Park and to Coorg just might have. We set out on a bouncy five-hour drive to Kabini Jungle Lodge, the former hunting lodge and grounds for the Maharaja of Mysore, now run by the local government. After a buffet Indian lunch (Indians love buffets just as much as the Scandinavians love their Smorgasbords), we divided into groups and climbed into jeeps. The ride was a safari through village life: past dhoti-clad old men herding unruly goats, women standing tall despite heavy loads of laundry on their heads, lazy cows napping in the middle of the road, and live chickens for sale at the village crossroads. The real jeep-stopping views came when we spotted little huts high in the bamboo trees. "Elephant watch towers," explained the guide. In these parts, cotton and rice farmers fear elephants trampling their crops during migration time. So they build tree huts and assign someone the very important job of elephant watcher. If an elephant—or two—strayed from the reserve and threatened the fields, the guard would bang on big tin drums to deter the beast. Apparently, this happened often; there were dozens of little huts dotting the bamboo trees along our route. Luke and David said we should adapt this idea to their tree fort in Maine to scare off deer—or crazy island invaders.

Late afternoon and early morning were the best times to elephant watch inside Nagarhole. We saw a family of elephants at the water's edge as the sun set, and were stunned silent. Such big bodies, such big ears, such big feet. Yet they stomped gracefully, as they walked to their next grassy snack. We saw both mama and baby elephants lift their back right legs, cross them over their back left ankles and hold the pose as they lifted their trunks to spray dirt and mud over themselves. We laughed at the thought of us trying those poses as a family.

The next morning, it was still dark out when a man woke us with a knock on our door and some hot tea in tin cups. We were so enthralled with elephant watching no one complained about the early hour, or the lack of breakfast. In the park the second time, we were ready and quiet when the driver cut the engine and pointed to the right. A herd of eight elephants emerged from the woods, slowly dancing through the dry grass, to a clearing where they bathed themselves in dirt. The guide warned us to keep still so they wouldn't be tempted to charge. When the small herd had sprayed enough dirt to cool off, they turned and walked down the road, tails swaying. We watched them leave in silence.

The coda, while not as much fun as elephant watching, was right up there in the "best personal Indian moments" category. We drove to a nearby lake and hopped out of the jeep. Most of the group opted for a motorboat ride to see more wildlife from the water. I took the floating basket option, a good way to grab a quiet moment to myself. With lush bamboo forests greening the distant landscape, birds flying overhead, my serene water guide paddled our basket boat close to a rock. "See madam," he whispered. "Water snakes for you."

After elephants, Dennis wanted to press on to Coorg, the largest coffee-growing state in India. Though Dennis has traveled through most of India, he had never been to Coorg, or *Kodagu* as it is called in the local dialect. This part of India, framed by the Western Ghats range, boasts some of the most productive land in India. A home-stay program on an organic spice plantation would be "educational," even for Dennis. The last 30 miles were brutal, the mountainous road under major construction. This was white-knuckle time—even for our driver. "Very bad road. Very bad road," he mumbled. When we arrived at the Rainforest Retreat, our driver hesitated, but the boys were already out of the car and scrambling through the jungle path to the check-in hut.

This coffee and spice plantation is owned by an Indian couple, both geneticists, who left New Delhi to rejuvenate the flagging operation using organic methods (the cardamom plants were besieged by disease and pests) using organic methods. Our room was in the first building across the path from the outdoor dining hut. We were surrounded by lush rainforest, tiny streams, pepper vines, coffee and cardamom plants. It was like living in a guide to companion gardening.

The next morning, an intern led us on an expedition over hills, across stubbled rice paddies, past more lazy cows and pecking egrets to the Golden Mist Plantation. Our challenge was to make it there before the daily power outage shut down the roasting machines. No problem. We hiked fast. We smelled the coffee roasting as we arrived. A fine reward, but not nearly as exciting as the tremendous spread of black, red and lime-green coffee beans drying in the sun. Golden Mist also grows tea, so we hiked further to the tea slope. I don't have the patience to be a tea leaf picker, but if I did, this beautiful spot is where I would pick.

By the end of the day, David, our intrepid gardener, added vanilla beans, pepper vines and cardamom pods to the list of things he wanted us to grow in Maine. We didn't want to discourage his botanical ambitions, so Dennis and I just smiled. "Why do we have to leave?" the boys grumbled. "How about we buy some spices to bring home with us?" I suggested.

I got pepper and coffee for grinding, and cardamom and

vanilla pods—secret ingredients to make my jams and chutneys sing.

Back in Maine, further convinced that gardens can nurture global passions, I returned to our beds with renewed determination to deepen our local roots. I planted sweet peas, and then more sweet peas. I can never have enough sweet peas, the flower of community. I planted delphiniums, and hoped their boldness and open heartedness would rub off on us. I believe in the dignity and elegance of dahlias. Breathe in all these sweet and powerful smells. Hold breath. Make it last just a sweet moment longer. Then take it with me wherever I go.

Our garden kept me growing. I learned how to take time to notice the plants, what works and does not. I wondered what the plants were telling me. What is the important news from the earth? An observation: Plants really sing, unless they need to sag. They are willing to take over, or lag behind, depending on weather conditions. Like weeds, they can be stubborn, go wild and crazy and want their own space. They are willing to take what they need from the earth and the air without asking. They aren't afraid to stand alone, tall like a sunflower. They welcome entanglements; they can climb higher that way. They are designed to shout hooray! They have bad years. They find a way to let you know that they need to be part of the garden.

When we came home from India, David insisted we grow lemongrass. Luckily, we found some in the herb section of the gardening store. We used the stalks in our curries and to make lemongrass tea. The next year, I skipped the lemongrass. I shouldn't have; we really missed it. I made a pledge to David: We will grow lemongrass, despite longitude and latitude differences; we just have to consider it an annual, not a perennial.

I saw my sons through the garden's lens. Year after year, we dispatched David to crawl through the tiny spaces between tomato cages to pick hard-to-reach drops of Sungold. But now he's grown too big for that. During high school, David started tomato seeds in April in his bedroom in Boston, adjusting the grow lights, nurturing the seedlings until he could get them into the ground in Maine. Now he's in England studying plant biology in graduate school. When we planted high bush blueberries along the deck, it was to keep the little boys from falling over the edge. We still pick the ripe berries in our pajamas, but the conversations have evolved: Luke is eager to discuss his summer work writing briefs about the most recent clash along the India-China border. As we fill our quarts, he snitches more than I do. But we are both snitchers at heart.

I credit the zinnia and the rest of my garden for leading me to "yes."

One Saturday in July, a neighbor stopped by and asked if we might donate flowers for the church that Sunday. We are not big summer churchgoers, preferring to be outside worshipping the beauty of the earth by hiking, gardening, or kayaking. But if the Great Cranberry Island Congregational Church needed flowers, why of course. We got cosmos, dahlias, and zinnias. Running on island time, I dashed up at 10:10 a.m. to deliver the bouquet to the altar by the start of the 10:30 a.m. service. Renita, the July minister, was in a tizzy. The pianist who normally played the hymns was ill. There was no one to accompany the singing. Renita sings and plays piano beautifully, but doing both on top of preaching was asking too much that morning.

"How desperate are you?" I asked. "Fairly desperate," she replied.

I volunteered that I was a decent sight reader. I had less than 10 minutes to zip through the hymns. The church bells pealed at 10:30 a.m., and I played the opening hymn. An oboist and flutist played with me—my first trio. It was also my first public performance since my dismal piano recitals decades ago. Undoubtedly, there were some flats not flatted, sharps not sharped. Luckily, this was a forgiving congregation. Renita and many others were wildly appreciative at the after-service coffee hour. My fellow musicians, Geoff and Laurie, congratulated me. Several Sundays later, I was invited back, to officially replace the other pianist. In a few years, David joined us on flute. Other summer visitors to the island, Figgy on violin, Susan on violoncello, swelled the group and our repertoire. Our music started drawing more and more people to the service. Who could ask for anything more?

Gardens are about tending, caring for the little things and hoping they add up, plant by plant, to something beautiful, nourishing and rewarding. The joy that makes the gardener-me smile comes from a simple discovery. Despite all the brokenness, I had within my reach the tools needed to make my own garden. Now, sometimes I squint my eyes and imagine our house in Minneapolis with well-tended hedges, April daffodils and May tulips, strawberry plants galore, like the ones my brother remembers having in Albert Lea, my birthplace. My mother loved peonies.

But what exactly was her favorite variety? As a gardener, I would like to know.

It helped tremendously that I picked Dennis, a great gardener, as my mate. But I also take credit for recognizing that if I wanted a garden, I had to plant one.

Chapter 28

On a cold winter night in Boston's South End, two women walked through the door of Studio 319. Oblivious to the other dozen or so First Friday art viewers in the room, one loudly exclaimed: "This must be the happy room." Pointing to a painting of a single bright purple tulip stem and then to one of an oversized pink zinnia blossom, her friend announced: "I just love all the bold colors."

I leaned against a bar stool next to my paint-spattered work table, wishing I could be simultaneously both invisible and visible. "Oh, are you the artist?" they asked. "Yes, I'm the artist," I replied, still surprising myself with my own answer. "And yes, this is the happy room."

This 400-square-foot studio space on the third floor of an old brick warehouse building on Harrison Avenue is where, in my fifties, I came to play with color. I dug through my collection of handmade papers, yarns, fabric swatches, shards of broken pottery and chips of glass, looking for the piece to spark my next mixed media creation. Sometimes the digging was slow, mostly because I hadn't organized or sorted my scraps in any systematic way. Sometimes the digging left me wanting; I trekked down the hall to investigate the trash. What overlooked gems languished in the recycling bin today? But always, when I worked in this sun-filled room, my windows overlooking the Pine Street Inn homeless shelter, I felt lucky.

The studio was a natural progression in my anything-but-logical budding art career. I had reached the limits of our dining room table. My messes encroached on our living space, annoying my family when I left them out, annoying me when I had to rush to clean up. My head was wrestling with whether to add orange to a corner section, or more turquoise? Or if the center read as muddled, or neutral? And the boys were asking: "What's for dinner?" Under these circumstances, a studio, while a stretch, seemed both plausible and wise. I lugged my bin of acrylic paints, a tool box of brushes, and assorted canvases down three flights of stairs from our Marlborough Street brownstone and hauled them to one of the hippest artist spaces in Boston.

I was doubly excited: for my new digs and unfolding identity as an artist. Still, the move was fraught with uncertainty and sprinkles of self-doubt. Arguably, it could even be considered premature. I had just barely finished a handful of adult education art classes and I dared to announce: I intend to be an artist, with my own studio, with creative work to do.

For some friends and family members, my artistic aspirations were questionable. As in, isn't this art thing going a tad off the deep end? "Where do you think this is going?" they asked.

I couldn't answer. I had never thought of myself as an artist. My eighth-grade art teacher at Ramsey Junior High School in Minneapolis saw to that. Mrs. Holmes threatened to fail me. Instead, she gave me a "C" out of pity. "Your older brother and sister were such fine art students," I can still hear her harping. "What happened to you? They must have run out of talent with the third one." I survived her cruel words. I deposited them in the bank of stupid and hurtful things teachers say sometimes and threw myself at studying what I was good at: foreign languages, history, politics and music. I forgot about Mrs. Holmes. Until 2007, when the clicking of her high heels, the nettlesome rubbing of her nylon stockings and her pale, wrinkly face came back to me in Italy. At a rustic villa outside Montepulciano, I joined a group of old pals from Tokyo to celebrate a Canadian friend's 50th birthday. Thanks to my sister, Kari, who generously volunteered to take care of my kids, I had eight days *sans enfants, sans* husband, *sans* responsibility.

Reunited in this midlife moment, we lingered over lunches of arugula salad, assorted *salumi* and wine. We pressed on with worldly discussions over late-night meals cooked by an Italian chef, who artfully dotted the dessert focaccia with dark red grapes. We reveled in our adult selves as we wandered through Etruscan museums and sniffed porcini mushrooms in the market. At the villa, like kids, we climbed fig trees and plucked the fruit: perfection with a thin slice of prosciutto for breakfast with our steamy cappuccinos. Not in charge of cooking, cleaning or anyone but myself, the demands of home quietened.

In the moments without my husband and our 8-and 6-year-old boys, I could hear my own internal voice again. It asked: for all the things I am and love being—wife, mother, reporter, writer, teacher—what else do I want to be? It wanted to know: what else am I going to do with my life? I made secret mental comparisons with everyone in the group. One dear friend from New Zealand had pursued a successful diplomatic career, climbing the ranks to become head of mission, even ambassador. With her husband, also a successful diplomat, she moved around the world, raising two amazing daughters. I calculated the years I'd stuck to my post in Boston, only to feel envious, and, well, stuck. Another friend had both a demanding two year old and a demanding career, but her husband stayed at home so she could work. This wasn't helpful. I wasn't in any of those boats.

After the birthday gathering, I stole a couple of extra days to wander Florence. It was odd being alone. Maybe I should have studied Italian not Japanese. Or maybe I had really been an Italian artist in my last life. These swirling thoughts were my companions as I stared at endless renaissance depictions of the Madonna and child and gorgeous gelatos. I took an inordinate time deciding to buy a bright orange jacket. Why not bright orange? On the flight home, instead of second guessing my purchase, I confronted the questions I had toted around Florence. "What would I do if I could do anything I wanted?" Take away all logical constraints: I don't have to be good at it, make money at it, and—this is important—to give a damn what anyone else thinks. What would I do? I made a list of possible new directions, held it close, and fell asleep.

Back in Boston, I took baby steps into the art world. Why not try what I am least likely to ever try was my new thinking. I signed up for a collage course at the Museum of Fine Arts. Most artists start with drawing lessons but I hate drawing. I hate drawing because it makes me feel inadequate. I signed up for collage, which is not drawing. Mixing paint on paper, applying magazine photos with glue—that sounded doable.

Walking through the museum to the studio classrooms, I sensed I was onto something, at least that's what I told myself as the nervous energy swelled. Clearly, those Florentine cherubs flying on the ceilings were still playing with my thoughts. But I had found the right new home for adult wanderers. The instructor asked us to "make a mark" on the paper. The act of making a mark, whatever that means, was the start. A mark didn't have to be anything. A mark was just a motion, a nonthreatening way into the otherwise formidable world of art creation. She prompted us to act like we were kids. Without lifting a brush, we made marks on paper with paint. We scraped lines using combs. We evoked ridges by dipping the cardboard sleeves from a coffee cup into paint and stamping it around on the paper. We crumpled newspapers, dipped them in color and went wild. No brush, no drawing, no realistic images were required. I was proud of my colorful marks, like a glowing kindergartner holding up an inspired finger painting at circle time.

The instructor refused to let us stop at kindergarten pride. "Pass the paper down to the next person," she said. We made marks on the paper. We passed it on. We did this for several turns. "Now, take the set of marks in front of you and rip it up." I tore with abandon, producing colorful scraps. "Dump your heaps into a pile on the center of the table." She tossed the pile gently, the way you would a bowl of fresh salad greens. "Now, you can begin." I was hooked. I managed to avoid drawing. "Greatness" and "artistic talent" were not required. Indeed, it was hard to even see where *my* marks were in the scheme of things. The ripping meant we couldn't hold onto our work: we had to give it up to others. Ah. We were all fish, swimming in a bigger ocean. Out of the offerings of the entire group, we fashioned our own first collage.

Fortunately, this did not turn into a "groupy" group where students bond like glue. Frankly, we were all too new and insecure at this art-making business to become friends. At first, we chatted about where we lived and what brought us to the class. There were two housewives from Wellesley who were meticulously made up, dressed in suburban casual and carrying designer handbags. They were empty nesters in search of distraction, purpose or both. Two other middle-aged women showed up only some weeks, suggesting they were not committed, but were not ruling art out either. There was a lone 30-something male computer techie type who said he always wanted to be an artist but somehow got sidetracked. And me: urban stay-at-home mom, minimal makeup, in search of a new outlet, decidedly non-techy and with poor taste in handbags. The instructor filled in the silent holes with tips on where to buy art supplies, upcoming museum events, different sizes of Mod Podge.

The eight-week course flew by. In a first, I signed up for the next session. I had never in my entire academic career repeated a course. An immediate benefit: the list of class supplies was so much easier to handle the second time. I knew where the art supply store was. Most importantly, I was comfortable making marks, playing with paints and inks, listening to the teacher. Slowly, needless self-judgment melted away. I banished "Am I good at this?" from my vocabulary—at least for now. Week to week, I gained confidence. I coveted my Wednesday afternoons at the museum. I arrived early and ate lunch at the café there. I strolled through galleries with new purpose and new eyes.

I was always home in time to pick up the boys from school but happy about how I'd spent my day. Dennis encouraged me to take it all in; he never once questioned whether I was being productive. He understood that reinventing yourself is not a linear journey; he'd had his own career zigzags. This was mine to explore. Only I could answer the question: "Do I have another artistic voice inside, one that just might have something to say?" I thought about how to visually create the stories running through my head.

People sometimes ask where artists get their ideas. I have no idea what goes on in other artists' minds. Navigating my own is treacherous enough. This is how it started for me. An ill-fated attempt to organize my dresser drawers led me to my Great-Aunt Mimi's sleek elbow-length gloves. Along with the fabulous ball gowns that she dressed up in to go to her Arthur Murray dance lessons, Mimi loved elegant gloves. When she died, I inherited a few pairs. I kept them in the right-hand side drawer of my mother's old dressing table, with Grama Nellie's silver brush, comb and mirror set. It was my way of keeping the Lindholm women together. I fixated on the gloves, until my brain stopped seeing Mimi's gloves and imagined a lavish family portrait. No faces, just gloves. I pictured my Dad's pipe-stained hands stuffed into his winter ski gloves. They were enormous. By contrast my hands were small, just comfortable reaching one note beyond an octave on the piano. My little boys' hands were even smaller. I visualized a clothesline with all our gloves hanging down. Or maybe it's a giant flower made up of gloves, all the different hand sizes represented. That winter, instead of throwing my sons' outgrown or single mittens away, I put them in a plastic bag for a future creation. Walking down the street, I stared at hands, their sizes and shapes.

Meanwhile, in art class I mustered a small collage with highly literal mitten shapes on a string. It hardly did justice to the amazing piece I pictured in my mind. There was such a gap between what I imagined and what I could pull off on paper. The teacher encouraged me: "I like how you are beginning to think."

For the next class, she asked us to bring copies of family photos, preferably old black and whites. Looking at photos of my grandparents and my mom and dad in their early married days reminded me of the uneasy strings still so easily attached to people no longer present. I squirmed at using images of dead relatives in my art. Still, I pioneered on. I would need a background that was not a canvas. I went to the kitchen cupboard and raided my tea collection. In class, I unfolded a Japanese box containing tea. Next, I smeared white paint over the green for a mottled background look. I formed a Japanese teapot out of paper scraps, mixing green tea leaves in with the paint, which I smooshed on the canvas. A collage about tea, with tea in it. How lovely! And literal. Then I reached for the black and white photos and cut out the tiny heads of Mom and Grama Nellie. I mod-podged them into the tea scene. The title for this creation popped into my head: "When Angels Come to Tea."

The dead women of my dreams found a space, a spot, determined solely by me on my modest-sized collage. It was a breakthrough, one that deeply altered my perspective on art, creativity and the power it holds to heal. This was not an artistic masterpiece, one others might ooh and ahhh over. It was a deeply personal moment of bringing past memories into my present existence in a new way: They died. I didn't. By inserting their faces, forever stuck in a moment of time, into a new fluid moment, I uncovered a new way to think about them. I got to choose where and how I wanted these women in my life. I look at the piece now; I feel a power surge. "I believe in the Energy of art, and through the use of that energy, the artist's ability to transform his or her life, and by example, the lives of others," the photorealist, painter and sculptor Audrey Flack wrote in her "Credo" on art. Oh, that makes complete sense to me now.

But dead women weren't my only hurdle. All this art-making dredged up other "stuff" that as an emerging artist I knew must be examined. The problem was red. I might not have known that I had a problem with red if it were not for my kids. When both boys were toddlers, we would sit for hours in our bay window at a little blue and yellow animal table with zebra stripes painted on the legs of the round stools. Happily, we colored, painted and ate animal crackers.

One day, as I sorted out the dead stubs from the still useable crayons, I asked David: "What color do you want next?" "Green," he said confidently. I offered him a green. "No," he immediately rejected it. I offered him another lighter shade; he rejected that one too. I dug for other greens. "No." He pawed through the pile until he found just the right shade: a Kelly green, quintessential shamrock, somewhere between jade and malachite. David's absolute certainty and joy at the right green blew my mind. He knew, even at this young age, what color meant to him. He detected differences in shades and values. He liked what he liked.

I turned my motherly observations on myself as a child. Might I have managed color thoughts at that age? Yes. There I was, lying in a hospital bed in Mason City, Iowa. I couldn't grasp how injured I was, that my mother was dying, that my life was never going to be the same, but I knew I needed a red crayon. I can still see the round bucket of 101 crayons by the bedside, a get-well gift from my mother's Aunt Gladys. Maybe there was some marketing gimmick in 1966: buy 100 crayons, get one free. Maybe the numbers were outsized on the package. Somehow, engraved in my brain was the number 101. But in that whole big bucket of crayons, which should have been enough to color the rainbows of the world, there was no red. Not one plain, perfect, red red. I searched. I dug. I came up empty. In disbelief, I cried: "There's not one single red." I was so angry about the missing red I refused to color. I stopped coloring. No more rainbows over stick trees for me. If nothing else, I took pouting seriously. I wanted red. No red? Try magenta, or scarlet or crimson. No. How could they have forgotten red? They had 101 chances.

Mostly, I just wanted to color with my mother.

For the first time, I saw clearly what the missing red crayon was about. It was how I got stuck, left behind in the color and art worlds. What is red if not the color of blood, scraped knees, death, fiery boldness? Denied the color I needed to express my rage, sadness and loneliness, I did not express it. To make matters worse for my color being, my sister chose red as her favorite color. Red shag carpeted her room. She wore red dresses, and everyone knew she loved red, so they gave her more red stuff for Christmas or birthday gifts. My green envy for red was not limited to my sister. My best friend, Kristi, also loved red. She too had a red room with red accents. When we knitted ponchos together in sixth grade, she knit a red one with white tassels; I settled on navy-blue and white stripes. Honestly, I did not blame them for loving red. But I certainly never let on I might be a girl who also needed red.

Instead, I chose yellow. Bright, sunny, happy yellow. Yep, that was me. The yellow girl: yellow bedroom, yellow roses, and later, even an eye-catching yellow house in Tokyo. But it turns out, I did need red. If only so I could move on to become a more fully rounded color person. I had glimpses of this in Tokyo. Far away from my past, I tiptoed into the red world. I bought a pair of red leather tie-up ankle boots. Crammed into a Tokyo subway car, I might be squished but I had happy red feet. Emboldened, I bought a red sweatshirt dress to wear over leggings. But I still had a long way to go. No one, not even me, realized yet that I stopped coloring after Mom died. Mark and Kari kept going to art classes. I did not go along, and demonstrated little aptitude or interest in making any art. I left that world to them, and went on to books and music, and a yellow life.

Unwittingly, I was probably following my mother's lead when I enrolled myself and 18-month-old Luke in a mom and toddler art class in West Roxbury. I acted on a tip from another mother at our local playground. Despite the 25-minute-drive, it was a good way to spend a winter morning with other moms and kids. I liked the creative projects the ever-so patient teacher came up with; Luke liked the snacks. After a year or so, Luke and I moved on to a mom and kids clay class in Brookline. The teacher was so great. "Mistakes are so interesting," she'd say to Luke. "Work with them. Don't throw it away because it doesn't look perfect." I kept going for years, bringing David when he was old enough.

With Luke in school, I could devote time just to coloring with David. I observed that while he knew his greens, his color story didn't end there. From Kelly green, he easily moved to blue and orange. I was there to color with him, to encourage his color choices, to make sure he did not get stuck too long on one color. I was there to fetch more animal crackers and apple juice. I was there to tape his masterpiece to the refrigerator door. Yeah for Kelly green, I cheered him. I cannot help but ask what kind of artist I might have become if I had a few more years coloring with my mother?

At the MFA, back in my collage class we progressed to wood block printing, mono prints, inks and brayers. We moved from paper to small canvas. Trumpets sounding proudly in my head, I graduated from beginning collage. My teacher suggested I look at the Massachusetts College of Art for my next course. My next course? Really? I love continuing education. I could be a poster girl for any adult education program. What I don't understand is why everyone isn't signing up. There are no grades. If you show up you are golden. I mean, honestly, no one fails adult ed. That's the beauty of it. And that's what gave me the courage to leap big. That and the fact I happened to notice a familiar name in the Massachusetts College of Art and Design course catalogue. Was the instructor the same Laurel who taught Pilates in Cambridge? It had been awhile since I'd seen her there. A phone call cleared things up. Yes, Laurel was an artist, as well as a Pilates instructor. She remembered me. Yes, I could join her class even though I had no prior painting experience.

Compared to the MFA collage course, Laurel's three-hour evening studio class was the big leagues. My sons balked when the babysitter arrived on Thursday night. "Why can't you go to school during the day like us?" they demanded. "Because this is the teacher and the class I want to take. It's important," I explained. Many of my studio art classmates were returning to painting, returning to art, after leaving it behind for their other "serious" life pursuits. They seemed to already grasp the fundamentals of composition and color theory. By comparison, I was starting fresh, which, it turned out, might have been an advantage. I had no expectations of what a mixed media Kathryn Graven painting should look like. I was not trying to return to a former artistic self, numbed by years in the corporate world. I was on a discovery mission.

Some of my early steps were more like toddler tumbles. Splat: face hits the sidewalk. In one class, we were exploring how to make found objects go in and out of a painting. I took the idea literally. I slit my canvas and wove a one-inch thick piece of rope through the holes. Momentarily channeling Jackson Pollock, I splattered on color. Then, I added glitter for glitter's sparkly sake. For me, just the notion of slitting holes in the canvas was daring, like I was a renegade pirate with a palate knife. So, I was caught off guard when I presented my piece for the class critique and my classmates delivered a harsh verdict.

"I'd think about putting that in the closet and revisiting

it in three months," said one woman. "How about painting the whole thing over in white," offered another. Stunned, I turned to the instructor to find some redeeming quality. "I don't think you need to resort to white," she said. "Maybe try yellow."

Definitely a low, low, low art class moment. "That bad?" I wondered out loud. "That bad," was the collective response. The idea that yellow might save me, burned even more. Whatever happened to finding something to praise first, and then diving into the "what went wrong?" With this class critique, I reconsidered my definition of brutal.

Lacking an alternative, I returned to my work area and regrouped. I talked to myself without making a sound. "If this is as bad as it gets, then, oh well. I still have my husband and two kids, friends and a good life. I'm fine. Who cares what anybody thinks about the work in a studio art class? Reasonable people disagree on the merits of a painting all the time. Isn't that what makes art, art? Anyway, I'll survive."

I had to. I'd already agreed to my first art show. And the show must go on.

Whatever my fellow Boston classmates thought of my work, their criticisms did not reach Great Cranberry Island in Maine. On small islands, it is possible to reinvent yourself many times, out of necessity or boredom. My island neighbor, Ruth, who was also the island's librarian, heard I was taking art classes. Out of the blue, I received this letter, which I will forever cherish for its unwavering support of both me and adult education.

January 25, 2007
Dear Kathy,

I am planning my next summer's exhibitions at the library. I am wondering if you might have some of your art which you would care to exhibit. If you are interested, I know a two-week period in July would be available. If this is something you might be interested in doing, I'd love to have you exhibit.

Sincerely,
Ruth Westphal

I was barely a month into my studio painting class. I showed the letter to Dennis. "Don't you think this is a little premature?" I asked. "But then again, this just might be my big break." We agreed: best not to miss the big break. A solo show struck me as too ambitious. Would Ruth consider a joint exhibition with my friend, Chris, an excellent photographer? She agreed and booked our show for the last two weeks in July. Hoots, laughter, disbelief, jokes abounded from all corners of my life.

I had six months.

Not only do small island communities love to support their own, they love to read all about it in the gossip columns of the *Mount Desert Islander*, a weekly newspaper. Our July art show made the column written by Barbara Fernald and Susan White.

"On Sunday, a large crowd attended the opening of Kathy Graven's and Chris Johnson's art and photography exhibition at the Great Cranberry Island Library. Chris is exhibiting photographs of

New England. Kathy is showing a colorful and whimsical collection of mixed media reflecting her many and varied interests. Ken Repp prepared a beautiful table of canapés and hors d'oeuvres. Kathy's husband, Dennis Encarnation, and their sons, Luke and David, helped host the event…"

A long-time summer salt on the island, Marilyn, arrived at the show early, and fell for a small acrylic mixed media piece. "I just have to have the blueberry one," Marilyn, also an artist, exclaimed. It was a riff on a Maine blueberry basket with pieces of a green carton attached to the canvas. "Music to my ears," Dennis whispered. Should I cash or frame her check for $75? Reviews by fellow islanders were also generous. "Love the colors." "Keep up the good work."

I loved Ruth for believing in me enough to offer me a show. I loved Marilyn for buying my first painting. I loved my island community for showing up. I loved Dennis for being the charming host. I couldn't give up now.

After returning to Boston, I advanced with courses in abstract art, and art as process. Months later, a new friend from one of my night classes, Barbara, introduced me to art studios in the South End. An oil painter, with a passion for orange lipstick, Barbara created lush large abstract oil works. Over coffee, she pushed me to give a studio a try. My reasonable side calculated that as a business plan, this was impossible. I would never sell enough paintings. Thankfully, the crescendoing artist in me made a different calculation on the way home: If not now, when?

Barbara introduced me to the artist in the studio across the hall from her. The MIT student who was half my age was looking for a studio mate. The $300 rent didn't seem too much to risk. I was thrilled to have one little corner to call my art space. I ignored her naked mannequin surrounded by precarious stacks of wooden stretchers, neither of which she ever appeared to use. What counted was I had someone else with me to greet visitors on the monthly open studio nights, making me feel less exposed. For six months, I painted during the day; my studio mate painted at night; our paths rarely crossed.

Ultimately, however, we were incompatible. She took up more than half the studio space, read wall display space, though I was paying half the rent. Selfishly, I wanted to make my own messes, not clean hers. The reality: I was too old to have a roommate. When another studio in the building opened, I tried to grab it. Too late. The building manager had already tapped the next person on the two-year waiting list. Discouraged, I unloaded studio mate stories on anyone who asked about my studio. I veered off my still fledgling artistic course and came dangerously close to becoming enmeshed in horrid studio and art politics.

On a winter break trip with my family, I vowed to turn my studio karma around, focus on my creative work, and sort things out with my difficult studio mate. Miraculously, while changing planes in Chicago on the way home, I received an unexpected voice mail from her. She must have picked up on my internal dialogue. "I'm going back to school full time. I can't keep the studio. Do you want the space?" Two weeks later, Studio 319 was officially mine.

On taking over, my first executive decision was to paint the old ceiling beams and one brick wall bright red. I claimed red as mine. This was my art room and it was going to have the right red, the red I couldn't find in that crayon box in the hospital room in 1966. I let nothing block my way. When a guy down the hall popped his head in to welcome me to the building, he said red was a terrible color on which to display artwork. I introduced myself and promptly showed him the door. I felt an unnatural affinity towards Nancy Reagan, who wore red dresses in the White House in spite of what the fashion critics had to say. While painting the three other walls white, my husband offered suggestions about ways to enhance the studio. "Shut up, this is Mom's room," said Luke. Bravo: My boys understood that this was my space, long before they were old enough to read Virginia Woolf. I stood and faced the red wall. Triumph washed over me. I let it. For a few days, I blissfully stared at the red wall. Then I realized that the guy down the hall was right. A solid red wall, however cathartic for me, would not serve my art. Knowing what was underneath, that the red sub layer would always be there, would have to suffice. I painted the brick wall white. I hung my work. I painted my name in an old repurposed frame. I opened the studio doors. I was an artist.

Happy rooms are not easy to find. To create them requires clearing and sorting. Then more clearing and more sorting. It takes the love and support of others. It required I learn to ask the angels to come to tea and for me to keep pouring, whether they showed up or not. People say I create happy paintings with bright colors. Some people like the work; some even buy a painting, take it home and hang it up. When that happens, I am a pink-cheeked ceiling cherub. It's right up there with newspaper byline joy.

Much of my artwork involves repurposing. I take old stuff: broken dishes, swatches of fabric, bits of leftover yarn, handmade papers from India and Japan, or maybe mesh from a bag of lemons, and see what mixes with my acrylic paint. My bag of broken pottery is almost as impressive as my pottery collection. It contains memories of trips to Mashiko with my Japanese sisters, excursions to Fiesole with Dennis, numerous trips to Mexico with my friend Wanda, birthday gifts from Martha who knows to stop in her tracks when the bright yellow and blue bowl in the market calls out my name. (I do the same for her with teacups; that's what friends are for.) At home, I don't just display pottery finds, I use them. Which also means I break them. But as an artist, I now think of a broken cup, or chipped bowl, as an opportunity, not a wrenching disaster. A favorite cobalt-blue and white Mexican plate? That beauty becomes part of a flower pot in a mixed media painting, a still life that isn't energetically still. Inside a painting of an oversized pink flower, I tuck snippets of Phyllis' dresses from the 1970s. The flower hugs viewers and showers love, whether they know it or not. Reusing what I have to create something new makes me smile.

But in the process of repurposing broken treasures, I kept hearing the same pesky internal voice that woke in Italy asking more pesky questions. The unnerving one: What happened to my Japan connection? How had almost ten years gone since my last visit? Why had I let it lapse? Kids, a husband with a global consulting business, were the easy answers. Combined with the bleak mood that enveloped Japan after the economic miracle bubble burst, it was hard to fathom why anyone would book a ticket to

Tokyo. For a while, I kept current on Japan matters by attending lectures in Boston and Cambridge. But even there, I detected lethagy and no great sense of urgency on Japan topics. The room of "Japan hands" felt tired, like a treasured screen whose gold leaf background was flaking. (The Fukushima nuclear disaster is a notable exception of an event that did re-energize interest in Japan.) It was easy to stop attending the seminars. Fewer students eager to unravel the nuances of Japan dimmed prospects for a resurgence. Why deplane in Tokyo, when the goldmine of opportunity for this generation awaited in Hong Kong, Shanghai and Beijing?

But these external justifications were only part of the story. Harder to express was the deep loneliness of losing both Otōsan and Okaasan. Repurposing old materials in my artwork, blending and mixing them with paint colors and textures, prompted me to give time to understanding the process of layering. The color I put down first peeks through later, depending on how thick something goes on top. Where and when do I want that to show through? When is a hint of something enough? Smearing a new color with a palate knife in hand, then using the point to scrape through to the bottom layer to bring out a contrasting line or shape, helped me think about my layers of grief differently.

I still needed to unwind my grief for the Maniwas, for Japan. Unwinding: arriving at the breakfast table and not hearing the rustling of the local newspaper and the "ano ne" of Otōsan, eager to discuss a headline. Unwinding: expecting Okaasan home from the drugstore any minute to cozy up under the *kotatsu* for dinner and a heartfelt talk and good laughs. But now, as an artist, I wanted not just to grieve, but to repurpose grief. I remembered the beautiful Japanese *furoshiki* Okaasan had bought for me on our first trip to Kyoto. To show her how much I loved the bold flowers on the indigo square cloth, I wrapped my school books in it. When my class mates oohed and ahhhed over it, I realized my big mistake. It was too special for everyday use. It was for wrapping and storing special treasures. I folded it, took care of it, kept it safe with my special fabrics. Now, I imagined using that *furoshiki* to wrap up my sadness. I'd tie it gently. I'd try to think of it as a new gift.

Japan, the people, culture, place, had been my gift. I needed to claim it, like I needed to claim red.

But how? First, I admitted I wanted Japan back in my life. Unlike Minnesota, or even California, I missed it. I was homesick for Japan. Then, I waited for the moment to turn things around. That moment was the *Jusan kai ki*. In Japanese, this refers to the 13th anniversary of someone's passing, as dated by the Buddhist calendar. Masae, the daughter in charge of family rituals now, invited me to Ohtawara for the ceremony at the temple and to the family reunion dinner afterwards. "I'll be there," I promised. In another phone call, Rie was charged with making sure I understood the protocol. "Kyashi-san, you can't wear bright colors," Rie warned. "We all wear black." I promised: "I'll wear black."

We gathered at the Maniwa house: Rie and Steve, Toshie, her daughter Yoko, Masae, Otōsan's sister, Otōsan's half-siblings Ayako and Satoru, various other cousins and spouses. The mood was relaxed; despite the black dresses, this wasn't a funeral. It was a family reunion, where the dead are first honored, and then invited back to join in the family gathering and feast. Together, we headed to the Tousen'in Temple, which belongs to the Soto sect of Zen Buddhism. The group behavior shifted slightly, became more reverential in anticipation of the ceremony. Passing the entry gate, we took off our shoes and stepped up into the inner sanctum of the temple. In a concession to modernity and aging legs, we sat on chairs on the tatami mat facing the altar. The chairs hinted the service might go on awhile. The priest lit incense and read sutras, as I sat in the second row gripped by eerily comforting smells and lulled by the sounds. It didn't matter I had no idea what he was chanting. I was here with my Japanese family.

With the official part of the Buddhist ceremony completed, we made our way to the cemetery. I noticed tall wooden slats with thick black characters behind the large family gravestone. I couldn't make out the kanji. "What's this?" I asked. *Kaimyo* are the new names for the dead, given by the priest, for them to take with them to their next life. How did I not know this? I loved this idea of entering a new life with a new name. I asked Masae to write the characters so I could translate them later.

The characters proved too difficult to decipher alone, so I asked my friend Toshio for help. I was relieved when Toshio's rendering of Otōsan's *kaimyo* did him justice. "Honorable Bright Philosopher Buddhist Layman who accumulated virtues to reach summit." I liked thinking of Otōsan's volunteer work for his Rotary Club elevated to Honorable Bright Philosopher. Yes, that would surely help him in his next life. Okaasan's *kaimyo* was also satisfying. "Beautiful Elder Sister filled with crystal-clear chastity who overcame difficulties." Indeed, Katsuko overcame many difficulties but never lost her clear essence and beauty. There was no doubt she was carrying that essence and beauty forward in new ways.

After throwing salt over our shoulders to prevent unwanted spirits accompanying us away from the cemetery, we retired to a local restaurant and our private dining room. At low tables on the tatami mat floor, I sat across from the priest. Behind him were the photos of Otōsan and Okaasan and lacquered trays for their food. Each dish brought in was first offered to the spirits of the deceased, then served to the rest of the family. The same went for the sake. At its heart, this sharing of the meal was like taking Christian communion. But instead of quiet contemplation, this was about boisterous connection. I poured sake for the priest, he poured for me. Refills were plentiful. It was also acceptable to get up, walk to the other end of the table and pour sake for someone else. Leg stretching disguised as polite hosting.

Hours later, the party continued at the house. Makoto's sister, whom everyone called the aunt from *Sakuyama*, unloaded bags of homemade pickles. We stabbed shriveled eggplants with toothpicks, joyfully piercing her claim to local pickle fame, as we sipped green tea. We laughed at yellowing family photos. Satoru fell asleep, just like Otōsan. He had another party later that night, which excused him to nap. Outside, in front of the house, we posed for multiple family photos. "*Ichi, ni, san: cheezu.*" My black dress blended with the group. My blond hair didn't. But it no longer got in the way of my belonging. "You must come for the next *kaiki*," Satoru insisted.

Side trips with Rie, Toshie and Masae to handmade paper and pottery studios, and Japanese craft stores ignited a spark, a new compulsion to bring Japanese materials into my mixed media art. I stocked various sizes of *furoshiki*. In my Boston studio, I went one step beyond wrapping my grief in beautiful Japanese *furoshiki*. I experimented with wrapping my paintings in them, revealing some of the abstract work, hiding other parts, then letting the viewer experiment with how to tie the *furoshiki*. After being wowed by Issey Miyake's Pleats Please line of clothing in Tokyo, I experimented with pleats. I painted on long flat canvases, then folded the canvas in pleats before stapling the canvas to stretchers. Why are canvases always stretched flat for the artist to add texture? Why not start pleated?

For other treasures from my prior Japan days, I headed across the Charles River to my overstuffed storage unit in Cambridge. I looked through boxes of old mementos and letters from my high school year in Japan. I touched my journals and flipped through a rice paper book covered in red floral *washi*. It was filled with raw poetry. From a pile of letters, I freed a 12-inch by 12-inch gold-rimmed *sayonara* card that the students and teachers signed for me. I remembered being overwhelmed when they gave me the card: happy about returning to America, anxious about finishing high school, dying to go off to college, impatient to make my life whatever it was going to be, sad to be leaving my school escort friend Kakuta-san, nervous about my obligatory farewell speech in Japanese. There was no way to absorb the messages then.

Now I was ready. Slowly, as a middle-aged woman, I read and savored their kind, thoughtful words. I fixed on a note from the art teacher. His message reassured me that what I was then is still who I am now, and who I hope to be as I grow old. In black elegant and perfect cursive ink, Nagashima *Sensei* had written: "Always be a beginner."

As a bow of gratitude to Nagashima *Sensei*, I made copies of my early calligraphy. Sheets of awkward hiragana and katakana alphabets would be the under-layer in a new piece. I color copied and enlarged beautiful Japanese postage stamps from the 1970s. I ripped handmade Japanese papers gathered on my recent trip. I layered and dribbled paint, only to scrape and uncover, and smoosh some more. Pleased, I signed the new piece in katakana: キャシ-. I heard Okaasan-san saying my name when I did. "キャシ-。" I thought of her beautiful calligraphy compared to my amateur script. I heard Otōsan saying, "Ano ne… so what is this painting about?" As I put the Japanese alphabet into the piece, I was surprised. This was the first time I had used letters in my art. And they were Japanese.

Repurposing begets further repurposing. Which leads to an exciting truth about aging. We have so much stuff, both in our minds and closets, to repurpose. The possibilities for repurposing them are limitless. What to do with those old scrap books? What use are those handkerchiefs and stained tablecloths? I visualize my life in a repurposed shoji screen, each divided pane its own beautiful story, a tiny abstract window on what has mattered. I paint that.

Chapter 29

How can I hear what I can never hear?

That's the question that has always loomed largest. Gardening helped carry me on a palanquin through my losses to happier times. Working the soil and playing with colors allowed me to open up, express my sadness, tickle my creative side and chase joy. But as effective as these activities were in healing my grief, they did not get at the deepest, hardest pain. Being visual and tactile, they could not fill the auditory void.

Our early family movies had no soundtrack. There were no answering machines on which to leave voice messages. Mom died long before everyday technology made it possible for the living to rewind and hear the dead, over and over. Before iPhones and YouTube made it easy to capture everyone joyfully singing "Happy Birthday."

If I close my eyes and listen hard to the inside of my brain, I think I can hear Mom tell me to "rinse the toothpaste spit from the sink" after I finish brushing. But no, really, it is only the words, there is no voice. Sometimes I think I can hear someone calling from the kitchen, "Don't pick on Kathy, she's only five." But no, in fact that's just the story retold by my siblings about how I lost my first game of Hearts. My brother threw me the queen of spades on the very first hand. I burst into tears. Mom always came to my defense.

I can conjure my father's deep voice scaring us with made-up stories of Algernon the Wolf. I can hear Gram's voice quivering on the high notes of "Skinnamarinky dinky dink, skinnamarinky do, I love you." I can feel the extra emphasis Phyllis put on the second syllable in my name when she called "Ka-*thy*." I giggle with delight hearing Okaasan call my name in Japanese with the diminutive "chan" attached to Kyashi. As in, "Kyashi-chan, *Ohayogozaimasu.*"

There is no doubt I can retain the voices of the dead in my head. Just not my mother's. So, how then did I find a voice for the gaping silence? I turned to music. I learned to imagine. And, well, I've had some long, perhaps unusual, conversations with pianos.

I don't remember hearing my mom play the piano. But the brown upright piano Gramps bought her to play growing up in Hayward always figured front and center in our family life. The black and white family photo used for my Dad's congressional campaign in 1962 featured my mom at the keyboard, flanked by my brother and sister. My Dad stands looking over her shoulder holding me. When we moved to Minneapolis, Mom placed the piano in front of the big window in the family room. The pianist had a great view outside to the basketball court in summer and the homemade ice skating rink in winter.

In due time, Mom pushed all three of us kids out the back door, across the alley to Mrs. Cooper's house for piano lessons. I started piano lessons when I entered kindergarten at four, which was too young, by most measures. But since Mark and Kari were already her students, Mrs. Cooper took me on, too. The baby grand piano, on the light-blue shag carpeting, hogged most of Mrs. Cooper's tiny living room. It almost swallowed me too. It felt like a tight squeeze to sit on the bench, my feet dangling above the plastic mat Mrs. Cooper put down to guard against drippy, muddy shoes.

After Mom died, and we were in the carrying-on-as-usual phase, we still went to piano lessons. When my sister was recovered enough, she vowed to practice harder than ever, as if to make up for the times she didn't practice when Mom had nagged her. Kari tried, but never enjoyed playing. Instead, she loved to color and paint. Dad said she could quit piano.

But somehow, music stuck for me and my brother. We liked to practice. Mark loved playing Debussy's "Golliwog Cakewalk." I loved Clementi's sonatinas, especially the catchy rhythm of Number 1 in C Major. I liked how purposeful I felt climbing our needlepoint covered piano bench, which opened to reveal a secret hiding spot for music. Every note I played was one tiny effort to fill the sound of silence, the missing footsteps on the pine floor in the family room, the chatting on the phone to friends in the kitchen, the hurry up and get your shoes on, sounds once made by my now-dead mother.

Eventually, the truth sank in. Practicing piano would not bring Mom back. But for me, playing piano became an important way to keep a private conversation going with her. In my mind, the notes, songs, melodies vibrating in the air sustained a musical connection with her I never talked about. In Sunday school, at church, people talked about hearing angel voices. If they could make up stuff like that, well then just maybe, my mother, whom Aunt Mavis said was now one of those angels, could hear my playing. Maybe, just maybe, she would visit?

Later, as I worked my way through piano books,

hymnals and sheet music, I'd come across old music of hers. I noticed that often she wrote the date she had studied or played a particular piece just above the key signature. In November 1949, she practiced Chopin's Prelude, Opus 28, No. 6. I imagined her playing legato in the left hand, softly in the right, pedaling to achieve the correct phrasing. In December, she progressed in the same John Thompson piano study book, to Tchaikovsky's short "Song of the Skylark." I pictured her, imagining the lark hovering and singing. Under the notes, she's penciled in the "and" count for the triplet sixteenth notes. Triplets trip me up, too. And in a way that makes sense to a motherless daughter, that music, that sound of Tchaikovsky's skylark, is as close as I can come to knowing her voice.

I never dared tell anyone about my musical moments, my private, real yet imaginary, conversations. By not telling anyone, they became something no one could steal. I don't ever remember my dad or piano teachers nagging me to practice my music. I just did it. Sticking with piano lessons had other benefits. Weekly lessons and daily practice gave structure and purpose to my free time. The routine of it was a relief in a household that lacked predictability and order.

Looking back, I realize it was Mom's piano that helped me through the dark phase of my father's lung cancer diagnosis. In Dad and Sally's townhouse, what reminded me most of the past was Mom's piano. When I played hymns and sang for Dad, just maybe, he had an inkling of what I long held inside: that playing the piano was the surest way to talk to Mom.

My move to Boston tested Dennis' commitment from

Day One. I was open and upfront with my one and only requirement for moving in with him: my piano came with me. As the movers unloaded my belongings outside his Marlborough Street apartment, they snarled at the endless stairs and absence of an elevator. When they realized there were five flights of stairs, and that the last one was a winding doozy, they balked. No way were they equipped to haul the piano up to "little Tibet." I shot Dennis a searing look.

He jumped on the phone to the Boston Symphony office and pleaded with a woman to help solve his urgent piano problem. The woman took pity on him and shared her contact at "Death Wish Movers." Within hours, heavily scarred, muscular guys arrived in black T-shirts. For the final fifth flight, the harrowing, narrow windy part with just enough clearance, they strapped my piano on the shortest guy's back. Slowly, step by step, he crawled my musical friend to our new home. Coinciding with our wedding a year later, Dennis and I bought a new condo further down Marlborough Street, still on the top floor, no elevator but with wider stairs. Naturally, our first call was to Death Wish Movers. Almost 30 years later, we are still in the same home, albeit after many nail-biting renovations.

Always, the piano has been central to our living space. Naked except for their diapers, as toddlers, both Luke and David climbed on the piano seat and made their own music. I let them bang freely. These were joyous musical moments. I vowed to get their music education right, not haphazard like mine. That proved elusive. They each took piano lessons at the Community Music Center of Boston.

They studied with different teachers to match their learning styles and personalities. So far, so good. But inevitably, there were meltdowns, then problems with certain teachers. Reluctantly, I switched their teachers. At home, despite my best "I will not nag" intentions, we battled over practicing. I told Luke he could quit piano lessons after sixth grade. When he started middle school and begged to quit, I confessed: "I lied. It is too soon to quit."

Having kids makes us do things we might never do for ourselves. As a little girl, I had a secret wish: someday I would sit at a big, beautiful grand piano and my fingers would move magically up and down the keyboard, and the room would be filled with the most perfect sound. I never dreamed about owning fancy cars, expensive jewelry or houses. But a grand piano was worth dreaming about.

On Dennis' strong nudging, we stopped by the Boston Symphony piano sale one September. We came home the proud owners of a Steinway A, one that had been used that summer at Tanglewood, the summer home of the Boston Symphony. "My boys will learn on a fabulous instrument," I rationalized as the crane hoisted the newest addition to our family through the bedroom window. I was also sick to my stomach—for days. I called friends and confessed I had fallen prey to horrible consumerist demons. Inside, I fretted that my piano playing wasn't good enough to deserve such a great instrument. My friend Harriet talked me down from the ledge of self-loathing. "Why not have something that makes you happy?"

With the new instrument crammed between the dining and living rooms in our loft space, my thinking changed.

Did I want to keep playing the same pieces I had studied twenty years ago? Would I still be making the same mistakes when I was 80? My kids aside, this new piano offered a chance to get unstuck musically. So, I did what a mother should never, ever do: I stole the boys' piano teacher. They didn't know I was stealing her, but that's what happened.

I began adult studies with a Debussy piece. Playing Debussy revealed my weakness for holding a steady rhythm. I don't know what steady is, I protested. My teacher suggested a new metronome. She told me to listen to my own heartbeat. It was a tough assignment, one that is ongoing. I revisited old friends Bach, Haydn, Mozart with fresh eyes.

Some weeks as I tackle composers new to me, like Clara Schumann, I puff up like a proud peacock. More often, I am deeply humbled. Can an aging brain ever overcome missed childhood learning opportunities? Occasionally, I have a breakthrough, one of those ta-da moments that makes my heart skip a beat. The added bonus: I've heard it skip.

One day, we came to a passage that had a long, tied note. It required holding the bass notes past the measure line, into the next bar. My teacher suggested, while the tied note deserved its full count, that I shift my focus from the sound of playing the note, to the sound the keys made when the fingers were lifted. The sound of letting go.

Whirr. Crash. Splat. Thud. Those were the sounds that came to mind when I thought of letting go. Dishes crashing to the floor, slipping out of wet hands. A steering wheel spinning out of control, a Wheel-oh flying through the air. The sound of letting go wasn't pretty. It was noisy and messy: disaster.

That night, I asked Dennis what he thought letting go sounded like. "Ahhh. Sigh. Whooooshhhhh." I was shocked to realize how negative my instinctual response to letting go was. I took a mental inventory of all I hold too tight. The list was long. I saw my grief, for my parents, for Phyllis and Warren, for Otōsan and Okaasan, as a long tied note. I had held it for the full count. I had held it beyond the next measure. As a musician, I was called to lift the finger, release the tie, play the next note with intention and precision. As a daughter, was I also not called to lift my sadness, release my grief and move on to my own melody?

At another lesson, this time working on a piece from Bach's French Suites, my teacher returned to the idea of how we as pianists end notes. Flutists and other wind players can finish notes with a stronger force of air than when they began, but once a pianist strikes a key, there is no way to make it louder. The only way to change the sound is through the release. "Paying attention to the release will help your playing so much," she asserted.

This letting go idea stuck, a life metaphor. How do we let go, and what sound does it make? Now I knew the new question I wanted to answer: What does grief released sound like? It was something to listen for.

That October, my teacher suggested I study Scarlatti. There's a "crispness" about the Italian-born, Baroque composer she thought I would appreciate. A contemporary of Handel, Scarlatti wrote sonatas known, experts say, for their combination of technical difficulty, harmonic audacity and adventurous modulation. I learned that later.

To get started on a piece, I flipped through the book of scores and the "vivo" tempo marking in K 113 caught my eye. I needed a little vivo right then. Lively. A Major. Sight reading the piece, I noticed sections where the left hand crossed over the right. Hmmm. Doable, but not easy. It takes concentration to land the crossovers. "It's all about focus," she insisted.

Right. This was not the time to think about walking the dog, or to remember damp clothes forgotten in the dryer. This was the time to have both sides of the brain present and fired. I sat straight and took a deep breath in and out. I practiced landing the high B and C natural crossovers with my eyes closed.

By measure 44, I was discouraged. The crossovers, the harmony and modulation had left me lost and confused. At my next lesson, I confessed that several measures seemed so beyond my reach I just might have avoided practicing them all week. "Then that's where we will start," she said. We went note by note, left and right hands separately, trying to understand the passage. "I just don't like measure 44," I whined. "You must keep playing it until you see its beauty," she said. "It resolves beautifully in the next measure. It's gorgeous."

"It may resolve but I don't feel satisfied," I said. In my confusion, I didn't think I just might be out of my league to question the motivation of the great Scarlatti. "Your ear wants to hear something else. Scarlatti doesn't give it to you. But you are right to be listening for it." That's high praise from this teacher. I left knowing I had work ahead of me but at least I was listening. Was resolving a passage from E minor to E major satisfying for Scarlatti and all the other pianists who play his pieces? Can we resolve an idea, a harmony and still be left wanting more?

Years of sight reading, practicing fingerings, finding my way to piano lessons, embarking on new composers, even watching my sons learn to play, have not been fruitless. In the quest to hear what I never can, I stumbled onto this: the sacred space in sound, the brief, but exact moment, when fear and sadness lift and the new energy required to move to the next note arrives.

Chapter 30

When someone we love dies, the grief rides with us for the rest of our life's journey. Will it ride softly, gently, next to us in the passenger's seat as a memory of love? Will it be pushed to the back seat, banished from clear sight—perhaps accessible through the rearview mirror? Will it be stretched in front of us, guiding us to our fear and acceptance of death?

How will I tend my grief? This is not a one-off question. It will keep coming up over and over, the longer we live, the more we love. It is front and center as we face a devastating global pandemic.

As this strange and scary COVID-19 virus took over the news, upended travel plans and social lives, and people of all ages became sicker and sicker, I found comfort in the steady foot pedal and non-threatening whrrrr of my Cortina sewing machine. Stitching and pressing seams, I escaped to the markets, stalls and little shops where I'd bought and collected these fabulous fabrics. Scavenging for elastics in Gram's sewing box, I came on leftover lace from the handkerchief quilt I sewed with such a heavy heart two decades earlier. I opened the little crocheted sombrero with my great-grandmother's silver thimble in it and put it on my finger.

I had survived having my first baby without my many mothers to help and guide me. I had another son and survived losing dear Warren. Every day, I feel lucky I had the chance to see both my sons off to first grade and every grade after, including college and graduate school. To their fidgeting dismay and embarrassment, I insisted on first day of school photographs every year in front of our Marlborough Street home. I needed to bear my own witness to this simple joy. My mother missed a lot.

Throughout my life, sewing helped me meet new friends, explore new cultures and nourished my creative self. Sewing helped me gather my tears and grief and move forward. Now in the midst of great uncertainty, looming fears and increasing isolation, sewing offered solace and more.

Sewing masks became my little effort to reach out to others. I tried to think who would like what color or fabric. I have a Norwegian friend who always wears bright red lipstick. I lined her mask in bright red cotton, in case she put on lipstick and then the mask. For another island neighbor in Maine who loves flowers and writes poetry, I chose a *tenugui* with a bird resting on a cherry branch. It was the closest I could come to a mask haiku.

After fun with *tenugui*, I turned to bold Marimekko fabrics, some from a collection I inherited from Phyllis, some from my stash. I sent those masks to Phyllis' daughters, and my Japanese family, who haven't met, but share an appreciation for Marimekko designs. I was thrilled to sew a dozen masks for Maria, one of Phyllis' granddaughters who owns a bakery in Virginia, passing on the love to the next generation. She sent me delicious cookies as a thank you.

One of my favorite set of masks was sewed with a limited edition purple and fuchsia-checkered fabric. I made a dress out of that fabric nearly thirty years ago to wear to the wedding of a guy I dated briefly. Its bold colors sang for me then, making me look and feel fabulous. I had enough scraps left over for a half dozen masks. I kept a couple for myself and sent the others to close girlfriends who would appreciate a mask that could make you feel both young and wise.

Inside each mask, I signed my name and offered a sweet something, a dose of cheer. My pandemic *odaijini*—a little bow of gratitude to *Okaasan*.

Sing!
Blow Bubbles!
Smile!
Time for a cookie!
Sunshine!
Be well!
Stay Positive!
I Love Flowers!
Breathe!
Let's Dance!

People loved the masks and the little messages. More and more requests came in. My efforts to connect to family and friends, I realized, were intricately tied to the post office. During the initial lockdown, I allowed myself two trips to the post office a week. Each time, I wore a mask. Soon, my masks were going global. "I made masks for my son and his flatmates in Scotland," I said proudly to the postal worker who needed to know for the customs form. "This one is for my family in Japan. This one is for friends in Canada."

"You're sewing masks?" She asked expectantly. "Did you

make yours?"

"Would you like some?" I offered.

"Oh yes, please."

"I'll bring some tomorrow," I promised.

On the way home, I bumped into my regular postal delivery woman. "Wait here a minute. I have something for you." I ran upstairs and grabbed a blue and white stripped *tenugui* mask from my sewing table and ran down to the street. "Here, I'm making masks. Would you like one?" Caught off guard, she accepted my mask with a quiet thanks.

The next day I saw her pushing her over-stuffed mail cart wearing the mask. "Hey, I love it," she said. "Everyone is asking where I got it." A few weeks later, she was wearing a standard light blue mask and stopped me to explain. "We have to wear these masks for work now. I still wear yours on weekends, though. It's my favorite."

So while the world was being suspended, upended and anxiety mounted, I made and sent masks to anyone who asked. Some offered to pay, but I said no, it was my effort at community service. I couldn't serve as a scientist or public health official or medical personnel, but I could make masks. Friends who ordered masks pushed me to come up with a worthy cause to donate to. But as we shuttered our lives through the spring and the economy stalled, there was overwhelming need everywhere. How to choose?

It was during my weekly piano lesson I found a way to connect my various passions with mask making. Months earlier, I had started studying in Boston with a new teacher—a talented collaborative pianist from South

Africa. She'd always dreamed of studying and performing in New York City and had been accepted to an advanced program at The Juilliard School with a scholarship. But it wasn't enough to cover her moving and living expenses and the pandemic was limiting her performing and teaching jobs. "I'll sew masks for you," I offered at the end of one of our Zoom lessons.

I announced my "Masks for Music" initiative on social media. I loved the responses. A long-lost Stanford friend who had worked with opera singers in New York ordered ten masks. A journalism colleague in Colorado sympathized, as her son was a talented, emerging musician. She ordered eight masks and we followed up with a long-overdue phone call. A woman from South Africa who knew my teacher emailed that she'd take as many masks as I could make for her daughter who lived and worked in up-state New York. Neighbors in Boston stopped me as I was out walking the dog and placed orders. My Japanese friend, Nahoko, who sent me the mask pattern translated my teacher's GoFundMe site into Japanese and my teacher posted it. The response was touching global support. Helping to send a young woman to New York to pursue her musical dreams filled me with joy. It gave her hope. My joy increased. She performed beautiful duets with mentors who also wanted to see her campaign succeed, including a virtual duet in Boston with cellist Yo Yo Ma. Now, that brought me happy tears.

I brought my sewing machine to Great Cranberry Island and sewed masks all summer for neighbors and friends. I found blueberry-themed fabric and wrapped my freshly made blueberry jams in a mask with matching fabric. It made me happy to see so many island friends wearing my masks on the town dock waiting for the ferry; it softened the physical distance we had to keep. At the end of summer, I fretted about my sons returning to their lives and studies in a pandemic world. But at least I sent each of them off with a pile of assorted masks—signed with supportive messages—with plenty of extras to share with friends.

My name has appeared on the front pages of national and international newspapers. I've brushed it artistically on the side of mixed media paintings. As a jar-filling enthusiast, I've scribbled it on labels for jams, pickles and hand creams. I've written it vertically in the Japanese alphabet. But signing the inside of my homemade masks brought me the sweetest joy.

For most of my lifetime, American society has been at a loss for how to grieve. We've been intent on brushing grief aside, craving something, anything, to numb the pain: wishing and willing it away. That approach won't stand up to the tsunami of loss our human family is experiencing as a result of this pandemic.

Perhaps the only thing worse than a funeral where no one is allowed to cry is no funeral at all. Gatherings of all faiths to honor the dead allow us a moment to collectively pull out our handkerchiefs and let the tears flow. They allow us to bury our heads in the warm embrace of others, taking whatever extra strength they have for our own; they give us permission to be sad, vulnerable and weakened. If only for an hour lulled by an organ, or for one day devoted to mourning, they allow us to be fully human. So many are denied that right now. Where will their grief flow?

There are some who understand that a moment of national, indeed international, mourning is required for healing. But anyone who has suffered a deep loss also knows that after the memorial candles are blown out and the hallowed strains of *Amazing Grace* faded, a profound emptiness remains. Everywhere in the world, when a child loses a mother or father, or a mother or father loses a parent or a child, or a grandparent loses a son or daughter, that family's fabric is ripped.

An Easter Sunday car accident when I was five-years-old shattered my family's life. Such brokenness might have culminated in sad defeat, if it were not for the grace of Helen, Phyllis and Katsuko. My loss gave each a chance to be more open, loving and caring. No one would ask for that opportunity but they were willing to step up when the universe asked.

More than a half century later, what would I say to a five-year-old girl who can never have what she wants the most: for her mother not to be dead, gone, never coming back? I would tell her that the world, for all its brokenness, is there for her. And I mean the whole world: from the neighbors across the alley in Minneapolis, to strangers in a small town in Japan, to villagers breathing the thin air of Tibet. I would tell her that you can't have your mother back but other women can and do step in and give you what you need. I'd concede that part of her will always understand, deep in her gut, what it feels like to be a motherless child.

I'd tell her that tending that grief is worth all the time, pain and effort. It's what makes finding joy possible.

I hope my story prompts others to expand their vision of family, to think in more global ways. The wider the constellation of examples we can choose from, the richer, the more interesting life we can aspire to. When we open ourselves to seeking and receiving love, comfort, and ideas from other cultures, we are better positioned to heal ourselves and this broken world. Let's resist the creeping discourse that makes us fearful of foreignness. Let's pass on to our children the courage and wisdom they need to plant themselves right in the thick of this grand world.

History has shown, and the global pandemic only confirms, that for years to come, our human family will face untold grief and need to cry gigantic puddles of tears. To heal ourselves and our torn world, it will take plenty of needles, many spools of thread. I await the next stitch.

Acknowledgments

My many parents gave me abundant love. I remember with joy: Arlene Lindholm Graven and David Graven; their parents Nellie and Oscar Lindholm and Helen and Henry Graven; Phyllis and Warren Sorteberg; and Katsuko and Makoto Maniwa.

So many families around the world opened their doors and embraced me. I honor my biological family. My colorful sister, Kari Graven, poured her heart into watching over me. My brother, Mark Graven, pulled me along when it counted. My aunts and uncles, Mavis and Stanley Graven and Lori and the late Lloyd Graven steadied us through tough stretches. Sally Graven cared so well for my father in his final days and has lived since with great resilience.

Kristi Sorteberg Reierson, David Sorteberg, Karin Kulzer and Mary Sorteberg made room for me around their dining room table and in the back seat of the family station wagon — thus stitching our childhood fabrics together. For the shared laughter and tears, you are forever in my heart.

Rie Proschan, Toshie Maniwa and Masae Maniwa have included me in their extraordinary Japanese family for more than four decades. Their individual and collective fortitude always lifts me. Happy memories of Tochigi outings and cozy meals sitting under the *kotatsu* sustain me. Their homemade *miso* and *umeboshi* inspire me.

My enduring love of Japan is inextricably tied to my wider AFS-Japan family. Special thanks to Kimie Kato, former head of AFS Japan, and her husband, Takeo. Kimie's unwavering support of global educational exchanges has transformed lives and the world. Tami Muto was not only the best advisor an exchange student could hope for, she has been a life-long mentor. Many AFS-Japan returnees guided me to a deeper understanding of Japanese business, culture and government during my reporting years. Toshio Fukuhara, an exemplary *"sempai,"* offered insights into Japan, good humor and, with his wife, Nozomi, generous hospitality.

The Tokyo Bureau of *The Wall Street Journal* was my work family for formative professional years. Thanks to fellow correspondents Marcus Brauchli, Damon Darlin, Masayoshi Kanabayashi and Yumiko Ono Murase for helping me become a better journalist.

Friendships born in Japan made living overseas incredibly fun and widened my horizons. Thanks to Deanna Horton, Janet Lowe, Carol Lutfy, Stacey Green Mason, Stephen Payton, Steve Proschan, Harriet Whiting and Louise Bullis Yarmoff for fabulous times in Tokyo.

A remarkable and irreplaceable group of mixed-faith friends helped Dennis and me create a new family in Boston. Thanks to Logan Brenzel, Martha Carter, Kenn Freed, Christopher Johnson, the Rev. David Killian, Dr. Barbara O'Neil, Ken Repp, Kristi Sorteberg Reierson and Wanda Reindorf for being amazing godparents and part of our Boston family.

With love and laughter, Martha Carter, dancer, choreographer and teacher extraordinaire, has kept me on my toes throughout my creative career. Her Canadian family—the late Howard, Marnie, Beth and James—

welcomed me to Vancouver in 1978, and have graciously offered me a home away from home ever since. O Canada!

I raise prayerful hands to the indefatigable Shukla Bose, the staff, teachers and students of the Parikrma School in Bangalore, India. Our time working and learning with you was truly a gift.

Seeking and accepting help has been critical to my life story. Over many years, a wise and wonderful team of women steered me through the deep work of healing body, mind and spirit. Thanks to Virginia Bunting, Tanya Geisler, Julie Gleason, the late Beverly Holt, Marcia Hood and Anne Kilguss.

I am grateful to all the readers who helped turn my story into a book. Louise Bullis Yarmoff improved early drafts with keen attention to detail, and Harriet Whiting sorted legal threads. Caroline Leavitt gave valuable narrative advice. Nahoko Hayashida, Steve Proschan and Rie Proschan corrected Japanese language mistakes. I take responsibility for any remaining errors. The poet, Susan Deborah King, listened, cheered and wouldn't let me give up. Without "Sam"—my "let's drink coffee on the porch in our pajamas" summer neighbor—this book would not be.

The excellent and supportive team at Cinnamon Press, Dr. Jan Fortune, Adam Craig and Rowan Fortune, gave this book a special editorial home. Their vision to publish stories of small miracles by distinctive voices resonated across the Atlantic Ocean. Thanks to Sophie Erb for wonderful graphic designs for the book cover and website.

My kind and loving sons, Luke Encarnation and David Encarnation, keep me growing and bring me immeasurable joy. Now making their way in the world, these curious, determined and funny young men give me hope for our fragile planet.

Finally, each day begins with coffee and a kiss and ends with a promise of more adventure thanks to my husband, Dennis Encarnation. With his abiding love and support, a beautiful family, surrounded by an even bigger global family, became possible. He gives me the space and time I need to write, create art, play music and garden. With love and gratitude, I dedicate this book to him.

Author Biography

Kathryn Graven is a writer, mixed-media artist, musician and a lifelong sewer.

Author photograph: Kathryn Graven by Paige Gilbert.

Fluent in Japanese, she began her journalism career in Tokyo at the ABC News Bureau, and then became a Tokyo correspondent for *The Wall Street Journal.* In the U.S., she reported for the WSJ from New York and Boston, and taught international business reporting at Boston University.

Kathryn graduated from Stanford University with a bachelor's degree in History and a master's degree in East Asian Studies. She graduated from Columbia University's Graduate School of Journalism in New York. She was a fellow at the Program on U.S.-Japan Relations at Harvard University, and was awarded an Abe Fellowship by the Japan Foundation.

Pivoting to a new career, Kathryn studied mixed-media painting and abstract art at Boston's Museum of Fine Arts and the Massachusetts College of Art and Design. She shows her artwork in monthly open studios and participates in solo and group art events.

Originally from Minnesota, Kathryn lives with her husband in Boston, and is mother to their two grown sons.

During the summer, she lives on Great Cranberry Island, Maine. Passionate about sharing and preserving the bounty of her Maine garden, she makes delicious jams and irresistible pickles.

Memoirs of a Mask Maker is her first book.

Please visit the author's website at www.kathryngraven.com for more information and photos.

Printed in the USA
CPSIA information can be obtained
at www.ICGtesting.com
LVHW090842011223
765223LV00003B/391